Fields of Deception

Fields of Deception

Britain's bombing decoys
of World War II

Colin Dobinson

METHUEN

Published by Methuen 2000

1 3 5 7 9 10 8 6 4 2

This edition published in Great Britain in 2000 by
Methuen Publishing Ltd
215 Vauxhall Bridge Rd, London SW1V 1EJ

Copyright © 2000 by Colin Dobinson and English Heritage
The right of Colin Dobinson to be identified as author of this work
has been asserted by him in accordance with the Copyrights,
Designs and Patents Act 1988

Illustrations © 2000 by English Heritage

Methuen Publishing Limited Reg. No. 3543167

A CIP catalogue record for this book
is available from the British Library

ISBN 0 413 74570 8

Design & typesetting by Roger Walker

Typeset in ITC Veljovic and Quay Sans

Printed and bound in Great Britain by
St Edmundsbury Press Limited, Bury St Edmunds , Suffolk

Papers used by Methuen Publishing are natural, recyclable products
made from wood grown in sustainable forests. The manufacturing
processes conform to environmental regulations of the country of
origin.

Contents

Foreword

This is the first in a new series of books arising from English Heritage's assessment of Second World War military remains. The series covers all the major monument classes from this period, beginning with books on three aspects of defence against aerial bombing: decoys built to deceive the enemy and detract from the intended targets, anti-aircraft artillery and radar. The material in these books is entirely new. Much of it wasn't covered in detail in official post-war histories, while some aspects of Britain's defence provision – notably bombing decoys – remained secret until recently.

The studies have their origin in work commissioned by English Heritage's Monuments Protection Programme (MPP), a national review of England's archaeological resources, started in 1986 and due for completion in around 2010. Among the statutory duties which English Heritage performs are the promotion of public enjoyment and understanding of the historic environment, and its appropriate and adequate protection. In the case of assessing Second World War remains, this has involved firstly original research, largely among records at the Public Records Office, to establish what was built, where, when and why; secondly protecting a selection of surviving sites, determined by, for example, their rarity, typicality and the quality of their remains; and thirdly disseminating the results of this work to a wide audience. This last is arguably the most important of these, as public support and understanding are essential prerequisites in assuring the long-term future of the comparatively few surviving sites.

Given the various objectives this survey has sought to achieve, the books contain both historical details, pertaining to the political and strategic developments of the time, and archaeological details of design, distribution and chronology. In each of the books a final chapter describes some of the very few sites surviving today.

Since the 1970s, and especially over the past decade, public interest in these often ugly and unprepossessing remains has grown significantly. Recently English Heritage has led the way in developing our knowledge of them and in protecting a selection of those sites that remain. Making this research widely available is the important final stage.

Sir Neil Cossons
Chairman, English Heritage

Preface

Students of the more clandestine arts of war are familiar with the notion that military deception can be conceived on two levels: the strategic and the tactical. The contrast between them is often sharp. Strategic deception is essentially a branch of intelligence work. It uses multifarious techniques to falsify the big picture of war, so misleading an adversary over the strength of forces, their dispositions, and what is likely to be done with them.[1] Operations typically extend over months or even years, laying a pattern of false clues across a continental canvas through the activities of agents and diplomats, signals traffic, and displays of troops and equipment, real and false. Strategic deception targets the higher command, and as an adjunct to diplomacy and politics in their broadest definitions can, and does, occur as much in peace as in war. Tactical deception, on the other hand, is a phenomenon of the battlefield. It works at the point of contact between attacker and attacked, playing on the susceptibilities of the fighting man and leading him to waste bombs, ammunition and possibly his life in attacks on bogus targets, or decoys. Strategic deceptions in twentieth-century wars have often been decisive in major operations, and this by itself explains the weighty volume of historical writing which they command today.[2] But tactical deception, though often equally successful in its own terms, has been less closely studied; and this is certainly true of Britain's bombing decoys in the Second World War.

In part this is explained by the sensitivity of the subject. At the end of the war it was ruled that information on military deception must remain secret, so while historians of the 1950s and '60s could mention that Britain had used decoy targets to divert German bombing, nothing could be said of their technology, numbers or locations. Secrecy lingered into the late 1970s. Though many official papers from the 1939–1945 war were released to public inspection in 1973, the decoy files remained closed for at least a further four years. Charles Cruickshank was the first to exploit the newly-opened material, if briefly, in his general study of Second World War deception published in 1979,[3] and subsequently decoy targets have been touched upon in several books and articles of more or less academic character.[4] But no full-length study has yet appeared, and still less one which maps the complete national system of decoys, explores their design and mechanics in depth, and – as this book does – tabulates the position of each site, and explores what has survived of them today.

Our interest in the modern survival of these sites is explained by the origins of this study, which began not as a conventional history, but more as a circumscribed project to assess how much had survived of Britain's wartime defence fabric in general. In the early 1990s, growing public and academic interest in this field led English Heritage, through its Monuments Protection Programme, to commission new research on twentieth-century fortifications, ultimately to permit a range of surviving sites to be protected under statute as historical monuments, just as we would protect Roman forts or medieval castles.[5] At first confined to England, this work began in 1994 with the aim of recovering gazetteers of locations and studying the structural characteristics of sites in several categories, decoys among them. Good returns from the English research led its geographical element to be extended to Wales, Scotland and Northern Ireland, with the result that we now have, for the first time, UK-wide maps of most of the major components of Britain's wartime defences, and more selective pictures of several others.

This book is the first of a series presenting the findings of this research. Together, the volumes show how the sites and structures of Britain's wartime defences were designed, how their geographical patterning evolved in preparation for and during the war, what part they played in operations, and – equally importantly – what remains of their fabric today. These aims are complementary, for it is the historical interest of these sites which ultimately justifies their preservation as monuments – unlovely as they often are compared to the architecturally distinguished fortifications of earlier eras.

The historical interest of the decoy programme rests partly on the immensity of its scale. In the Second World War decoys were provided for a huge range of targets, beginning early in 1940 with the RAF's airfields and extending over the following three years to embrace towns and cities, naval and army installations, industrial and communications targets, oil refineries and, ultimately, the embarkation points built to serve the cross-Channel amphibious operations which culminated in *Overlord* during the summer of 1944. Altogether, some 797 sites were occupied by decoys in the United Kingdom, among which were distributed around 1100 decoys of various types. And they worked. Calculations made at the end of the war suggested that, weight for weight, around 5 per cent of the German bombing effort against the UK had been diverted by decoys, in operations ranging from minor diversions to heavy raids almost completely displaced. Though no one knew so at the time, those whose lives were saved by diverting this weight of bombs – more than 2500 people, by the Air Ministry's calculations – owed some of their thanks to the cinema technicians who had entertained them in the years immediately before the war. Much in the decoy programme was unorthodox, and nothing more so than the arrangements under which the sites were designed and built. Dummy aircraft and buildings, artificial fires and deceptive lighting all stemmed from an Air Ministry team working jointly with Sound City Films at Shepperton Studios. The decoy programme thus gives us one example of the collaborative effort between military and civilian typical of twentieth-century conflict, and in no small part their technology reflects how the arts in peace came to serve the art of war.

Acknowledgements

Among the many people who assisted in the preparation of this book, I owe a particular debt to five whose work is directly represented in its pages. Naomi Tummons and Geoff Harrison acted successively as research assistants for the original project on which the book is based, from 1995 to 1997 handling the cartographic work on English site locations represented in Appendix I. Neil Redfern extended this work to the remainder of the United Kingdom in 1997–98, both by processing data and undertaking a substantial body of original research.[1] Michael J Anderton of English Heritage's Aerial Survey Team at Swindon then undertook follow-on work to investigate the survival of sites on the ground (as described in Chapter 8) and, as one result, identified most of the aerial photographs which appear in these pages. Just as the plates owe much to Mike's research, so the line drawings are to the credit of Allan T Adams, of English Heritage's office in York, who despite joining the project at a late stage set an impeccable standard of draughtsmanship for the series as a whole.

Research among primary sources was undertaken largely at the Public Record Office, Kew, and in secondary materials at the Cambridge University Library, to both of whose staff I owe thanks. The PRO also gave permission to reproduce the Crown Copyright photographs appearing here as Plates 2, 6, 8–10, 14–17 and 19. Further assistance was kindly provided by the Royal Air Force Museum, by Colonel M R Cooper of the Royal Engineers Institute (who arranged for the supply of Plate 1), and by the British Film Institute. Within English Heritage the project was overseen for the

Monuments Protection Programme by Dr John Schofield, while Jeremy Lake represented the Listing Team. For their support throughout I also owe debts to Dr Geoffrey Wainwright (formerly Chief Archaeologist), Graham Fairclough (head of the Monuments Protection Programme) and Val Horsler, of Publications Branch. I am most grateful to Sir Neil Cossons for contributing the Foreword. Others who assisted in various ways were Carol Pyrah and Fred Nash, together with Max Eilenberg and Eleanor Rees at Methuen. Roger Thomas kindly supplied Plates 22–25, while the remaining photographs are derived from the National Monuments Record. Lastly, I join with English Heritage in expressing warm thanks to the Royal Commission on the Ancient and Historical Monuments of Scotland, Cadw (Welsh Historic Monuments), and the Department of the Environment (Northern Ireland) for authority to publish the results of the research which, under their sponsorship, extended the geographical aspect of this study to the remainder of the United Kingdom.

Colin Dobinson
North Yorkshire
July 2000

List of figures

List of plates

List of Abbreviations

AA	Anti-aircraft
AHB	Air Historical Branch
AOC-in-C	Air Officer Commanding-in-Chief
ARP	Air Raid Precautions
ASQL	Assault QL
AWAS	Air Warfare Analysis Section
C&D	Concealment and Decoy
CAS	Chief of the Air Staff
COSSAC	Chief of Staff to the Supreme Allied Commander
COXE	Combined Operations Experimental Establishment
DCAS	Deputy Chief of the Air Staff
FUSAG	First United States Army Group
GCI	Ground Controlled Interception
HE	High explosive
IRA	Irish Republican Army
K (site)	Day decoy airfield
KGr	Kampfgruppe
LCA	Landing craft assault
LCS	London Controlling Section
LCT	Landing craft tanks
MoHS	Ministry of Home Security
MPP	Monuments Protection Programme
MQL	Mobile QL
Q (site)	Lighting decoy for airfields
QF (site)	Small fire decoy
QL (site)	Lighting decoy
RAF	Royal Air Force
RFC	Royal Flying Corps
SF	Starfish
TI	Target indicator
TSF	Temporary Starfish
USAAF	United States Army Air Force
VE	Victory in Europe (Day)
VISTRE	Visual Inter-Services Training and Research Establishment
WAAF	Women's Auxiliary Air Force

CHAPTER 1

Substance
and shadow

MAY 1938 – AUGUST 1939

The war of 1939–45 was the first in which Britain operated a nationally co-ordinated system of decoy targets to mislead enemy bombers. As far as such judgements can ever be made, it will probably be the last. The decoy sites which began to appear throughout the British Isles from spring 1940 were designed to meet a form of attack in which aircraft operating in numbers delivered bombs on a range of targets and in which – most importantly – the majority of those bombs were visually aimed. World War Two was distinctively, and predictably, that kind of war. Preparations for attacks of this kind started during the mid 1930s, when Britain's air defences began their long haul of expansion to meet the rise of Hitler's Luftwaffe. Civil defence planning got under way in 1935, radar reached an elementary operational state in the following two years, and by the time war was declared Britain could call upon a serviceable layout of anti-aircraft guns and barrage balloons. Throughout the late 1930s, the Royal Air Force itself was steadily enlarged. But tactical deception was almost entirely overlooked. It was summer 1938 before any government department began to study the value of decoys in a future war.

The Air Ministry was the first to do so, followed by the Home Office, but it was only after the Munich crisis in September that either made any headway with preparations. In many ways it is surprising that they left it so late. These departments were responsible for the two main groups of targets – respectively the airfields and the cities – which by 1938 had long been recognised as Germany's prime bombing objectives. The deepening fear of government and people alike in the late 1930s was that the next war would begin with shattering air attacks, delivering a 'knock-out blow' which would neutralise the RAF and leave the cities in ruins and the morale of their people broken. The portents were grave enough. Germany launched 103 air raids against Britain in the Great War, in which 300 tons of bombs left around 5000 casualties.[1] On average, each ton of bombs killed sixteen people, and for all that these were mainly civilians, the death-toll was trivial by the standards, say, of the Western Front. Yet the figures mislead, as averages always do. More than 800 people had been harmed in just two especially sharp raids on London in summer 1917, when the average for those killed or injured by each ton of bombs rose to 121. Twenty years on, Air Ministry analysts believed that 600 tons of bombs might fall daily in the next war – double the weight dropped in the whole of the last – yielding slaughter on a massive scale. Early in 1937 the Air Staff foretold 200,000 urban casualties weekly from bombing, a third of whom would die.[2] Worse, it was believed that with herculean effort the Luftwaffe might lift and deliver a fearsome 3500 tons of bombs in the first 24 hours. This, if it fell, would be the knock-out blow.

One reason for the neglect of decoy planning until the year before World War Two can be found in the resistance shown to the technique during the Great War, at least in the home theatre, which left little solid experience to draw upon. By spring 1916 Zeppelins had been raiding Britain for more than a year, time enough for the Royal Naval Air Service, who took charge of Britain's air defences for the first eighteen months of war, to gather impressions of their habits and weaknesses. Bombing visually and carrying minimal aids to navigation, Zeppelins showed themselves to be easily misled. Writing to the Admiralty in early March 1916, the Rear Admiral Commanding at Immingham reported his impression that vessels making landfall across the east coast were 'frequently quite uncertain as to their exact positions, and having once made land were inclined to steer for the first group of lights and drop their bombs there.'[3] This tendency, argued the Admiral, could readily be exploited by laying out lighting displays replicating towns to act as bait. In practically every respect – including the idea that railway signal lamps could be used to represent marshalling yards – this far-sighted plan prefigured a type of urban decoy lighting introduced in 1941, known as the QL site. But pre-figure was all it did, for the Admiralty appears to have done nothing with the scheme during the war.

The Immingham plan for decoy towns was only one of several suggestions reaching the Admiralty in 1916, all of them working towards similar ends. In mid March another came in from the naval base at Lowestoft, whose staff had found that flares lit on the navy's night landing ground at Holt had drawn numerous bombs from a passing airship. Though airfields were not in themselves prime targets for Zeppelin attacks, it was argued that dummy airfields laid out with flares would probably draw opportunistic attacks.[4] Supporting evidence came later in the year. In early August the night landing ground at Burgh Castle on the north Norfolk coast was lit as bait for a Zeppelin hovering in the area, so enabling an aircraft loitering overhead to home in on the raider.[5] The ruse worked, and while the landing ground was lit chiefly to lure the airship into the fighter's path, it again confirmed that airfield flares (real or otherwise) could attract Zeppelin commanders. The Admiralty went as far as to investigate this incident, which was paralleled by another at Redcar, but resistance remained.

It is possible that the Admiralty may have done more with these suggestions had their responsibility for domestic air defence continued, but, as this duty was formally transferred to the Royal Flying Corps in February 1916, by the time the recommendations were made to the Admiralty matters were already passing out of their hands. There is no evidence that the RFC used dummy airfields in Britain, but their value was amply demonstrated in the harsher climate of the Western Front, when in 1918 the men of 54 Night Bombing and Fighting Wing began to lay false flarepaths to deflect night attacks from their landing grounds. Sited around two miles from their genuine 'parent' stations, lit with paraffin flares and accompanied by small clusters of softly-illuminated dummy buildings, these decoys attracted many bombs, though supervision reportedly proved 'dangerous and nerve-racking' for their six-man crews.[6] Dummy airfields for daylight use, too, were built across the Channel, and proved practicable largely through the simplicity of their genuine counterparts: with no permanent buildings or solid runways, these stations could be mocked up with tents, hutting and a few derelict aeroplanes on a suitable field. Apart from vindicating the basic idea of decoy airfields, the French experience established the principle, only slowly overturned as World War Two approached, that these contrivances were a local responsibility, not a matter for central control.

Although World War One demonstrated the tactical value of decoys, after the Armistice no fresh study of the technique was made for nearly fifteen years. In 1932 the Air Ministry convened a conference on decoy matters whose main result was a technical paper summarising the wartime work in France.[7] Authoritative as it was, once written this treatise was simply filed and all but forgotten. Until 1938 the idea that decoys might be of use in a future war only seldom arose. One instance came in January 1937, when Alexander Korda of London Films approached the Air Ministry with the offer that his staff and studio at Denham might be embodied into a part-time air defence unit, such as an anti-aircraft battery or searchlight company, of the kind then forming widely in the territorial forces. Korda's public-spirited proposal was quashed by bureaucratic quibbles (such units could form only at established drill-halls), but on visiting him to discuss the idea Air Ministry representatives were struck by the alternative potentialities of Denham Studios, whose vast workshops, stages and 2000 powerful lights could plainly be pressed into some kind of war service, likewise the expertise of its staff. 'These men are specialists at "make believe",' reported the inspecting officers, 'and [in] deception in defeating both the eye and the camera. They possess the workmen, material and shops to build jerry constructions for deception purposes.'[8] So they did, and in time the film industry would provide the technical know-how underlying Britain's entire decoy programme. But not yet. The most instructive outcome of the visit was the attitudes discovered among the many foreign nationals to be met around Denham early in 1937. Believing war to be imminent, many expatriate staff were living with their 'bags packed'. One German girl told disturbing stories of developments in her Rhineland home, where everyone – including women and the elderly – had been allocated a war job and the young men told where to join up.

Although the report on the Denham visit was carefully filed away for reference, more than a year remained before the Air Ministry would capitalise upon it in drawing up plans to protect the airfields which, by the late 1930s, were looking increasingly vulnerable to attack. In order to understand the problem facing the Air Ministry at this time we need to look briefly at the type of service which the RAF had become in the period from 1934, when expansion to meet German rearmament began.[9] This was largely a bomber force, shaped by the belief that offensive operations were the proper business of independent air forces, and that defence against the bomber could never be more than partial, at most. Rooted in the experience of the First World War, this doctrine was developed by theorists of the 1920s to the point where, by the early '30s, the self-defending bomber formation was widely seen as a more or less irresistible instrument of war. It was Stanley Baldwin who voiced this orthodoxy most famously when he warned in November 1932 that the bomber would 'always get through'; there was 'no power on earth', Baldwin declared, that could prevent the British people from being bombed: security lay in maintaining a counter-force able to retaliate in kind.[10] By the 1930s this was the RAF's *raison d'être*.

That said, the military value of the RAF expansion schemes of the mid 1930s is today widely questioned.[11] Their main weakness was aircraft. Once the Baldwin government was committed to maintaining 'parity' with the expanding Luftwaffe, squadrons had to be equipped simply by ordering whatever was available. Many new units of 1935–37 formed with obsolescent aircraft, while the force as a whole included many types poorly matched to their war role – Hawker Hind light bombers, for example, commanded insufficient range to operate over Germany (or at least to do so and return), and in any case lifted a tiny payload. Britain's new generation of war-winning monoplane fighters began to trickle into the squadrons only at the end of the 1930s – Hurricanes from December 1937, Spitfires in August 1938[12] – while the most advanced bombers available before war broke out were twin-engined Hampdens, Whitleys and Wellingtons. The four-engined heavy bombers which would devastate Germany's cities in the later war years entered service only in 1941, by which time most of the aircraft which had equipped squadrons in 1935–37 had long been scrapped.

Despite the shortcomings of the RAF's early expansion schemes, rearmament in 1935–37 did give the RAF one sturdy asset destined to serve it well for years to come: a huge stock of new airfields, which opened in numbers from 1936 onwards. Before the expansion programme the RAF's squadrons were spread between fewer than 50 flying stations, practically all of them in permanent fabric and many of Great War origin, if substantially rebuilt. By early 1938 around 40 new airfields of 1930s design were either complete, under construction, or awaiting development. Added to its pre-expansion stock, by the time war began the RAF could call upon over 100 permanent airfields, the majority designed for bombers and the larger share originating in the previous five years (Fig 1). Building up a bomber force to fly against Germany gave an eastern orientation to the new stations, which by gradual accretion came to dominate the counties from Suffolk to Northumberland, with concentrations in Lincolnshire and Yorkshire. Though surfaced only with grass and distinctly cramped by later standards, these new stations were at least seedlings for the growth to come. And that growth was huge: by 1945 there were 740 military airfields in the UK.

Protecting the new stations against air attack was a growing concern throughout the expansion period, and while the most determined measures belonged to the eve of war itself, safeguards against air attack were embedded in their fabric from the start. Station defence relied partly on conventional camouflage – 1930s airfields were generously planted with trees and Virginia creeper chiefly to soften the outlines of their buildings – but more so on the principle of *dispersal*. Since the mid 1920s new RAF stations had been planned with generous separations between buildings, which individually were kept small to restrict casualties from a direct hit. During the 1930s these structural measures were enhanced by introducing dispersal for parked aircraft, both within and between stations. By early 1936 it was accepted that hangar buildings would have only limited use in war, since aircraft gathered together under one roof might be destroyed wholesale by a single well-placed bomb. Instead, they would be dotted around the perimeter of the airfield at prepared points – soon known as 'dispersals' – which later came to be supplied with hutting, shelters and hard

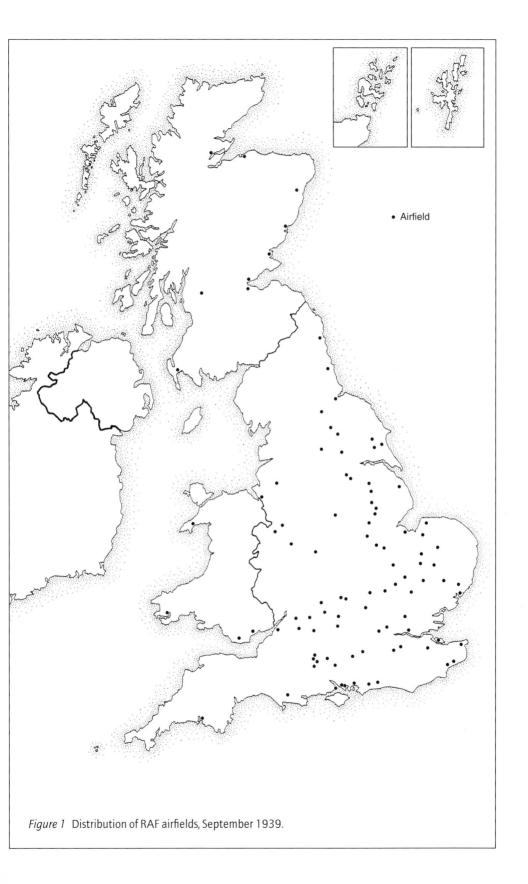

Figure 1 Distribution of RAF airfields, September 1939.

surfaces linked up to runways and perimeter tracks. At the same time it was decided to carry dispersal to its logical conclusion by finding sites for complete secondary airfields – 'satellites' – to which aircraft could be hurriedly scattered under threat of war.[13] At first the Air Ministry expected to find satellites from among Britain's growing complement of civil aerodromes, which brought the obvious advantage of being ready-prepared for aircraft. Where no civil airfield existed within ten miles of a permanent station, however, it was accepted that 'farmers' fields' would be earmarked and, in war, given basic facilities for aircraft. As things turned out, the civil aerodrome building boom expected during the 1930s never fully materialised,[14] so unprepared fields came to be widely selected as satellites. By the summer of 1938 most of the sites had been found.

In the later years of the expansion programme the security provided by camouflage and dispersal was supplemented by new measures, notably the redesign of buildings to resist bombs, the building of air-raid shelters, and the provision – at first only in theory – of anti-aircraft guns. And it was in this climate of quickening preparation that in May 1938, Group Captain F J Linnell, the Air Ministry's Deputy Director of War Operations, suggested that the time had come for the Air Staff to settle policy on whether decoy airfields would have a place in a future war.[15]

Made four months before Munich, Linnell's suggestion began a debate which would run for nearly eighteen months before any decoy site was actually commissioned, and during which time two branches of the Air Ministry began to study the problem independently. For the first six months nothing happened – Linnell did not even receive a reply to his question,[16] which was cast as an official minute – and it was only when the Munich crisis broke in September 1938 that serious thinking began. When it did so it was the RAF's operational formation which provided the impetus. At the end of September Bomber Command's 4 Group sought guidance on what, if anything, was to be done about decoys, only to be assured by their command headquarters six weeks later that building dummy airfields would be impracticable in a future war.[17] In this same week, Coastal Command approached the Air Ministry advocating that a policy of building daytime decoy airfields should be adopted without delay.[18] On the model of the previous war, the prevailing assumption in this correspondence was that any decoy measures deemed necessary would be arranged locally, by RAF units, rather than under central control. In these circumstances it was clear by December 1938 that stations must be told exactly what was expected of them. Formal discussions accordingly passed between Air Ministry officials in December, before the question was referred to Sir Cyril Newall, the Chief of the Air Staff, in January 1939. Newall was positive, and in the first week of February word duly came down from his office that the RAF should plan to establish daytime decoy airfields near its operational stations, using fields and open spaces scattered with dummy or obsolete aircraft, and that a 'system of lights' should be developed for use at night. Elementary as it was, Newall's ruling marked the Air Ministry's first commitment, at least in principle, to using decoy airfields in the coming war.[19] That war, by now, lay seven months away.

As these discussions were taking place, however, decoy planning of another kind was also under way elsewhere. Although Linnell's successor would not learn of these developments until the following spring, in the late summer of 1938 the Air Staff decided to investigate the technicalities of producing dummy aircraft – rather than sites, lights or other devices – to serve an as yet undefined daytime deception plan for airfields. The Air Ministry's usual procedure when introducing a new item of equipment was to invite tenders from commercial firms against a specification, and on 14 September 1938 a brief for the design of dummy aircraft was duly produced in draft. As it happened this was the day before Chamberlain made his first visit to Hitler, and the distraction of the events surrounding Munich may explain why the document was not recast in its final form until the middle of December.[20] Elaborated and refined, Specification 23/38 was issued by the Directorate of Technical Development on 6 January 1939, at this stage only to aircraft manufacturers and others already bound by the rules of confidentiality governing secret contracts.[21] Firms were invited to tender for three types of dummy: a fighter, to resemble the Hurricane, a light bomber, based upon the Fairey

Battle, and – the most ambitious – a twin-engined bomber resembling the Whitley. The basic requirement was for cheap and durable dummies, easily erected and dismantled, which looked right and cast realistic shadows.

Whether Newall himself knew that tenders had already been invited for dummy aircraft is unclear, though nothing in his ruling given in February 1939 suggests that he did. More certain is that the officers responsible for taking the decoy project further were unacquainted with progress on this front, and towards the end of February the idea was abroad that Maintenance Command might be approached to advise upon or supply dummy aircraft.[22] That confusion aside, in putting details to the policy the Air Staff's first problem was to decide what sorts of stations, in which locations, could be replicated by decoys given available funds, manpower and time. An early decision, never revoked, was that mimicking the permanent stations in which the RAF had become so richly provided over the previous five years was simply impractical. With their complex layouts of hangars, buildings and roads, these places were impossible to shadow with day decoys without massive investment in time and materials. In any case, the Germans already knew the whereabouts of the permanent stations, and also that they took two or three years to build. New sites appearing overnight, like mushrooms, would be self-evidently bogus. The satellites introduced under the dispersal policy of spring 1936, on the other hand, offered better models for daylight decoys, and in this respect the shortage of civil aerodromes for this purpose now appeared to be an advantage. Since the farmers' fields chosen in some numbers since 1936 would metamorphose into satellite simply by the arrival of aircraft, tented accommodation and a few lorryloads of equipment, faking them was a practical proposition. And, it was believed, they would probably draw bombs. The Air Staff assumed at this time (wrongly, as it turned out) that attacks against the RAF on the ground would hit satellites as hard as permanent stations, so dummy satellites equipped with fake or obsolete aircraft therefore made good tactical sense. And, unlike the permanent stations, the positions of satellites would remain secret until war began: assuming good security, German intelligence would have no way of distinguishing between a newly-occupied satellite and a decoy from prior information.

Night decoy airfields were a simpler proposition. From the start the Air Staff realised that misleading hostile aircrews in darkness would be much easier than by day, just as it had been in the previous war, but potentially at the cost of serious confusion to RAF pilots. Relying merely on a pattern of lights aping those of a true airfield, night decoys could be laid out more or less anywhere. Communications (probably a telephone) were necessary to co-ordinate lighting at the real airfield and its shadow, which the preliminary thinking of spring 1939 saw functioning together, with the decoy doubling as a kind of holding point for aircraft waiting to land. Flying actually in progress around a decoy, with aircraft orbiting as if in the 'circuit' which pilots generally fly before lining-up on the runway, would add to the ruse. This kind of thinking suggested that every airfield likely to operate in darkness would need a night decoy, possibly co-located with the day site, but more likely separate.

These were the Air Staff's initial thoughts, committed to paper in late February 1939 and circulated to Bomber, Fighter and Coastal Commands for comment in early March.[23] Only one response was at all negative.[24] Responding for Fighter Command, Air Chief Marshal Sir Hugh Dowding argued that, while decoys might be all very well, 'the substance should be provided before the shadow', and real airfields brought fully up to scratch before surrogates were begun. He had a point. As Dowding was careful to explain, Fighter Command in spring 1939 remained under-provided with satellites, no permanent airfield had yet been provided with a solid runway allowing all-weather operations, and four front-line stations – Turnhouse, Usworth, Kenley and Hendon – urgently required extensions to operate Hurricanes or Spitfires. Dowding was also troubled by the threat which decoys might pose to civilians, especially for stations such as Kenley which were already embedded in suburban sprawl. Dowding, as we shall see, would later become mildly fixated on the Air Ministry's decoy arrangements, and in particular on the priority given them relative to other things. But in the circumstances of spring 1939, his anxiety that effort might be diverted from readying his airfields for war was prudent enough.

Others were more positive. Although Coastal Command shared Dowding's concern over the relative priority given to decoys and real airfields, they enthusiastically endorsed the idea of night dummies and declared themselves ready to begin searching for sites immediately.[25] Day decoys, they felt, might usefully be combined with genuine satellites, the site alternating between a decoy or a real landing ground as circumstances required (an idea that the Air Ministry immediately ruled out, though it would later reappear). Coastal Command were the first to suggest that decoy provision should be bounded by definite geographical limits. Their recommendation – a decoy area east of a line linking Portland with London, Glasgow and Montrose – was expanded by the Air Ministry to a border running from Southampton up to Birmingham and thence to Perth. Perhaps because some kind of decoy system was now Air Staff policy, Bomber Command reversed their thinking of November 1938, when they had dismissed decoy airfields as impracticable.[26] Night decoys, they recommended, should have electric lights replicating the full range found on a real airfield, together with an operating shelter with telephone, while day sites should use purpose-built dummy aircraft rather than cast-offs from the squadrons; further, a special organisation should take care of decoy sites to lessen the burden on station commanders, and central equipment stores should be established up and down the country. All of these ideas would later be assimilated to Air Ministry practice.

Operational commands had been asked to return their views on the Air Staff paper by the end of March, and as these were coming in Linnell's successor, Group Captain R P M Whitham, sought the advice of the Directors of Equipment and Operational Requirements on the supply of dummy aircraft.[27] It was at this point that the two independent strands of development – one of sites, the other of dummies – began to converge. Rather, we must imagine, to Whitham's surprise, on 27 March Group Captain Robert Saundby, then serving as Director of Operational Requirements, forwarded a copy of the September draft of Specification 23/38 with the news that at least two sets of prices for the Hurricanes, Battles and Whitleys had already been tendered.[28] At this news, the staff who had been husbanding decoy policy realised that what had hitherto been a looming problem was already some way towards solution. But not quite. As tenders continued to flow in during the late spring it became clear that the prices offered far exceeded the budget likely to be available. They were also wildly varied. The cheapest quoted were £377 for the Whitley, £116 for the Battle and £105 for the Hurricane, though one firm had costed the Whitley dummy at more than £1800 and another had suggested that a Battle mock-up could not be supplied for under £800. Even the lowest of these figures was about double what the Air Ministry, at the end of May, decided it could afford to pay. The problem, simply, was that aircraft manufacturers knew how to make aircraft, not dummies. Fabricating something to resemble an aeroplane without the complexity and expense of conventional airframe engineering was something they had never previously been called upon to do.

Faced with these costings, at the end of May Group Captain D P Stevenson suggested that film companies should be asked to assist in drafting a new specification for the dummy aircraft and, perhaps, even to tender for their manufacture.[29] The early work in this direction was now recognised as something of a false start. That aside, however, assimilating the responses of the commands enabled Air Staff policy on decoy airfields to be settled formally in early June.[30] Decoys, it was decided, would lie east of the Southampton–Birmingham–Perth line, where day sites resembling satellites would be built for each permanent station and night sites for airfields of all kinds. Positions would be chosen before the outbreak of war, avoiding villages and other settled areas – a concession to Dowding – and would be operated by crews supplied by their parent stations. Dummy aircraft production would also be re-examined, while night decoy lighting systems would be given practical trials. In June 1939 no one knew with any certainty how much time remained for this work, but there was little sense of urgency. In another concession to Dowding, the Air Staff decreed in June that readying satellites and real aerodromes must come first.

A fortnight or so before the Air Ministry settled its policy on decoy airfields, the Home Office began its own independent trials of deceptive lighting to protect the cities from night bombing. In doing so they, like the Air Ministry, were making a laggardly start. By the summer of 1939, preparations to harden the cities against the knock-out blow had been underway for more than four years. An Air Raid Precautions Department had been formed by the Home Office as early as April 1935 with a remit to study structural and other protective measures against incendiaries, high explosive and poison gas, though for a variety of reasons – chiefly the absence of legislation obliging local authorities and others to act – civil defence preparations before Munich were often piecemeal and half-hearted. From an early stage, however, the ARP Department took a keen interest in lighting restrictions as a means of masking towns, and targets within them, from the eyes of hostile bomber crews. Trials with blackouts and restricted lighting were held in 1936 and 1937, with some success, and in February 1938 local authorities were advised that the outbreak of war would bring a general 'darkening' of cities, in which householders, businesses and factories would be responsible for masking their own lighting. There was never any expectation, however, that blackout could be perfected. Heavy manufacturing processes which could not readily be interrupted were almost impossible to conceal, along with marshalling yards, while houses, shops and factories would always be liable to some 'leakage' of light, despite the wearyingly keen attentions of Air Raid Wardens. Lighting restrictions would always be something of a compromise.

In years to come the inherent imperfections of blackout – through 'exempted' and 'leaky' lighting – would be played upon in the design of sophisticated decoys for towns, much as recommended in 1916. But the Home Office's first foray into deceptive lighting exploited these weaknesses in a rather different way. Rather than mimicking the pilot's view of an imperfectly blacked-out town – so 'displacing' the target in the direction of the approaching bomber – these first trials were designed to conceal the faint pinpricks of light showing from a town by smothering it in an array of artificial lights spreading for many miles around. This 'baffle lighting' technique saw its first tests around the Humber on the night of 20/21 May 1939, when no fewer than 4000 hurricane lamps were laid out on a grid (at half-mile intervals) on either side of the Estuary, stretching well into eastern Yorkshire and Lincolnshire.[31] A Whitley bomber was sent out from Dishforth to observe the result, which the crew and representatives from the ARP Department found strangely convincing: chinks of light

showing from Beverley – specially darkened for the experiment –
proved indistinguishable from the hurricane lamps, whose regular
layout gave the odd sense of 'flying permanently over a large town
which had not been successfully blacked out. A most confusing situation was produced by the impression that the town moved along
with the aeroplane as it flew [. . .]'.[32] Buoyed by this result, the
Home Office was keen to run further tests, ultimately with the
idea of establishing a national baffle system to smother the entire
country with a carpet of twinkling lights. But nothing further was
done, and a moment's thought is perhaps sufficient to grasp why.
Though it may not have been the most eccentric air defence
notion of the pre-war years – this was an era of lively inventiveness
– the scheme to supply the whole island with a half-mile grid of
hurricane lamps was plainly ludicrous. The Home Office's lighting
experiments were suspended on the outbreak of war, to resurface
later in more practical form. Dubious as they were, however – and
simple to the point of naivety when compared to the lighting
decoys which eventually protected Britain's cities – the Humber
lamps did mark the first practical tests of deceptive lighting held
by a government department before the war. Oddly, and despite
the involvement of an RAF crew, the Air Ministry seems to have
known little about them.

Back at the Air Ministry, the airfield decoy policy settled in early
June 1939 was allowed to languish in the three months remaining
before the war. A new specification for dummy aircraft was drawn
up at the end of the month,[33] but little or nothing appears to have
been done with it during peacetime, and as July turned to August,
and war seemed increasingly imminent, some officials in the Air
Ministry were becoming restive at the prospect of bombs falling
before any decoy arrangements were in place. Though commands
had been acquainted with the Air Staff decoy policy in July, no
personnel had been made available, no one had been trained, and
no specialist equipment had been designed. In these circumstances on 25 August Group Captain Stevenson asked somewhat
desperately whether there was 'any hope' of finding material to
make ad hoc preparations for simple night decoys.[34] But this came

to nothing. As Dowding had wished, substance eclipsed shadow in the summer of 1939. At least six new permanent stations opened between June and early September, while building was accelerated at others authorised under the final peacetime expansion schemes. Further satellites were acquired, and work begun on the long-awaited project to furnish fighter stations with solid runways. Added to a host of lesser war preparations, activity on all of these fronts nudged decoy planning to the sidelines.

On 29 August 1939 the Air Ministry warned operational RAF commands that in the event of hostilities breaking out – hostilities which now lay four days away – a much attenuated set of airfield decoy measures should be put in hand. With nothing done to supply dummy aircraft or any other props, day decoys would be deferred. Instead, working to the Southampton–Perth line, commands were instructed to shadow each airfield with an improvised night decoy using obsolete paraffin flares. Such was the position on 8 September 1939, when, five days after Britain entered the war, decoy arrangements were formally activated by an Air Ministry signal. Reporting heavy air attacks on aerodromes and aircraft factories in Poland, the Air Ministry urged Fighter, Bomber and Coastal Commands to 'press ahead' with the 'urgent provision' of decoy airfields in line with the latest Air Ministry instructions.[35]

Despite sixteen months' planning for this moment, the instructions in force on 8 September 1939 called for a layout of decoys which was actually far less sophisticated than that used in France in 1918. And in many respects – such as limiting decoys to night sites based only on flares – these orders significantly modified the agreements struck with commands only six months previously. In those circumstances it was unsurprising that some officers questioned their orders. At Bomber Command, Air Chief Marshal Sir Edgar Ludlow-Hewitt referred them directly back to the Air Ministry, reiterating his view of November 1938 that flares were of dubious value in night decoys and urging that day sites should be kept within the plan.[36] On 17 September Dowding authorised his group commanders merely to 'grant or withhold' permission for stations to use dummy paraffin flarepaths as they saw fit.[37] By this time at least one had already done so. This was Wittering, where Dowding warned other commands that a dummy flarepath had been laid, and that the crew would flash a signal at any RAF aircraft which, mistaking it for a real airfield, might attempt to land. But, as Ludlow-Hewitt soon reminded the Air Ministry, the warning specified – a steady red light – already had a different meaning in the vocabulary of RAF signalling. By mid September a situation was developing in which commands were working independently (if they were working at all) without procedures for advertising their actions. It was plain that duplication of effort, waste and accidents would soon result.

It was in the midst of these exchanges that Air Chief Marshal Sir Wilfrid Freeman suggested to a routine Air Council meeting on 13 September that the Air Ministry might consider providing decoys for RAF airfields, as well as factories and other targets.[38] On the face of things it is difficult to credit that the Air Council, as late as the second week of war, was unaware that decoy planning had been active in the Air Ministry for more than a year. Yet the sense of Freeman's contribution leaves little doubt that this was so. In fact, the officers working on decoy policy had long intended to refer a paper to the Air Council; they had last mentioned doing so in mid August, though for some reason never did. But once the RAF's supreme governing body examined the question, as they did only briefly on 13 September, the practicalities of decoy organisation were immediately settled. Ludlow-Hewitt had earlier suggested that decoy matters 'might well be placed in [the] charge of a retired officer with drive and initiative and organised independently of any RAF command'. And in this, the Air Council concurred.

Plate 1 'Dictator of dummies': Colonel Sir John Turner.

CHAPTER 2

Colonel Turner's Department

SEPTEMBER 1939 – MAY 1940

In September 1939 Colonel John Fisher Turner had recently retired for the second time.[1] Born in 1881 and educated at Rugby School, Turner had been commissioned into the Royal Engineers in January 1900 to begin a colourful and varied career. He served briefly on the Gold Coast before moving to India where, apart from a spell in Mesopotamia during the Great War, he remained throughout his time in the army. Turner became Assistant Commander Royal Engineers at Ambala in 1922, beginning as he did so a long association with the civil engineering services of the RAF. By 1928 he had reached Chief Engineer to the air force in India, a post he held until his retirement from uniform at the age of fifty. His second career, as Director of Works and Buildings at the Air Ministry in London, followed immediately. Taking up this civil service appointment in the summer of 1931, Turner remained for the whole of the RAF expansion programme – an unusually lengthy tenure, at a time of unprecedented activity – overseeing the design and construction of buildings and stations and retiring, for the second time, only a month or so before the outbreak of war. Now, at fifty-eight and with no wife or family to call upon his time, he was available to begin a third career.

Turner's qualifications to take charge of the Air Ministry's decoy programme were impeccable. His knowledge of airfield planning was unrivalled. The greater part of the RAF's airfield stock as it stood in 1939 had been crafted under his supervision (not to mention special projects such as the RAF College at Cranwell) and, as a qualified pilot, Turner knew these places as well from the air as the ground. For all that, however, Turner's had not been the first name to occur to the Air Council as a candidate to head a central decoy organisation. They had first asked Lord Trenchard, who declined.[2] With hindsight it is probably as well that he did. For all his resourcefulness, by 1939 the RAF's first Chief of the Air Staff had been in retirement for almost a decade, and was certainly out of touch with the modern Air Ministry. Trenchard and Turner, however, did have one qualification in common: they shared a practical ability to get things done, and in not dissimilar ways. Turner was widely admired for his energy and efficiency, and in nearly twenty years with the RAF had become known for forthrightness and what one contemporary described as 'difficulty keeping patience with those, whatever their rank, who seem to him to be obstructive.'[3] He antagonised some, and could make enemies; but equally he enjoyed recounting the rebukes earned for overstepping the line. He enjoyed his nickname, too: 'Conky Bill' was a tribute to his strong features, and he used it himself. Turner's wiser colleagues came to identify the irascible streak with an unusually strong sense of purpose. The novelist Dennis Wheatley, who worked in strategic deception and knew Turner in the later war years, found him a 'quite exceptionally forceful and determined personality'.[4] He was usually determined to do things his own way. Years later colleagues remembered how, in India, he had somehow contrived to supply the RAF with accommodation far superior to the army's. That kind of thing won popularity. There was nothing of the bureaucrat about Turner.

Drive, initiative, readiness to work outside the system, and close familiarity with the Air Ministry's workings would all be essential to Turner's task of heading a new branch, with a novel and secret role, and building it up from scratch. He accepted the job immediately, asking only for a few days to put his affairs in order.[5] Returning to duty on 22 September, Turner was given a room in the Air Ministry's premises at Aerial House on the Strand, though for the sake of secrecy he would never enjoy an official title. In the months to come the staff which grew up around him was known simply as Colonel Turner's Department. But Turner had no staff at all in the first days, when he had principally three things to do: to set objectives for the numbers and types of sites required; to design, make and test equipment; and to arrange personnel. Probably the simplest of Turner's jobs in his first days was to read the paperwork accumulated in the decoy files. That would have taken less than an hour.

In late September 1939 no one in Britain knew that the prophecy of massive air bombardment at the start of the next war would be proved false, nor that a breathing space of nine months remained until serious attacks began. So with the knock-out blow still daily expected, the sense of urgency surrounding decoy preparations now became acute. Happily for Turner, responsibility for dummy aircraft was soon put in the hands of the Air Ministry's Director of Equipment, who in line with Stevenson's earlier suggestion asked for a new specification to be drafted jointly with Denham Studios.[6] But no sooner had these discussions begun than the Air Ministry's Research and Development (Technical) Branch revealed that they had already arranged for new tenders to be submitted against the specification of the previous December.[7] By now, designs and costings were being assembled by several firms – among them Warner Brothers and Gaumont British Studios – for dummy Hurricanes, Battles and Whitleys. Once again, poor liaison between Air Ministry branches meant that the dummies were more advanced than some involved with the job had realised. Embarrassing as this undoubtedly was for those concerned, it did mean that Turner would have the products earlier than expected.

It was to avoid such hitches that the Air Council had appointed a single officer to mastermind the decoy programme, and true to this thinking in the first weeks of his tenure Turner held a busy round of meetings with the RAF's frontline commanders to settle tactics. Discussing the question with Bomber Command on 27 September, Turner made it clear that working to a rigid policy of one day decoy airfield for each station would be impractical at first. Instead, Turner proposed to start by laying out day decoys for some of the forward bomber stations in East Anglia and Lincolnshire – the territories of Bomber Command's 4 and 5 Groups – while leaving the number of night decoys open for the time being. In an important departure from the provisional Air Staff policy, Turner decided that clearances between genuine airfields and decoys should be raised from one mile to five or six miles. There were two reasons. Crowding day decoys too close to real satellites would result in both appearing on the same German reconnaissance photograph, which might compromise the decoy by inviting direct comparison between the two. Night decoys would be kept clear of their parent stations to prevent the real airfield, though blacked-out, being exposed should an intruder drop a flare over the dummy before attacking. So, already by late September 1939, subtle tactical considerations were reshaping expectations of how decoy measures would work on the ground. Instead of closely shadowing real airfields, Turner envisaged a largely discrete pattern of sites.

These and other ideas were pulled together in Turner's first specifications for day and night decoy airfields, issued for comment in mid October.[8] Although equipment had yet to be designed and prototype dummy aircraft were still being assembled, Turner was nonetheless able to outline the general principles on which his decoys would work. Day sites, he explained, would be of two kinds, replicating either a simple 'all-way' grassed flying field, in which take-off and landing were allowed in any direction, or the more specialised 'tracked ground', usually to be created on terrain of heather or gorse, where aircraft movements were channelled onto defined strips. Sites of the first type need be no more than 800 yards square – though larger if possible – while tracked grounds could be formed from two 700 by 200 yard strips at right angles. Either type would have ten dummy aircraft, together with simple features aping those found on satellites: disturbed areas representing dumps for petrol and bombs, worn tracks suggesting activity, a windsock and 'smudge fire' showing wind direction, shelters for the crew, and machine-gun posts. On a clear day these contrivances were expected to produce a decoy 'reasonably conspicuous' from 10,000 feet at six miles' distance. Simple as these requirements sound, however, Turner was under no illusion that they would be easily fulfilled. By late 1939 many suitable sites had already been taken for airfields and satellites in the expansion schemes of the 1930s, and although the Air Ministry's periodic anxieties that the landscape was nearing 'saturation' had always proved premature, it is true that sites were becoming scarcer. Added to his difficulties in finding suitable grassed fields, Turner had to contend with alternative demands on land. Once the war began much pasture was turned over to arable, with the result that Britain's stock of grassland was daily shrinking, and with it the freedom to site decoys according to strict tactical desiderata. For these reasons Turner accepted that day decoys would often be shuffled onto to marginal land, probably on sites criss-crossed by ditches and hedges. But ditches, he explained, could always be covered with brushwood, while standing hedges might even act to advantage. Many RAF airfields had by this time been overpainted with dummy hedge lines for camouflage. If the real hedges on decoys could be made to simulate poorly-executed dummy hedges on real airfields, argued Turner, then the deception would be all the more complete.

Turner's plans for night decoys were simpler. Paraffin flarepaths were rejected in favour of electric lamps replicating the full lighting of a genuine airfield. The main feature would be a set of yellow lights imitating the T-shaped wind direction indicator – the 'wind T' – of a real airfield; four alternative wind Ts would be laid out in a cruciform pattern, with a switch to change between them according to wind direction. Four red lamps would represent the obstruction lights used to mark higher buildings and other flying hazards, while a single 'recognition light' – probably flashing green and yellow – would be lit if a friendly aircraft mistakenly attempted to land. Finally, there would be a set of car headlamps, suggesting the taxiing lights of an aircraft or a set of floodlights. In Turner's thinking of October 1939 these would be used as bait: the most powerful of the lights, they would at first be manipulated to attract a raider's attention but then be doused when an attack began. All of this apparatus would be controlled from a sunken shelter.

Unlike day sites, the night decoys could be put anywhere – even on arable, with the lights raised on poles – without regard to topography, ditches, or other features not normally visible from the air in darkness. The basic requirement was for a site five or six miles from the parent station on the expected line of a raider's approach, though there might be exceptions. Turner acknowledged that some stations near London would be hard put to find sites clear of housing, and that Coastal Command stations would need flexibility to allow for the position of the coast. Much was left to the discretion of station commanders, whose responsibility it would be to find the night decoy sites (the more exacting day sites would be found by Air Ministry teams). At some point between

Turner's drafting the site specification and its dispatch to commands on 19 October, the night lighting decoys gained a name. Presumably on the model of the navy's 'Q ships' – warships disguised
as merchantmen – the night decoys were now officially designated
'Q lightings'. They were usually known as 'Q sites'.

Although Turner's plans drew heavily upon ideas already circulating between the Air Ministry and commands, as late as October 1939 their details remained largely abstract. No lighting sets
had yet been tested, and dummy aircraft prototypes had not so far
been scrutinised from the ground or from the air. This being so, as
scouting for sites began in November, Turner's attention shifted to
equipment. Once the plans for day decoys had been settled in September, the requirement for dummy aircraft types had increased,
with the result that four separate companies were now at work on
five designs. And not all were equally successful. Touring the
country to inspect progress towards the end of October, Turner
found that only one firm had produced really convincing prototypes at a realistic cost.[9] Two engineering companies had either
overdone the detail or failed to come up with something much
resembling an aeroplane. A dummy Whitley built by North-Eastern Aircraft Components of Gateshead was found to be over-engi-
neered, with workmanship which Turner found 'far too elaborate'
and a price, quoted at £700, greatly in excess of what was afford-
able. In fairness to the company, however, it was recognised that
the firm had worked to the original, more demanding specification
– among other refinements the dummy was fully wheeled – so
Turner gave them another chance. Another engineering company,
Green Brothers of Hailsham, near Eastbourne, had built a Hurricane sound enough in basic design but with a poor covering, if at a
reasonable price. Though Warner Brothers and Korda's London
Film Company at Denham had been included in the early discussions on dummy aircraft, neither gained contracts for prototypes
and only two film studios were still working on the project. Gaumont British had come up with a moderately convincing Battle,
but by far the best offering was a Wellington built by Sound City
Films at Shepperton. 'A good job,' reported Turner, at a very afford-
able £225. The Wellington was one of the two dummy types introduced since the original specification of 1938. Sound City had
recently won the contract for work on the other – the Blenheim –

which had yet to start when Turner visited. On the model of the Wellington, though, Turner was confident of the result.

Turner's inspection in late October 1939 appears to have been his first visit to Shepperton Studios, fifteen miles west of London in what was then still a rural patch of Middlesex (and is now in Surrey). Though no one knew so at the time, a year later it would become his permanent headquarters. What lay behind this improbable convergence between a Royal Engineer colonel and a film studio was Turner's immediate admiration for Sound City's technicians, whose expertise was exemplified by the Wellington model, and for their general manager, Norman Loudon.

Nearly twenty years Turner's junior, by 1939 Loudon was already a businessman of substance. Early ventures in accountancy and merchandising had brought him, by 1925, to the managing directorship of the Camerascopes company at the remarkably young age of twenty-three.[10] While at Camerascopes Loudon had diversified into manufacturing little flicker-books for children – their images animated by flicking the pages with the thumb – usually depicting sportsmen. Loudon himself shot the stills for his flicker-books, which by 1928 had made him enough money to invest in his real interest, which was cinema. In that year he bought Littleton Park House at Shepperton, a dwelling of medieval origin rebuilt in the 1900s, with a view to founding a studio. His timing was astute. Only a year earlier the British film industry had been practically dead on its feet, unable to compete with the prolific output from Hollywood. But the situation had been saved by government intervention in the shape of the 1927 Cinematograph Films Act, which for the first time obliged exhibitors to show a specified proportion of British-made (or Empire-made) pictures, and to direct the profits back to the domestic industry. It was the resulting demand for British films which Loudon, in 1928, was poised to exploit. At the end of 1931 he expanded his base at Littleton Park House by buying up a substantial tract of adjoining land and, with this deal complete, in February 1932 founded Sound City Film Producing and Recording Studios. Loudon's choice of name advertised his facilities. The 'talkies' completely supplanted silent films in the early 1930s, and Sound City was one of the first British studios purpose-built to produce them.

In some ways Sound City was an odd studio, and many in the trade at first tended to dismiss Loudon's venture as a gaggle of dilettantes with a bit of money to waste. Certainly, Sound City's staff were unusual: no fewer than five ex-naval commanders worked there in the early days, and with its centre in a Victorian mansion, the studio had a country-house feel. Adrian Brunel, the first professional director to make a film there, found the staff to be mostly 'intelligent amateurs, sometimes kidding themselves that they were "in films" and at other times wondering whether they were not living in a world far more make-believe than the flicks.'[11] Old hands dubbed it 'Sound City for Sons of Gentlemen'. But, tough Campbeltown Scot that he was, Loudon was first and last a man of business who drove his staff hard. Brunel was forced to concede that 'Norman's vision and enterprise were justified', and so they were. Riding on the surge of demand following the 1927 Act, Sound City soon settled to making what Loudon called 'modest second features', productions known to the industry, more prosaically, as quota-quickies. Quickies made by in-house directors were Loudon's bread and butter, though from its earliest days Shepperton could attract illustrious names. W P Lipscomb's *Colonel Blood* was made there in 1933, and Korda's *Sanders of the River* in the following year. *Sanders* was one of twenty-five films made at Sound City in 1934, giving Loudon an accumulating reputation and the scope to expand. Further enlarged, Sound City was relaunched in June 1936 as a studio serving independent film-makers. From then on, Loudon produced no films himself, but let his extensive sound-stages, exterior lots, technicians and craftsmen to freelance producers and directors.

Martha Robinson joined Sound City in its infancy, working first as a secretary but soon as a continuity girl, the title which she gave to a revealing memoir published in 1937.[12] One of the surprising themes running through *Continuity Girl* is exhaustion, physical and mental. Robinson's book draws a vivid picture of young people, desperately keen for the lustre of being 'in films', living at the limit of endurance to satisfy the studio's insatiable demands for motion pictures. Today, this account of prodigious work relieved by parties and pranks has a familiar ring. At first difficult to place, it most closely recalls the war memoirs which would appear a few years later – especially those from younger hands, such as Guy Gibson's *Enemy Coast Ahead* or the more cheerful passages of Richard Hillary's *The Last Enemy*. The danger is missing, though even that was not unknown – an extra died from exposure on one of Sound City's exterior lots in the mid '30s. The truth of Martha Robinson's account is not in doubt, for it was well-documented conditions such as these which caused the film industry to become increasingly unionised during the 1930s. By 1936 Sound City's output was averaging a film a fortnight, mostly quota-quickies. Scripts could be finished barely hours before filming began. Economy, tight timetables and the resulting need to control conditions meant that film-making was largely confined to the studio, with little time for the indulgence of 'location' work. Complex sets were often built overnight, to stand for only a day.

The significance of all this is that, by the mid 1930s, staff at Sound City were already working under a regime which many in less driven occupations would not meet until wartime. Set designers, carpenters and painters became adept at contriving visual illusions cheaply and at great speed, such that scenes which would today be filmed on location – an African village, the deck of an ocean liner – were instead assembled at frantic pace as studio sets, or erected on one of the outside lots.[13] It was the veterans of these campaigns, led by Loudon's works manager, Percy Bell, that Turner met when he arrived at Shepperton in October 1939 to look over the Wellington. What he found were technicians who commanded skills identical to those of the military engineer: practical men who prided themselves on building more or less anything, more or less instantly (Turner, indeed, would always speak of Sound City's craftsmen as *engineers*). And Loudon and Turner had much in common as individuals: a shared enthusiasm for shooting, a hardy disposition – which buttressed Loudon's appetite for glamour and high living – and a strong practical sense.

In Sound City and Norman Loudon Turner found the technical bedrock on which his decoy work would rest in the following five years. And it was also true that by 1939 Loudon desperately needed new work. Sound City's output dropped sharply in the year before the war, thanks to legislative changes which reduced the demand for quickies. Ever the entrepreneur, Loudon had considered alternative uses for the Shepperton plot. His most ambitious wheeze, the Sound City Zoo and Wonderland, might have become Britain's first theme park had war not intervened. But as it was, the last pre-war film made at Sound City was Mario Zampi's *Spy for a Day*, one of only three pictures issuing from the studio in 1939. Turner discovered on his visit that Loudon had 'a large idle staff' more than ready for whatever work he could give them.[14]

Once Turner had examined the dummy aircraft prototypes in the manufacturers' works the next stage was to assemble them on real airfields to compare their appearance with that of genuine aircraft. Such was Turner's faith in Sound City's work that he immediately entrusted Loudon with scrutinising the other contractors' products on the Air Ministry's behalf. Loudon accordingly visited Green Brothers on 10 November to advise on improving the skin of their Hurricane (which was otherwise 'quite a practical job') and to Northolt, on 13 November, to look at the Battle. Loudon was less impressed with this dummy, which was fragile and poorly designed for disassembly and transport, and undertook to advise Gaumont British on refinements.[15] At the same time North-Eastern Aircraft Components' redesigned Whitley was carted down the A1 to RAF Dishforth, where it was assembled and photographed from the air alongside the real thing.[16] Together with the Gaumont British Battle, Sound City's own Wellington (Plate 2) was delivered to the bomber station at RAF Harwell, where it proved so convincing that Turner ruled that airfield trials of their Blenheim were unnecessary.[17] With these tests complete, production runs for all but the Whitley began towards the end of November. Sound City were contracted for 100 Blenheims and 50 Wellingtons – the largest order given to a single company – while Gaumont British began work on an order for 60 Battles and Green Brothers on 100 Hurricanes.

With Loudon handling the dummy aircraft, during November Turner was free to get on with testing prototype lighting systems for the Q sites. By now the RAF's commands had had time to consider the ideas circulated in mid October, and with one exception had accepted them practically without demur. The exception was Fighter Command, where Dowding was worried that realistic

Plate 2 Dummies on trial: RAF Harwell, 28 November 1939. The aircraft nearest the camera is a genuine Vickers Wellington bomber, the next is a Sound City Wellington, and that beyond, a Gaumont British Battle. Harwell was an early expansion period bomber airfield, and it was the size and complexity of permanent stations such as this which prevented their replication by day decoys.

electrical decoys might confuse his own pilots, unlike the paraffin flarepaths which had been improvised by some of his stations since the first week of war. Dowding's fears, however, were answered by a detailed letter from Turner, and for the time being that appeared to be that.[18] The first experimental Q lighting set was tested at Abingdon on 13 November, when despite low cloud Turner found that the dummy wind T was both convincing as a decoy and – a point to answer Dowding – could readily be dimmed and brightened as a warning not to land.[19] Not all was yet perfect. The trial showed the flashing red and yellow warning light to be a 'complete failure', and the motor headlamp used as bait needed further thought. But the system was essentially sound.

As production began on the lighting sets for Q sites, attention turned to the questions of personnel and maintenance for the programme as a whole. In the middle of November Loudon told Turner that Sound City would be glad to look after the general upkeep of the dummy aircraft, and over the following weeks a plan took shape whereby depots would be established for storing completed aircraft kits pending issue to the sites, and for training crews in their assembly. Early in December Loudon visited the RAF's No 2 Balloon Depot at Hook, near Chessington, to check what capacity might be available for storage there.[20] Conveniently placed for Sound City's base at Shepperton, Hook was soon chosen as the central training station for day decoy personnel, and three other balloon depots, at Kidbrooke, Stanmore and Newcastle as storage centres for the dummy aircraft (the last for the Gateshead-manufactured Whitley). By the first week of 1940, Sound City had established its Target Plane Section at Hook, ready to receive the first dummy aircraft, and the first intake of trainees.

Since mid October Air Ministry staff had been active in finding sites for the day decoys, and after two months' work Turner was able to report to the Air Council on 12 December that fifteen 'probable' sites had been found from a total requirement expected to lie between 33 and 38.[21] With contracts in hand for the aircraft dummies and Sound City handling arrangements at Hook and elsewhere, Turner was confident that this aspect of the programme was developing well. The Q sites, however, were a different story. Equipment had been ordered following the Abingdon trials, and most of the lamps and wiring were already available for installation; but the stock of sites had been slow to accumulate, with the result that by mid December Turner had a reserve of equipment in hand but nowhere to put it. Most of the RAF's commands had been slow in getting to grips with the job; but, though Turner did not say as much to the Air Council, one command in particular was proving especially troublesome.

Turner's unstated difficulty at this time was the increasingly intransigent attitude of Fighter Command towards the technicalities of Q site design. Once Turner had completed the trials at Abingdon he had written to Dowding to confirm that the system worked and, emphasising that Bomber and Coastal Commands had shown a preference for electrical lighting, had tried to persuade the AOC-in-C Fighter Command to do the same.[22] Dowding, in fact, had earlier reassured Turner that he would accept the majority view, if only to ensure uniformity. But by early December Dowding had switched tack, and continued to insist upon lighting his own decoys in his own way. Though rooted in a disagreement on technical points, it had become clear to Turner by the end of December that the dispute was developing in other directions, and that Dowding was actively obstructing the selection of Q sites for Fighter Command airfields. Building upon the legitimate delays in site-finding met elsewhere – this was an exceptionally harsh winter – Fighter Command's awkwardness was threatening to jeopardise the night decoy programme as a whole.

This, at any rate, was the gist of the problem as Turner explained it in a private letter to Newall, the CAS, at the end of December.[23] Matters had come to a head a couple of days after Christmas, when Turner had been summoned by Sir Kingsley Wood, Secretary of State for Air, to receive what sounds from Turner's own account to have been a gentle reprimand over the rate of progress in the decoy programme. If meant as a general judgement, this would certainly have been unfair – Turner's achievement since mid September had been huge – but Turner himself had conceded to the Air Council a fortnight earlier that the Q site programme was 'very unsatisfactory' without going far into the details. Once the matter had been aired by the Secretary of State, however, Turner was obliged to say something in exculpation. And what Turner had not revealed before was that Dowding had been awkward from the start. Visiting Fighter Command during his round of consultations in September Turner had found Dowding out of his office, but his plans had won general agreement from senior staff. A few days later, however, a telephone message had arrived saying that until officially notified of Turner's appointment Dowding would not recognise him, and that Turner was barred from visiting Fighter Command's stations or group headquarters, for any reason, until the two had spoken personally. When they did, Dowding had said, in Turner's account, that he was 'not much interested in the day dummies provided that he had nothing to do with them', and that he wanted flares on the night sites, not electric lights, though he would go along with the other commands if their views differed. It had been at this point that Bomber and Coastal Commands had reiterated their wish for electric lights and Dowding had, after all, declined to fall in line. This was difficult enough, but Turner's more immediate problem at the end of December was that Fighter Command had ceased to respond to his correspondence. Letters sent several weeks earlier seeking approval for specific sites had remained unanswered, while a telephone call to one of Dowding's staff had brought only the whisper that 'things were difficult'. In Turner's plaintive account to Newall, Dowding's attitude was such that 'there is little prospect of any reasonable progress on sites in his areas'.[24]

Described in this way, Dowding's conduct seems almost gratuitously obstructive. Turner, indeed, was not alone in meeting this kind of thing from the AOC-in-C Fighter Command in autumn 1939; even the official historian of the air war, usually reticent on the foibles of senior commanders, noted that in these very weeks Dowding's absorption in operational problems led him 'neither to understand other arguments, nor to compromise, nor even to accept with good grace the decisions that went against him.'[25] But Dowding's problems at this time were almost intolerably weighty; and, after all, it was he who had insisted on substance taking precedence over shadow. It is not for us to pass judgement, but we should note that this spat between Dowding and Turner delayed the Q site programme, that its ripples were felt for months afterwards – as late as March 1940 Turner's officers were treated as pariahs by some fighter station commanders – and that it would not be their last.

At first Turner had expected to see the Q sites commissioned before the day decoys, but by the New Year of 1940 the delays in site-finding had switched them around. And for the day sites, at least, all was running smoothly. On 2 January Turner told the Air Council that 36 would be built, 22 of which were 'more or less definitely' sited.[26] In Turner's vocabulary the detailed planning of a site was 'getting out a scheme', and schemes were by now out for nine, and almost so for three more. There was much progress, too, on other fronts. By now, Air Commodore Andrew Board – another retired officer recalled to duty – had taken charge of personnel, and would soon be joined on Turner's staff by an equipment officer and four 'area officers' to oversee arrangements in the regions. All being well, Turner explained, the dummy aircraft would be marshalled at their storage centres before being moved simultaneously to the first batch of day sites to be commissioned. D-Day for this operation, so to speak, was set at 15 February, and the full complement of 36 sites was expected to be operational by the end of March. Beyond that, Turner reported that lighting sets had been obtained for most of the 50 or so Q sites planned, with sufficient wiring, so far, for 25 of those. Franker now than previously, Turner added that 'certain difficulties' with Fighter Command over the night decoys had 'not yet been overcome.' Air Marshal Peirse, Deputy CAS, who was already acquainted with the problem, offered to approach Dowding on Turner's behalf.

The first dummy aircraft arrived at Hook next day, 3 January, when Loudon's Target Plane Section received the first Wellingtons and Blenheims from Sound City safely into store.[27] By the middle of the month deliveries had settled into a regular stream, as kit-parts of Hurricanes from Green's at Hailsham and Battles from Gaumont British rolled through the gates at Kidbrooke and Stanmore, as well as at Hook. The timetable for training site crews hinged upon these deliveries, since ideally specimens of the full range of dummy types had to be available at Hook before instruction on their assembly could begin. There was a snag with the Whitley, which throughout January was held up in Gateshead for redesign, so Turner decided to go ahead with the first four types alone. Time was short. By early January nineteen men had been allotted to each day decoy (one sergeant, three corporals and fifteen aircraftmen), all of whom required three days' instruction. Three detachments were put through the course simultaneously, 57 men graduating twice weekly. The first intake began training on Monday, 22 January, around the same time that Turner came up with a codename for the sites they would occupy. From the end of January, as a counterpart to the 'Q' terminology of the night decoys, day decoy airfields were known as K sites, while the ground organisation established to serve them – Board's four officers – was divided into four regions, known as K Areas. Area K1 served Scotland, Northumberland and Durham, with a headquarters at Pitreavie Castle, Dunfermline. Yorkshire and Lincolnshire made up K2, headquarters Linton-on-Ouse. K3 was East Anglia, based at Mildenhall, and K4 the south-east, controlled from Uxbridge. We do not know why 'K' was chosen as the theme for the sites and their organisation, but a play on 'Conky' is an entertaining possibility.

Some time earlier in the month Turner drafted a standard introductory lecture for the K site crews, presumably to be given by Pilot Officer G M D Roberts, the officer in charge of the target plane courses, who arrived at Hook on 21 January.[28] Though one paragraph was scrapped and begun again, the virtual absence of corrections in this five-page handwritten text reflects Turner's finely organised thinking.

> I have brought you here today [wrote Turner] to give you the reason for the training you are undergoing and to tell you what you will be doing in the future. In giving you this information, I am putting you on your honour not to mention anything I say outside your own detachments, not even to other RAF personnel. The success of the scheme which you will be operating, and many lives[,] depend on the utmost secrecy being maintained. So secret has the matter been kept up to date that Colonel Turner who runs it at the Air Ministry has no official title. He is merely known by his name and all correspondence on the subject of his work is 'secret'.
>
> We do not know what form of attack on this country the future will bring and we have to prepare for all possibilities. One very probable form of campaign will be a continuous attack by the

Figure 2 The Sound City Wellington, showing (upper view) the dummy's sectional construction, with the model resting on the timber trestles used for assembly and (lower) the complex scaffold frame which supported it when on display. A fabric cover was supplied for the cockpit area to avoid the need for a perspex canopy, while the tailfin was held in place by bracing wires.

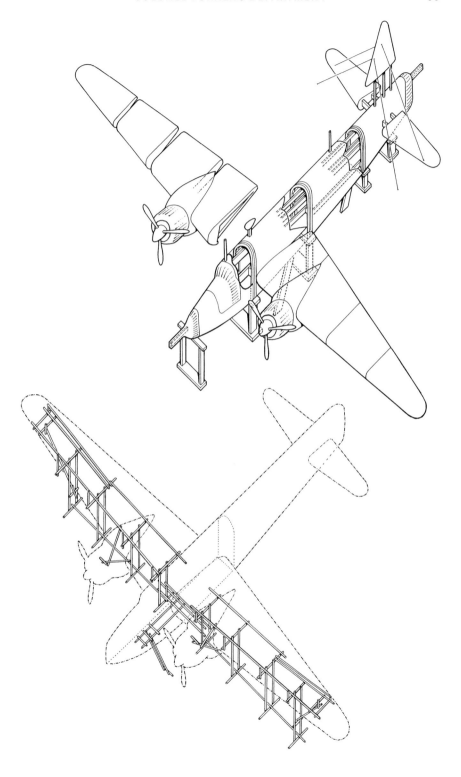

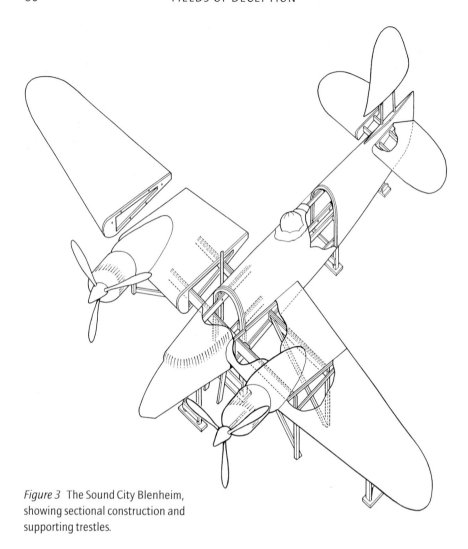

Figure 3 The Sound City Blenheim, showing sectional construction and supporting trestles.

Germans on our fleet, ports, and shipping by mine, torpedo, and bomb combined with an attack on our aerodromes. It is with the attack on our aerodromes that we are concerned this morning. This can be met by air defence[,] ie fighter aircraft, ground defence on aerodromes with machine guns etc[,] and deception in the form of dummy aerodromes which it is hoped the enemy will attack thinking they are satellite aerodromes and thereby fail to bring their full resources to bear on our true aerodromes. You, in future, will be responsible for manning these dummy aerodromes, and your training here on erecting and dismantling dummy aircraft is being carried out to enable you to do your job efficiently. Obviously, if it leaks out that we are making dummy aerodromes and if in particular the positions of those dummies reaches German ears, the whole scheme will break down, and the full attack with increased losses will fall on our stations and satellite aerodromes.[29]

Keen to muster his crews as quickly as possible, Turner had accepted inexperienced men for training at Hook, usually drawn from the RAF's less specialised trades. Their work would not be complex – little more than shifting the dummies regularly to suggest activity, and looking after the general upkeep of the site. As the drawings show (Figs 2–3), the dummy aircraft were simply bolted together in sections, though the sizeable Wellington was supported by a complicated scaffold framework which required rather more work than the other types.

Though Turner was keen to arrange machine-gun training for the detachments – few of whose members had even been trained on rifles – it appeared that a dull time might lie ahead. 'After a while you may get bored', explained Turner's lecture. 'All warfare consists of long periods of boredom and discomfort interrupted by short periods of much work and risk.' Turner encouraged the men to use these spells for games, and for shooting practice, but recognised that they would still have time on their hands. Conscious that this regime could jeopardise efficiency and weaken morale, Turner arranged for his men to spend their nights at their parent stations, where they would benefit from company and from RAF discipline, rather than billet them closer to the sites.

During the last week in January crews began to pass to the stations where they would remain until the first K sites were commissioned. The first three sets to graduate went to the frontline Bomber Command bases at Marham, Honington and Feltwell, and in the following week the next two intakes were sent to Wyton, Detling and Thorney Island, and then Benson, Tangmere and Linton-on-Ouse.[30] These were the first nine stations for which day decoys had been sited by the Air Ministry teams at work since the previous autumn. By now, however, reconnaissance for the day sites was also suffering from the worsening weather. Much of Britain was blanketed in snow, making survey of potential grounds all but impossible, with the result that only 20 K site positions had been found by the middle of February. Six further sites were in hand, but ten still remained to complete the total of 36 and in some areas of Lincolnshire and Yorkshire the competing demands of agriculture – much as expected – were tightening the availability of land.[31] In these circumstances Turner's plan to commission a large proportion of K sites simultaneously on 14 February was dropped in favour of a more piecemeal programme spread over the following weeks.

The first two K sites entered service towards the end of February, after which the number occupied rose steadily, passing thirteen in mid March to reach 25 by the third week in April, when the first Qs were commissioned.[32] The evolving layout of day decoys in this period broadly followed the sequence planned earlier in the year, which itself had governed the flow of trained men from Hook to the stations. The first two opened appear to have been those parented by Marham and Feltwell, respectively at Swaffham and at Lakenheath (one of several later converted to a real airfield). These were two of six sites in East Anglia to use Sound City Wellingtons, mimicking aircraft of Bomber Command's 2 and 3 Group squadrons in the area. The other Wellington K sites were Thetford, parented by Honington, which opened in late March, and Cavenham, Boxford and North Tuddenham, assigned respectively to the bomber stations at Mildenhall, Wattisham and Watton, which were occupied by late April. These six sites absorbed the total Wellington order placed with Sound City earlier in the year.

The K sites using Wellingtons were the only type to form a reasonably tight geographical group. Of the six decoys equipped with dummy Battles, the first three, opened by mid March, were at Gautby (for Waddington), Haddenham (Wyton) and Pyrton (Benson). These were followed in April by Folkingham (for Grantham), Swayfield (Cottesmore) and Grendon Underwood (Bicester). The first sites using Sound City's Blenheims were parented by a mixture of Fighter and Coastal Command stations, and were similarly scattered. Overlooking Chichester Harbour, West Wittering (destined to become one of the most successful day decoys), was assigned to the Coastal Command station at Thorney Island, while Lenham was parented by the fighter station at Detling and Hollesley by Martlesham Heath, on the Suffolk coast.

All active before mid March, these sites were soon joined by Craigie, parented by Leuchars – the first decoy in Scotland – Grangetown (for Thornaby), and Coxford Heath, Fulmodstone and Sarclet (for Bircham Newton, West Raynham and Wick).

Decoys using the Green Brothers' Hurricane were mostly for stations in 11 Group, Fighter Command's forward battalion covering Portsmouth to south Norfolk, which would bear the brunt of

Plate 3 A day dummy airfield: site K10(a), Cold Kirby (for Dishforth), 3 May 1940, using dummy Whitley bombers built by North-Eastern Aircraft Components of Gateshead.

the fighting in the Battle of Britain six months hence. First to be occupied, in early March, was Bulphan (for Hornchurch), followed by Lullingstone, Gumber, and Nazeing, respectively for Biggin Hill, Tangmere and North Weald. All of these decoys were occupied by late April, together with Menthorpe, serving the 13 Group station at Church Fenton, to the south of York. The remaining Hurricane sites were occupied soon after. Acklington, in 13 Group, had its K site at Long Houghton, while the 12 Group stations at Duxford and Wittering parented decoys at Horseheath and Alwalton (though the last, in Turner's account to the Air Council, was 'held up by Fighter Command for a long time').[33] Northolt, another 11 Group station, gained a Hurricane K at Barnet, though not without difficulties – in fact those anticipated by Dowding – in distancing the site from suburbs. In a disturbing portent of the future, both Northolt's and Acklington's K sites had met vigorous local objections.

The final six of Turner's 36 K sites used the Whitley developed by North-Eastern Aircraft Components. This dummy was the last to reach a good standard and as late as mid February 1940, following further critical judgements by Loudon and others, opinion in some quarters of the Air Ministry was that production should be placed elsewhere.[34] In the event, however, two Whitley-equipped K sites were occupied by mid March, at Bossall, for Linton-on-Ouse, and Toft Grange, serving Hemswell, respectively in Yorkshire and Lincolnshire. Skipsea (for Driffield), Cold Kirby (Dishforth) and Owston Ferry (Finningley), completed the Yorkshire layout of Whitley sites, and Hagnaby (Coningsby) that in Lincolnshire. The bomber station at Coningsby, however, remained some way from completion in spring 1940, and did not open until January 1941.[35] Parentage of Hagnaby was soon transferred elsewhere.

As the dummy aircraft arrived at these sites, so the work began which would gradually transform them from anonymous fields to distinctive places, with their own characteristic sets of built features. The first to be provided were the dug-outs for the crews – essentially rudimentary air raid shelters – together with disturbed areas of soil representing the fuel and ammunition dumps which a hostile crew would expect to see on a satellite. Tracks were created, representing the pattern of activity typical of a satellite airfield newly carved from a tract of farmland: particular care was needed to form worn tracks to the dummy aircraft dotted around the site perimeter. The most time-consuming job was forming the landing strips called for by Turner's 'tracked grounds', that is K sites on heather or gorse. We cannot, in fact, be certain how many sites used this method (though one to do so was West Wittering), but those that did so required the surface foliage to be cut back to expose at least one would-be landing strip. All of this work was done by the site detachments, under supervision from their area officers, in the first weeks of occupation.

Throughout their operational lives K sites would be continually modified to enhance their deceptive value, and moves in this direction were made almost as soon as the first were complete. Once dummy aircraft were in place stations routinely sent aircraft up to take a look at their new K sites, finding when they did so that the decoys were strikingly convincing at lower altitudes but tended to vanish above about 10,000ft. This, in fact, had been the upper limit at which Turner had expected the sites to be seen, but once they were in place ambitions grew and much was done to improve their appearance from high and low altitudes. Guided by Turner and Air Commodore Board, in May the site detachments under their sergeants got to work on further tricks to make the deception more sophisticated.[36] Hard standings were laid out for the dummy aircraft, using light coloured gravel dusted with clinker to suggest prepared areas darkened by spilled oil and use. Mimicking the improvised fighter pens used on satellites, earth traverses were thrown up to surround some of these standings on three sides, and made to appear patchy, in imitation of camouflage, by laying irregular dumps of chalk or light soil across them. Efforts were made to emphasise the landing trackways on those K sites which used them. Native heather, gorse or whatever foliage came to hand was heaped in lines along the edge, and lorries raced up and down to give the appearance of wear by aircraft. Smoky bonfires were kept alive to draw attention and suggest *activity*, which in time would emerge as the key desideratum for all day decoys. With the same aim in mind, crews were entreated to keep their dummy aircraft continually on the move, turning them daily through at least a right angle. Early in March Turner decided that activity should be taken a stage further by using at least some K sites as 'secondary satellites'

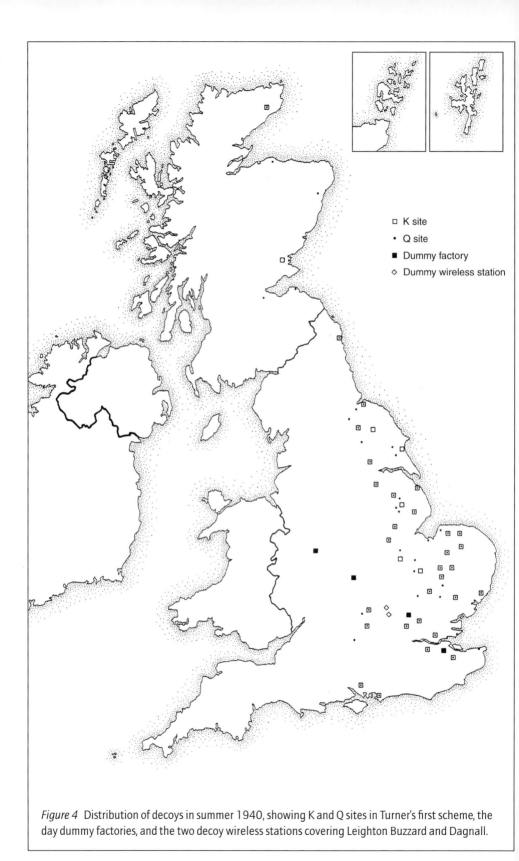

K site
Q site
Dummy factory
Dummy wireless station

Figure 4 Distribution of decoys in summer 1940, showing K and Q sites in Turner's first scheme, the day dummy factories, and the two decoy wireless stations covering Leighton Buzzard and Dagnall.

– that is, for operating real aircraft from time to time – which apart from offering extra dispersal airfields would prevent the 'local spy or chatterer' from realising that the site was a decoy.[37] This idea, it may be recalled, had been proposed by Coastal Command in March 1939, when the Air Ministry rejected it out of hand; but now it had its day.

The commissioning of Turner's 36 day decoy airfields was virtually complete by the time the first Q sites came into operation in April. The night decoys were laid out and constructed under arrangements largely separate from their daytime counterparts, with the lights and other equipment installed by electrical engineers from the Air Ministry's Directorate of Works. With more of the groundwork in the hands of the stations, for some time Turner had difficulty keeping track of how many Qs had been finished and were operable, but by the last week of April reports pointed to eleven completed from the 55 by then listed.[38] Despite a late start, Turner was confident that all could be completed by mid May, little more than a month after the first had been built. In the event, all but three Q sites were operating by mid June, though the target had by then been shaved down to 54 sites.[39]

Stretching from Wick in northern Scotland to Thorney Island on the Hampshire coast, the layout of Q sites was both broader and denser than that of the day decoys (Fig 4). Unlike the K sites, the night decoy airfields would eventually grow in number, and substantially so; but this first group was confined to the Southampton–Birmingham–Perth line fixed earlier in the year. No fewer than 30 of the 54 Q sites in place by June were co-located with their day counterparts – leaving 24 Qs and only six Ks as single-function sites – while in two cases parent airfields were given a pair of Qs rather than the usual complement of one. In Turner's early practice, single-function sites were known simply by their names, while night lightings overlying K sites were suffixed 'Q' (making Menthorpe Q, and so on) and secondary night sites by 'QX'. Since two airfields had both a Q and a QX, only 52 stations parented the first group of 54 decoys. Bomber Command airfields accounted for 25, Fighter Command's stations eighteen and Coastal Command's ten – two of which, at Thornaby and Bircham Newton, parented the QXs. Additionally, one decoy belonged to a Training Command airfield. This was the joint Q/K at Hagnaby, originally assigned to the bomber base at Coningsby but temporarily given to the Manby armament training station.

The pace at which the Qs were commissioned in April and May 1940 reflects their simplicity. The basic lighting kit used was that trialled at Abingdon in November, with the main difference that the wind T was enlarged to 22 lamps by lengthening the stem of each of the four figures (Fig 5).[40] Continuing experiments at Abingdon during February and March had also modified ideas on how

Figure 5 Comparative plans of Q site lighting arrangements, 1940–43: the T-Type, Drem and In-line Hooded flarepaths.

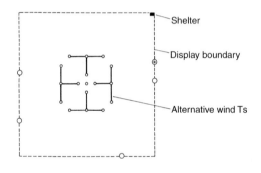

T-TYPE

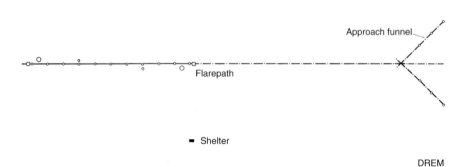

DREM

IN-LINE HOODED

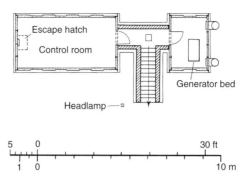

Figure 6 The first design for a sunken Q site shelter, early 1940. Designed by the Directorate of Works and Buildings at the Air Ministry (to their drawing 3395/40), this building was widely used for the early T-Type Q sites until frequent flooding led to the adoption of surface-built shelters for the Drem Q of 1941 (see Figure 36, page 152).

the headlamp should be used to draw a raider's attention. In these new trials Turner had arranged for a lamp angled slightly above the horizontal to be swung carefully through an arc, so as to represent the movement expected from the headlight of taxiing aircraft. This had worked, the momentary pinpoint brilliance of the lamp as it swung into line with an observing aircraft being sufficient to catch the eye from five miles distant.[41] Translated to the operational Q site of 1940, the lamp was mounted on a fixing immediately outside the shelter, which had been designed on Turner's behalf by the Directorate of Works early in the year. This partly sunken brick and concrete building contained a generator to power the full range of lighting – the wind T, the red obstruction lights, and the headlamp – with the switches to select between the Ts and a dimmer control to vary the lighting intensity, as well as a telephone linking the site to the operations room at its parent station (Fig 6). This cold concrete box was also home for the two-man crew, where they would wait on duty through the night and shelter in the event of an attack.

The relationship between a Q site and its parent airfield was much closer than that for a day decoy. Where the personnel for K sites were a distinct cadre, trained at Hook and answerable to Board and his K Area officers, the two men based on a Q site were drawn from the parent station, on whose strength they remained. The men chosen were aircrafthands, though it is not clear whether they were volunteers (either literally or in the traditional military

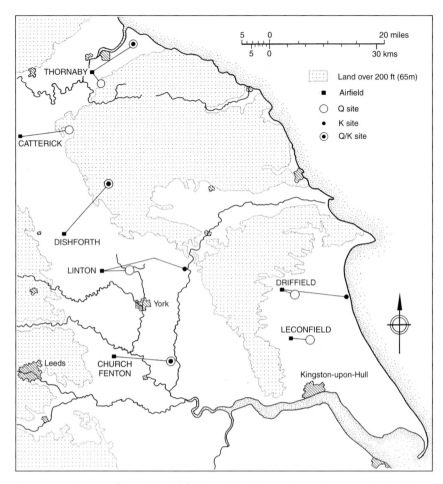

Figure 7 Landscape of deception. Airfields and their decoys in north-eastern England, June 1940. Parentage of decoys is indicated by linking lines.

sense). Tactically, too, the Q site was intimately connected with its parent. Whereas a K site was simply left to draw attacks as it might, Qs were designed for a more active role in the defences of their parent stations. They were controlled by the station commander, who could activate his lights when and how he thought fit. In time, much thought and research would be devoted to how this was best done, but at the start Turner set down the procedure for which the site in its pristine form was designed. 'Let it be assumed', he explained in a circular to station commanders, 'that the parent station wants his night dummy lit up and that there is an air raid warning out.'

The operations staff at the parent station will ring up the night dummy. Here there will be two men provided each night by the parent station taking watch and watch [ie alternate watches]. One will probably be asleep. The man on watch wakes his companion and starts up the generator. [. . .] When the generator has been started up, one man goes to the control panel and switches on the correct T, the obstruction lights and the head lamp. The two men take it in turns to manipulate the head lamp [. . .] until an aircraft is heard approaching near enough to pick up the landing T. They will then switch it out and stand on watch. If the aircraft is a friend and signals by a Very light he wants to land, ie mistakes the Q lighting for a real aerodrome[,] the lights are switched off [. . .]. If it is an enemy, who starts to attack[,] the obstruction lights only are switched off [and] the T flare path is left because on stations and satellites T flare paths cannot be extinguished in a sudden attack without great risk to personnel. The two men then take cover in their dugout and report.[42]

Building on the Abingdon trials, Turner gave precise instructions on the headlamp's use: first, rotate through 90 degrees in five seconds, then switch off for 40 seconds or so, then switch on again in a different direction and repeat the five-second sweep. Manipulated in this way (so the idea ran) the lamp would suggest a taxiing aircraft pivoting on one wheel as it turned. This, really, was the only taxing job for the Q site crew – unless we include summoning the presence of mind to sit in a field, defenceless and miles from anywhere, goading the Luftwaffe to attack.

A look at the distribution of airfield decoys at a regional level shows how their siting in relation to parent stations also played its part in inviting bombs. As the map (Fig 7) shows, in June 1940 nearly all the existing RAF stations between the Humber and the Tees had decoys: from Church Fenton in the south to Thornaby in the north, seven airfields parented five Ks and eight Qs, distributed between ten separate sites. K sites had no regular geographical relationship with their parent stations, whose function with respect to the decoy was chiefly administrative. But the positions of Q sites, chosen by station commanders under Turner's guidance, were selected with more direct reference to the position of the parent station, and its topographical context. A number of general principles were brought into play. One principle, of course, was that decoys should always lie in the general direction of enemy approach, as these are; but more subtly, the officers siting night decoys were advised to identify the landmarks which incoming bomber crews would probably use as guides, and then to exploit this specific routing. Two further principles were that decoys work best when they offer the enemy what he already expects – and hopes – to see; and secondly that crews flying at night (in aircraft of 1940) seldom knew with certainty exactly where they were.

The basic problem in this latter respect was that the aircraft's speed through the air, and its heading, could be read from instruments, but speed and track over the ground was a different matter: the difference was a product of the strength and direction of the wind, which despite the availability of forecasts was seldom known with confidence when operating miles from home. It was the navigator's job to fix his position by identifying as many landmarks as possible during the sortie, and to establish wind strength and direction by comparing airspeed and heading – measured inside the aircraft – with the groundspeed and track calculated either from visual 'fixes', from star-shots with a sextant, or from the Luftwaffe's still rudimentary layout of radio beacons. Later in 1940 the Germans began to use more sophisticated electronic aids to overcome the weakness of visual navigation, and even without them they were better served than their Zeppelin predecessors of World War One; but even so, for much of the time bomber crews were to a certain extent lost.

The art of siting decoys was to exploit this uncertainty, and a look at the distribution of Q sites in the Humber–Tees region shows how it was done. Near the coast, the Qs for Driffield and Leconfield lay only three or four miles east of their parents, presumably on the assumption that an incoming crew intent on one or the other station would obtain a fix when they crossed the coast and so be reasonably sure of their position by the time they reached the vicinity of their target, little more than ten miles inland. Putting either decoy much further east would not have worked. Further inland, however, the separations between Q sites and their parents were greater, reaching eleven miles for Church Fenton–Menthorpe, and twelve for Dishforth–Cold Kirby. Though large, these separations can also be explained by tactical principles. A bomber crew intent on Church Fenton would probably rely on picking up the mouth of the Humber and flying due west, eight miles north of the narrowing estuary. Approaching Menthorpe Q, they might be surprised to see airfield lights glimmering under the nose quite so soon, but would probably explain this by an unexpected drop in headwind. Add a measure of inexperience, or a nervous disinclination to linger, and the crew would be even more likely to bomb the decoy and swing for home. The Q for Linton-on-Ouse, on the other hand, is much closer in, at about five miles; but this site is not far from the City of York, which on a clear night (blackout notwithstanding) might offer a 'fix'.

It must be stressed that we do not know for sure whether the Yorkshire Qs were sited with these specific thoughts in mind; the foregoing is an attempt to analyse the map in the light of general principles. It is certainly true that large separations between parents and Qs could come about for other reasons – sometimes merely from difficulties in finding sites closer in, and sometimes through the caution of station commanders, some of whom believed (on no evidence whatever) that decoys might actually draw attacks on their stations. But the general rule, at first, was that the further a parent station lay from some identifiable landmark, the greater was the latitude in siting the night decoy. As we shall see, once attacks on Q sites began in the summer of 1940 it became clear that the Luftwaffe was not so much being diverted from specific airfields, as bombing anything visible; but no one expected this at first, and early Qs were accordingly sited with some care.

Although most of Turner's work during the spring of 1940 was taken up with the airfield decoys, these were not his only problem. Early in the year the Air Council had considered the possibility of providing decoys to replicate aircraft factories, and as the K and Q sites came into operation in April and May, this scheme gradually converged with more general ideas on decoys for civil targets fomenting at the Home Office. Though busy enough with other matters, in mid February Turner had told the Air Council that he could readily contrive dummy aircraft factories for daytime use, provided the sites were made available and the Air Ministry would accept the heavy costs, which might be as much as £20,000 apiece.[43] Turner also stressed that a dummy aircraft factory presupposed an adjacent dummy aerodrome, and that finding sites of sufficient size in the right places – replicating specific existing works and their airfields – would be no simple task.[44] Nonetheless, the Air Council instructed Turner to begin planning the scheme, by identifying six factories which might be decoyed on the assumption that the Treasury would play along. By the end of March Turner had a shortlist of nine – in fact all the large works of the major aircraft firms – and had found good sites for decoys at four. These were Short's factory at Rochester, De Havilland's at Hatfield, Boulton & Paul's at Wolverhampton and the Bristol Aircraft Company's works at Filton.[45]

Had Turner been allowed to go ahead with these schemes in March 1940 it is probable that several of Britain's vital aircraft factories would have been shadowed by established daytime decoys when some actually came to be bombed a few months later. Almost immediately, however, the programme became stalled by uncertainty over departmental responsibility for sites of this kind. On 5 April the Camouflage (Policy and Organisation) Committee, a newly-formed interdepartmental body under Lord Swinton, issued a paper recommending experiments in night decoy lighting for urban and industrial targets, but making no mention of day decoys for factories.[46] These lighting trials duly went ahead later in the year, but by the end of April the Committee had queried the policy of building daytime dummy factories at all.

For Turner, these developments were a source of justifiable and unconcealed frustration. Swinton's committee had been formed expressly to enable the service and civil ministries to liaise over camouflage policy, which was taken to include decoy policy. For all practical purposes, however, the committee had begun again from scratch, without reference to what Turner had already achieved; and if this were not enough, in April they suggested that Turner should seek the advice of the Home Office's own panel of visual camouflage artists before taking his thoughts on dummy factories any further. An added frustration was that the Treasury had queried Turner's plan to build the experimental factory already authorised simply by placing an order with Sound City, rather than putting the job out to competitive tender. Turner was therefore called upon to justify taking what is known as a single tender action on the contract – a procedure which, *prima facie*, should have appeared amply justified by the threat of imminent attack on the targets to be protected, coupled with Loudon's proven expertise. That problem was overcome and an experimental dummy factory was erected by Sound City staff north of Banbury, but by the end of April Turner was in the awkward position of having suspended ploughing on the five sites already chosen for the factory decoys without the necessary authority to requisition the land formally. Turner laid the facts before the Air Council bluntly on 23 April.

> If the Air Council want these sites in any reasonable time [wrote Turner] it is quite hopeless referring to the Central Camouflage Committee at the Home Office who know very little about camouflage and nothing at all about deception. Deception is an engineering matter and the question of materials is vital. The only people who can design deception of this sort are engineers in the film trade and this is what we are employing. A second factor is essential for speed. I have authority to carry out this experiment with a single tender contract. I must have the same authority to carry out all these sites on a single tender contract because Sound City, who have been working with me on aircraft and in preparing the experiment, are the only people who know anything about the requirements.[47]

Turner, of course, got his way, and Loudon his contract. Swinton's committee reversed its decision chiefly on the understanding that since dummy aircraft factories required dummy airfields, they must fall within a common remit with K sites, and were thus a matter for the Air Ministry alone. But it was late June 1940 before any was begun.

In the three months between the opening of the first K sites in late February and the near completion of the initial programme at the end of May, the Second World War passed two landmarks which together signalled the close of Britain's nine-month reprieve. On 9 April Germany invaded Norway and Denmark, and at dawn on 10

May opened her assault in the west by advancing upon Belgium, Holland and France. Both campaigns offered a disturbing insight to the tactics which, before long, would surely be turned against the British Isles. Building on their experience in Poland, the Germans forced their way into Scandinavia and the Low Countries by Blitzkrieg: the technique of 'lightning war' relying on deep penetration by airborne troops delivered by parachute, aircraft and glider, supported by fast armoured columns breaking through the frontiers. As late as early May 1940 Britain had made virtually no tangible preparations against this form of attack. A huge programme of emergency land defences was begun, designed to meet tanks landing on the beaches and troops who, on the model of tactics in Norway and Holland, might arrive by transport aircraft or glider on any open space. Airfields, for the first time, were defended against capture by these methods, using rifles and whatever else could be made available to bring fire to bear upon the flying field itself.

In the week after the Germans' advance into the Low Countries it became clear K sites might play a critical part in the coming battle against Britain, but in a wholly unexpected way. If the Germans were bold enough to attempt landings on occupied airfields, then K sites – at least those which had fooled the Germans – would be vulnerable by the same token. In early summer 1940 none of the RAF's airfields was geared to meet this threat, but with only nineteen men and a lorry driver the K sites were virtually defenceless, even though the men by now had been trained to handle light anti-aircraft machine guns. The means by which those weapons should be used were discussed by Turner in a circular issued on 18 May, when K detachments which had not already done so were instructed to build machine-gun positions to meet low-flying attackers.[48] Turner also had a good deal to say about dealing with parachutists and enemy aircraft which might attempt to land. What his advice amounted to, however, was to keep shooting and call for help.

The problem of defending K sites from capture was not the only sign that real war was approaching towards the end of May. Two months earlier the Air Council had suggested that Turner's newly-won expertise might be drawn upon to build decoy airfields across the Channel. In April Turner duly took a call from Air

Commodore F P Don, head of the British Air Forces in France,[49] to which he wrote a lengthy and encouraging reply. On 29 May, however, Turner minuted an Air Ministry colleague that the situation across the Channel was 'so chaotic' that deception measures would be pointless. What Turner evidently did not know when he wrote those words was that the Battle of France was already over as far as British forces were concerned. News of the Dunkirk exodus was made public on that same day, 29 May. More than four years would pass before Colonel Turner built any decoy airfields in France.

CHAPTER 3

Into battle

JUNE – OCTOBER 1940

German air operations against Britain began to bite a few days after the last boats returned from Dunkirk. On the night of the 5–6 June a force of 30 aircraft was dispatched against airfields and other targets on the east coast; and they visited again 24 hours later.[1] Several of these sorties were drawn to decoys. 'Information is still very vague', reported Turner on 10 June, 'but it is certain that at least five of the "Q" lightings have been attacked during the last few days'.[2] Lincolnshire and East Anglia had borne the brunt. Donna Nook, Q for North Coates on the north Lincolnshire coast had been bombed; so too had Folkingham (for Grantham), Lakenheath (Feltwell), and Coxford Heath (Bircham Newton). In just two nights Watton's Q site at North Tuddenham had been hit twice. Some parent stations had also suffered, for despite lighting its Q site the bomber station at Hemswell had drawn an attack. But it was an auspicious start. Turner straightaway arranged for stations to report incidents systematically.[3] He also saw to it that bomb craters were quickly filled, lest untended damage should betray a site as a dummy. Documenting successes and maintaining deception against post-raid reconnaissance would always be pressing concerns.

These early attacks were followed by a brief lull until the German victory in France was secure. Resuming in mid June, hostile operations remained light, but troublesome. Q sites were attacked almost nightly in the following weeks. Lakenheath was bombed for the second time on 18 June, and Skerne (for Driffield) and Cold Kirby (Dishforth) on the following night. On 19/20 June a small force operating over Cambridgeshire bombed the towns of Ely, Chatteris, March and Benwich. Blacked-out and invisible, the nearby airfield at Upwood escaped attention, but its Q site at Benwick was lit and drew several poorly-aimed bombs. Owston Ferry, for Finningley, had its first attack in the early hours of 20 June – when several hapless pigs became the first casualties of the decoy war – and Cavenham (for Mildenhall) on the 21st. By the end of June a single attack had been recorded on Depden (for Stradishall), while Swayfield (Cottesmore) and Otmoor (Upper · Heyford) had both been bombed twice, Driffield's Q at Skerne had drawn its second attack and Qs at Fulmodestone and Massingham Heath (both for West Raynham) had been bombed – the last being one of two additional Q sites established in late June. All of these sites were parented by stations of Bomber Command, for whose decoy operations itemised records survive;[4] but the action extended more widely, and by the end of the month no fewer than 36 attacks had been drawn by Q sites nationally.[5] Some were heavy. The raid on Otmoor Q on 25/26 June, for example, drew over 2000lb of high-explosive, more than half the payload of a Heinkel 111 bomber. Four days later seven high-explosive bombs and around 100 incendiaries had fallen in the raid on Cottesmore's Q at Swayfield.[6] Their parent stations had barely suffered, though airfields *without* decoys were harder hit. In the official historian's account, published in 1957, sixteen industrial targets and fourteen ports were bombed in this phase of raiding, together with thirteen airfields, but while most of the bombs dropped were aimed at the aerodromes, 'some fell harmlessly in open country'.[7] Indeed they did, but the official historian was not at liberty to reveal why.

36 attacks drawn in the first month of operations was an impressive haul, but as ever in the decoy war, the significance of the figures needs to be judged with caution. Everything depended upon how attacks were measured. The first problem, evident even in these early weeks of action, was that many bombs were falling sufficiently far from Q sites to raise doubts over whether they had truly been targeted. Despite evidence that some attacks plainly directed at *genuine* targets had themselves been way off the mark, Turner preferred to err on the side of caution, and soon directed that only bombs landing inside a half-mile radius of the site would be counted as aimed at it. Nor was there room for complacency in

measuring the larger military value of the attacks. Although the first Q sites had been conceived as part of the active air defences of their parent stations, it was obvious that in practice they were not so much decoying those airfields in a one-to-one correspondence as simply presenting the Luftwaffe with a *general* array of anonymous targets. It followed that in most cases a raid upon a Q site had not actually deflected a specific operation against its parent, with all the savings in life and property which that would imply, but simply enticed the Germans to squander bombs on a farmer's field. Their effect, therefore, was more to waste German explosive than to save definable caches of British *matériel*. That of course was valuable in itself, and in general these early raids provided comforting evidence that the blackouts at genuine airfields were working very well. But it was not clear how long this would last, particularly since much of the present bombing appeared to be surprisingly opportunistic and loosely controlled. So Turner was not sanguine in the face of these early successes. 'Too much confidence should not [. . .] be placed in our "Q" lighting', he wrote on 23 June. 'There appears to be considerable evidence that many of the enemy pilots appear to be lost and to be inclined to bomb anything they can see, especially lights.'[8] Turner guessed that these raids were being flown by novices, either because they were training for something bigger, or alternatively because the Luftwaffe was already losing its more expert crews in their continuing operations in France.

Turner's first judgement was actually very close to the mark. These were indeed training sorties, designed to familiarise the Luftwaffe with night flying over Britain and to allow selected crews to experiment with the new electronic navigation aid known as *Knickebein*, of which we shall hear more later.[9] Poor bombing accuracy led to minimal damage, and in general the main effect of these raids was nuisance. Frequent air raid warnings disrupted production and intimidated the civil population, though they came about largely because the warning system was highly sensitised, allowing sirens to howl in places where the chance of attack was remote. From late June these warnings were given more sparingly. For Turner's staff, on the other hand, the effect of this first skirmish was positive: too light to do much harm, the raids of June 1940 were nonetheless frequent enough to vindicate the night decoy principle as a whole, and to reveal some of the subtleties which should be allowed for in future. With the Germans in control of bases across the whole of northern France, towards the end of June orders were issued to expand and diversify the layout of sites.

In the six weeks or so remaining before concerted attacks on the RAF began in mid August – and with them the Battle of Britain proper – the decoy programme began to grow in several directions simultaneously. Technically the simplest was the addition of new sites on the existing model, both west of the Southampton–Birmingham–Perth line, and within the original boundary. The push west shadowed the expansion of occupied territory across the Channel, and paralleled a thickening density of operational airfields in the western counties. As approved by Newall in the last week of June, the policy was confined at first to Q lights. Though several day decoys sharing sites with Qs had been damaged at night, none had yet been attacked in its own right and any decision to expand their numbers was deferred until the existing sites had been proven in action.[10]

Turner's second job in early summer 1940 was to contrive a wholly new form of decoy. By mid June the frequent use of incendiaries in attacks on Q sites had suggested that controlled dummy fires might draw attacks from aircraft approaching a target they knew – or believed – already to have been bombed. An experimental decoy fire was accordingly built at Toft Grange K site (parented by Hemswell), and lit on the night of 21 June, when Turner went aloft to inspect it with an experienced Bomber Command crew, who compared the result favourably to what they had seen of their own work over Germany.[11] This experimental fire consisted merely of burning creosote in tins with lengths of roofing felt suspended above, to give bursts of greater intensity as they dropped into the flames.[12] These basic ideas were soon refined, however, and by early July the new decoy type – soon to be known as a 'Q fire', or 'QF site' – could call upon four kinds of apparatus (described later), evolved by Sound City technicians to give subtly different visual effects.[13]

Turner's policy for siting QFs was settled in consultation with commands and others during July, but at the beginning of this new round of work he identified four RAF stations and twelve aircraft factories as likely recipients for the first equipment. The inclusion of factories reflected progress in the third line of decoy work under way in the summer of 1940, which was the development – at last – of the day dummies for these targets discussed in the early weeks of the year. By early July it had been decided that just four aircraft factories would be duplicated, at least at first, though to these were added two smaller-scale day decoys for the especially sensitive Air Ministry wireless telegraphy stations at Leighton Buzzard and Dagnall, making six day dummies in all. The four factories decoyed were Short's works on the Medway at Rochester, Boulton & Paul's at Wolverhampton, De Havilland's at Hatfield, and Armstrong Whitworth's at Baginton, near Coventry; dummies for these places were respectively at Chatham, Coven, Holwellhyde and Leamington Hastings, each a few miles from its target. Begun in late June or early July, all six sites were completed by late summer.[14] Their design and construction was given to Loudon's men, whose creative skills were keenly adapted to architectural work. The wireless stations consisted of little more than dummy aerial towers, but each of the factories was finished as a full-scale replica, complete with such niceties as derelict vehicles in car parks and dummy aircraft parked out on the airfield, as if awaiting dispatch. The factory scheme also added a fifth dummy aircraft to Turner's fleet: Defiant fighters were faked to serve the decoy at Coven, covering the Boulton & Paul factory at Wolverhampton where the real thing was built. As experience would show, however, the challenge of giving perpetual life to such a complex and specific decoy as a factory was probably too much even for Sound City. Daytime raids on these sites would never be numerous.

As Sound City's engineers began the dummy factories, yet another new type of decoy was taking shape elsewhere. The Home Office's forays into decoy work had been in abeyance since the baffle lighting experiments on the Humber in 1939, but on 8 May 1940 – just two days before the Germans began their advance in the west – the Civil Defence Committee of the Ministry of Home Security finally judged that the time had come to investigate decoy lighting for towns and cities. Detailed planning began in early June, when it was decided that MoHS technicians and artists attached to the Civil Defence Camouflage Establishment at Leamington Spa

Plate 4 The dummy factory (site M1) at Chatham, decoying the Short Brothers' works at Rochester, seen on 1 June 1942, the month in which this and the other three such sites were abandoned.

would make night flights over Sheffield and Crewe to record impressions of industrial area lighting. At the same time experiments would be mounted, again at Leamington, with fires.[15] Launched independently from Turner's work on fire decoys, by the first week in July these trials had reached the first, full-scale layout to decoy a real target. Originally intended for Newcastle upon Tyne, the MoHS experiments eventually took place at two sites on moorland to the north-west of Sheffield, and in the vicinity of Glasgow docks. The more northerly of the Sheffield systems, on the Sheffield Moors, and was intended to suggest a row of furnaces, two stretches of factory roadway, and four marshalling yards. The southern system, on Big Moor and Eaglestone Flat near Chesterfield, replicated a marshalling yard and a factory road. Both

Plate 5 The dummy wireless telegraphy station (site M6) at Dagnall, seen on 20 December 1945, when the bases for the aerial towers remained in place.

included dummy fires. The scale of these works was vast – much larger than anything attempted by the Air Ministry, either before or subsequently. The Sheffield system reportedly occupied several miles of moorland and needed 70 soldiers, supervised by three officers, to operate it. The size and exact character of the Glasgow shipyard is uncertain, but like the decoy at Sheffield it was reportedly nearing completion in the first week of July.[16]

Whatever their individual technical merits, the cumulative result of running so many plans and experiments simultaneously was that Britain's decoy arrangements were in danger of losing force for want of co-ordination. Not only were two departments beginning to duplicate one another's work, but to make matters worse the absence of a recognised deception authority was giving rise to outbreaks of independent action, as diverse military units began to improvise crude decoy schemes of their own. At the end of June, for example, Turner got word that troops encamped in the Norfolk heathland had recently ignited decoy fires in response to air attack; and, not for the first time, he was sent copies of correspondence circulating in another department recommending that lights, fires, and so on should be improvised widely under local arrangements.[17] The writer of that note was aware that the Air Ministry was up to something in connection with airfield decoys, and it was perhaps creditable to Turner's security precautions that he did not know exactly what. But Turner was furious that 'promiscuous fires' had been lit by the soldiers, and that anyone had thought of displaying lights on an *ad hoc* basis. 'If every yarhoo [*sic*] starts showing lights all over the country when he gets a yellow warning', wrote Turner on 2 July, 'he will wreck the whole complicated system of night dummy landing grounds which I have evolved.'[18] Indeed he would, and this by itself advertised the need for co-ordination.

The first steps toward setting up a national decoy authority were taken a few days later. On 4 July Archibald Sinclair, Secretary of State for Air, approached Sir John Anderson, his opposite number at the MoHS, recommending that liaison between their departments on decoy matters should be given a more formal stamp. Sinclair had in mind particularly the idea of developing a national urban decoy lighting strategy following from the Sheffield and Glasgow experiments – then beginning – which plainly would benefit from pooling expertise between the Leamington establishment (under Dr R E Stradling) and Turner's department.[19] The following Wednesday, 10 July, was duly set for a round table meeting. The day before the conference, Turner briefed the leader of the Air Ministry delegation on his ideas for how a co-ordinating authority should work. Unsurprisingly, perhaps, these plans were essentially a statement of his own practices enlarged to the national case. Decoy co-ordination, argued Turner, should lie within the Air Ministry, whose staff knew the air defence picture and understood Luftwaffe tactics, and the work should be driven by a sense of urgency: 'The time for experimenting is passed. Immediate action is required if any use is to be made of dummies. No dummies that take months to prepare are of any value.' Turner argued further that a recognised individual should be at the head of decoy work – a 'dictator of dummies' – with a proper staff and the freedom to award contracts by special procedures. Turner did not go so far as to suggest a candidate; but he did advocate 'a working man with experience', adding, in an obvious and well-deserved jibe at the Swinton Committee, that 'It is useless putting in a "name" who is ignorant. It merely wastes time.'

Turner's official appointment as dictator of dummies was more or less immediate. Meeting on 10 July, with Stradling in the chair, the interdepartmental committee – representing the three service ministries, and Ministries of Supply and Home Security – agreed that the Air Ministry should be home to a co-ordinating staff for decoy work along the lines which Turner wanted.[20] These proposals were duly sent up to the Deputy Chiefs of Staff Committee, where they were endorsed on 21 July with instructions that plans for a national decoy strategy should now be assembled without delay.[21]

In binding together the strands already spun by the MoHS and the Air Ministry, Turner's first problem was to secure higher approval for urban decoy lighting of the type under trial at Sheffield and Glasgow. This issue was raised with the Civil Defence Committee on 31 July,[22] where despite some hesitation arising from the incompleteness of the experiments, decoy lighting for industrial areas and 'vital points' was approved.[23] For Turner, this decision carried far-reaching implications, since it represented the first formal notification that he should now allow for five decoy types rather than four – in other words for Q and K sites, the day dummy buildings then under construction, the new QFs (none of which was yet active), and now urban lights, which would come to be known as 'QL sites'. With this decided, Turner's provisional plan for co-ordinating schemes was referred to the Air Ministry on the next day, 1 August, and thence to the Civil Defence Committee a few days later.

> The paramount factor [declared Turner] is the necessity for speed. Large scale attack may come tomorrow and if decoys are to be of any value they should be started at once in as many places as possible. It is necessary therefore to work on the information and results now available, to aim at simplicity, and to spread the work. This does not prevent the continuation of experiment nor the extension of schemes at a later date. A considerable factor in the situation is the apparent ease with which the enemy pilot is now deceived but we must recognise that once they recognise a decoy

as such, the value of that type of decoy is greatly diminished and we must keep ahead of such discovery by continual change and improvement.[24]

Though Turner now had authority to *co-ordinate* decoys nationally, it is important to stress that the origination of schemes under these arrangements remained with the departments concerned. Thus the MoHS would define civil requirements and the Admiralty those for naval installations, while the War Office would select targets to be decoyed on behalf of the army. In addition, a recently mooted plan from the Petroleum Board to provide fire decoys for oil tank farms would be handled by that body itself, Turner providing technical advice and, in common with all other departments' schemes, filtering proposals for sites through his office. This, at least, was Turner's view of how the system would work when fully established, as he explained:

> Representatives after working out their policies in their departments will put forward proposals for decoys. In the early stages they will be largely dependent on the Air Ministry for information on decoys and on the selection of sites. Later on it is hoped they will be able to put up definite schemes. The Air Ministry as co-ordinator will check the scheme to ensure that it does not interfere with other decoys or defence. The Air Ministry will not be responsible for the policy of the scheme but they may give advice especially in the early stages both on the scheme and its cost. If the scheme is approved the Air Ministry will issue funds from a block grant to cover the anticipated cost. [. . .][25]

After which, construction would be handled by different bodies according to whose scheme the decoy belonged: the army and navy would take care of themselves, the MoHS would probably need to call upon army or RAF works services, and the Petroleum Board's decoys would be left to the oil companies whose premises they were intended to protect. Sites would be selected under rigid criteria, particularly respecting civilian interests. Standard safety distances were defined, similar to those used for Q sites: no light or fire was to lie within 400 yards from a building, 800 yards from a village, or about a mile from a small town. Railways, too, had to be avoided, as well as hospitals – especially mental hospitals – together with standing crops, food dumps and other sensitive points. Approved in full by the Civil Defence Committee on 7 August and circulated widely on the 13th,[26] this was a practical solution to the problem of co-ordination – not to say a diplomatic one in its handling of the other service and civil departments. Rather than cleave all responsibility to himself, Turner had conceded the other departments considerable freedom in what was, in practice, a fairly decentralised system.

Nor, in fact, did the system embrace every decoy to be built in the country. In early summer 1940 the War Office authorised coast artillery and anti-aircraft batteries to lay out tactical decoys near to their sites as part of their general camouflage arrangements.[27] Though these were day decoys and, in that sense, comparable to the Air Ministry's dummy factories and wireless stations, they differed in being a purely local expedient, never brought within central control under Turner and perhaps more closely comparable to the dummy pillboxes, roadblocks and other deceptive devices widely improvised by local army commanders. Interestingly, they do not seem to have been in place for long and – equally so – Turner wanted nothing to do with them.

By coincidence the policy paper setting out these new arrangements was circulated on a landmark day in Germany's air offensive against Britain. For the Luftwaffe, 13 August was *Adlertag*, 'Eagle Day', the appointed time to begin the systematic destruction of the RAF in the air and on the ground. Eagle Day marked the end of a two-month period in which German raiding had been comparatively light and scattered. Following June's night operations against airfields and other targets, in the following month the Luftwaffe made fewer penetrations inland, instead concentrating their attention on Channel shipping and ports. Attacks on Q sites consequently fell in July, dropping to only eleven from the 36 recorded in the previous month – or, strictly, in the second half of that month, once systematic reporting had begun.[28] Ks were less successful, and with only one daytime attack recorded by mid July Turner urged K detachments to introduce general untidiness to enliven their sites' appearance.[29] Two more Ks were bombed in the fortnight after these orders, and by 26 July attacks had fallen on

Skipsea (parented by Driffield), Coxford Heath (Bircham Newton) and West Wittering (Thorney Island).[30] These were all coastal sites, well placed to draw the attention of Luftwaffe crews operating against shipping and ports. Turner remained confident that K sites would have their day when the main offensive began.

The relative quiet of July also gave an opportunity for technical refinements among the Q sites.[31] To build on the early attack record Turner encouraged station commanders to accentuate the contrast between stations and dummies, cutting the real airfield lights to the barest minimum and paying fastidious attention to blackout, while at the same time nudging the dimmer switch on the Q site a few notches upwards. Stations were also urged to begin searching for secondary Q sites, which could be brought into action quickly by laying out initially with flares. Though technically a retrograde step, this in Turner's thinking would give fluidity to the layout – which in its original area had now been in place for several months – and prevent the electrically-lit dummies being spotted as fixtures and possibly, therefore, as fakes. In a further attempt to heighten realism the station commander at Bircham Newton arranged for aircraft to feint landings at his Q site, so raising the general level of activity around the decoy. More attacks followed, and Turner encouraged others to play the same game. Nothing was left to stagnate.

By the last week in July the search for sites in the west was about half complete, and was already reaching into areas beyond those delineated earlier in the month. Allowing for further extensions into north-western Britain, about 40 new Q sites were called for in all, 26 of which had by now been sited. To bring these sites into operation quickly, Turner had fallen back on goose-neck flares for the Q sites pending the installation of their electrical lights and the building of shelters. The result was that, as July turned to August, the majority of the new Qs were operating in some form. Less had been done with the QFs, and though nineteen had been sited from a requirement of around 40, work had begun on only five. Twelve of the QFs were for aircraft factories, including the four provided with day dummies, which by early August were almost complete. Turner's chief difficulty in planning this extended programme lay in the fluidity of RAF deployments, as stations changed occupancy and new airfields were commissioned in quick time. Priorities for new decoys were often difficult to define, and liable to rapid revision. This problem applied equally to the east of the country as the west, and was compounded there by the thickening density of airfields and other military sites, all of which needed care in their avoidance. 'I have to dodge satellites, Fighter Stations etc', wrote Turner at the end of July, 'and the checking up of a mass of detail is not too easy'.[32] Nonetheless, by the time the Germans' main offensive began on 13 August the decoy layout was in a serviceable state to meet it.

Germany's objective in this new phase of attacks was to crush the Royal Air Force and win the command of the air necessary to launch an invasion. The first strike had originally been planned for 10 August, but was foiled by the weather; heavy raiding did take place on the 12th, however, when Ventnor radar station was bombed out of action and the Luftwaffe mounted its first concerted raids on fighter airfields. Attacks on Eagle Day itself, by contrast, were again disrupted by weather and were poorly co-ordinated, but on that night a second prong of the Luftwaffe's tactics was revealed in the start of systematic raids against aircraft factories – the very targets which Turner was at that moment attempting to cover with QFs. Although the factory QFs were among the first to enter service, they were completed too late to play a part in this campaign, which in the next fortnight delivered raids on most of the major complexes. In the event, however, the lack of QF cover hardly mattered, since with a few exceptions the night raids were wildly inaccurate. But a few daylight raids were diverted by the recently-completed day decoy factories. The first to be hit was Coven, covering Boulton & Paul's works at Wolverhampton, which drew a heavy attack on 14 August,[33] and by mid September three of the four dummy factories had been bombed, one of them twice.[34] No fewer than seventeen attacks were drawn by night decoys for the factories before the end of October.

The value of Q sites during the fighting of August and early September was limited by most raiders coming in the long daylight hours: thus were fought the famous air engagements of the Battle of Britain proper, in which the RAF's Hurricanes and Spitfires defeated the Luftwaffe by the narrowest of margins. The more limited night operations in these weeks gave the Q sites a score of just 28 attacks in August, compared to 36 in June – and this with more sites in place – though a further 20 incidents were recorded in the first half of September, when the switch back to night raids began. Nor, as things turned out, did K sites add much to Britain's defences in the weeks when the battle was at its peak. Just thirteen attacks were recorded on eleven sites between early July and mid September, meaning that fully two-thirds of the 36 Ks drew no bombs in the period when the Luftwaffe was expressly targeting airfields by day. Their parent stations, however, were hard hit. Sixteen of the 36 were attacked before mid September, in 27 separate raids (these figures of course exclude attacks on those *without* Ks).[35] The reason for the relative weight of attack between Ks and parents is simple: contrary to the expectations of 1939, the Luftwaffe's offensive was directed very largely toward disabling permanent stations, not the satellites which the day decoys were intended to replicate. Indeed, in many raids they appeared to be targeting the solid fabric of the stations – the buildings, manoeuvring aprons and hangars – rather than the aircraft dispersals, which in itself suggested that this was a campaign against bricks and mortar as much as flying fields and aircraft. Few stations were put out of action for very long, though the damage was occasionally grave: Kenley, for example, lost most of its hangar roofs and Driffield was so battered as to be temporarily evacuated.

Though K sites themselves played only a minor part in the Battle of Britain, their dummy aircraft did gain an important secondary role at the height of the fighting. In spring 1940 Turner urged commands to adopt a new tactic in which aircraft at permanent stations would be hidden entirely and dummies dispersed on the airfield perimeters in substitute. All the commands rejected this idea on first hearing (Dowding was especially dismissive), but a few months later had begun to come round.[36] The first dummies were installed on a true airfield in late July, at Drem, where the station commander exchanged dummy Hurricanes for his fighters, which he managed to hide in a wood bordering the airfield. The eight Hurricanes supplied to Drem swallowed up the reserve stock of this type, and suspecting that a new demand was looming – and that Dowding had changed his mind – Turner ordered 50 extra Hurricanes and 50 more Defiants as insurance. Some of these were soon in place among fighter stations at Manston, Rochford, and Lympne, while a supply of dummy Battles was sent to Eastchurch.

In mid September Turner was asked whether he could improvise dummy repairs to hangars, such that stations bludgeoned to
the point of abandonment might be quickly remade to serve as
decoys. Driffield in particular was examined with this in mind,
though the scheme was dropped after Turner argued that so dras-
tic a step could be justified only when a site was irretrievably
wrecked, as Driffield was not.[37] But dummy aircraft were used
here, in a rather different way. Following the attack of mid August,
Bomber Command asked for fourteen dummy Whitleys to be
parked at Driffield to conceal the station's evacuation. Ten were
duly brought over from the Skipsea K site (where Hurricanes were
substituted), supplemented by four from reserves. This deployment was arranged less to draw attack, than to persuade German
intelligence analysts that the station remained in commission. In
a minor way, the Driffield feint could be seen as Turner's first venture into strategic deception, since these dummies falsified the
pattern of RAF deployment, more for the benefit of intelligence
staff than attacking pilots. Dummies displayed at real stations
drew no attacks in 1940, but eleven were recorded in the first five
months of 1941. Later in the war displays of this kind became the
main function of dummy aircraft.

On 7 September the German air offensive turned toward
London, and the Battle of Britain began to merge into the Blitz. With
the growing volume of German night activity the graph of Q site
operations swung upward: 37 raids were recorded in September and
23 in October, bringing the cumulative total in the first week in
November 1940 to 135. By now, the extension of the layout to the
western parts of the country coupled with the addition of sites in the
east had brought the number of Qs nationally to almost 100, though
many of the newcomers were still operating with flares alone.
Among these, only eleven of the original 56 sites (54 of the first plan,
together with two more added in June), had not drawn at least one
attack, and some had been regularly hit. Parent stations with Qs, by
contrast, had drawn only 55 night attacks over the same period,
meaning that seven in every ten night attacks on airfields *with* Qs
had struck the decoys.[38] In measuring the value of that statistic we
should, of course, be mindful of the caveat discussed earlier – that a
Q site attack could not automatically be chalked up as one deflected
from a specific station – but the record was still impressive, both for

the volume of bombs which the Luftwaffe had been induced to squander, and the false picture which so many Q site raids was drawing for German intelligence officers: returning crews, after all, were presumably reporting each of these operations as a valid airfield attack. K sites, too, began to do better in the autumn, drawing seven raids in September and ten in October, their best month of the war.[39] And for all this, casualties had been light. Two members of a K detachment perished in one of the daylight raids, but there were no serious injuries on Q sites (at least not to humans) and as far as it was possible to tell no civilians had been harmed. It seemed that decoy work was safer than many had expected.

Although Q and K sites drew only moderate numbers of attacks at the height of the Battle of Britain, when the extended period from mid June to the end of October is considered it is clear that their contribution to the British victory was respectable enough. Few, certainly, had been compromised during summer and early autumn. Evidence of this fell into Turner's hands in early November, when maps recovered from a crashed German aircraft were discovered to show no Q sites marked as decoys while three Ks were annotated as genuine airfields, together with one curious site where no decoy or airfield existed. This evidence was consistent with the testimony drawn from captured aircrew, several of whom claimed knowledge of a complex system of decoys in the south of the country, in areas where none existed, but appeared entirely ignorant of the real layout. The misidentified decoys were often described as dummy villages – Turner suspected these were genuine army camps – and fires, which in Turner's interpretation may have been dry grass ignited by stray incendiaries (a common occurrence) or perhaps 'promiscuous' decoy fires lit by the army (he looked into that). The prisoners also confirmed one of Turner's early hunches, namely that Luftwaffe crews were indeed under orders to bomb lights opportunistically.[40]

Since urban diversionary lighting was approved as a general policy as late as August 1940, the only cities with decoys in place when raiding swung towards the cities in September were Sheffield and Chesterfield, which were covered by the experimental MoHS lighting systems built in July (the continuing use of the Glasgow system is uncertain). These lights did well in trials during the summer. Observations showed the layout to be practically undetectable from the air by day – so it was safe from photo-reconnaissance – and that the decoy at night resembled what it was supposed to resemble, even if the displays rather lacked 'body'.[41] In mid August the site began to collect bombs. Three fell on the night of 18/19th and more on three occasions in early September, before 27/28 September brought a bag of 500 incendiaries.[42] It was far from certain, however, that these incidents could be seen as raids diverted by the decoy; more likely they represented aircraft dispatching odd bombs at unidentified lights, as many were by now known to do. Turner, for his part, knew the main weakness of the Sheffield decoy to be its position: situated nine miles north-west of the city, the site transgressed the principle that decoys must intercept the enemy's line of approach and was effectively in exactly the wrong place. This and other considerations led Turner, in the face of some resistance, to close the site once experiments were complete towards the end of October.[43]

Turner's authority to suspend work at Sheffield reflected his new status as co-ordinator of the national scheme authorised by Cabinet in early August, and with the London Blitz now fully under way it was this programme which claimed his attention. The targets now under consideration for decoys varied by department. The Admiralty were studying schemes for dockyards and Fleet Air Arm airfields, and the War Office a range of military sites such as barracks, ordnance factories and ammunition depots. At the same time, the Petroleum Board were examining the special requirements of decoying oil tank farms and the MoHS the wider range of civilian targets – factories, industrial areas, railways and cities generally. Each of these departments had appointed a liaison officer, whose duty it was to assemble deception plans in line with the general rules issued by Turner. These plans would then be referred to Turner's department for checking and, in particular, for co-ordination with the geography of schemes submitted by others. The point where these diverse plans converged was a master map, kept in Turner's office at Aerial House, showing the sites sanctioned for each department. This was Turner's chief tool in avoiding clashes and overseeing the evolution of the national plan.

Though this map would only gradually fill with markings over the coming year, by the middle of November plans made earlier in 1940 were coming to completion, and a few sites for the national layout had been approved, if not yet begun. The Air Ministry's new system of QFs authorised in early July was now fully operational, with 32 installations spread across the original decoy area of 1939 and its westward extension. Four covered the day dummy aircraft factories built earlier in the year – Coven, Chatham, Holwellhyde and Leamington Hastings – and a further six protected aircraft works without day dummies: these were at Wisley (protecting Hawker's works at Brooklands), Shurdington (for Gloster's at Brockworth), Chinnock (for Westland's at Yeovil), Bretton (for Vickers' at Hawarden), Longford (for Hawker's Langley works) and Mottram (for the Avro factory at Woodford). The remaining 23 sites shadowed airfields or important Air Ministry support bases. Most of the first airfield sites protected Fighter Command stations in the south-east, and included three added to joint K and Q sites, promoting these to the first triple-function positions: thus Nazeing (for North Weald), Bulphan (Hornchurch) and Lullingstone (Biggin Hill). Others covered airfields in the same area omitted from the original programme, but now generally provided with Qs, such as West Malling, Redhill and Kenley (which uniquely had two QFs, at Woldingham and Walton Heath). Several were for aircraft storage units, where the RAF husbanded its precious reserves – thus Quedgeley, Burtonwood, Cosford and St Athan – or special function sites such as the balloon station at Cardington or the packing depot at Sealand. The distribution of these QFs is shown in Figure 8 on page 72.

In the following year the technicalities of fire decoys would see enormous advances, thanks to the programme of large urban diversionary fires unexpectedly required in the winter of 1940–41 – the subject of the following chapter. But these early QFs were small and rudimentary. They were developed from the first experimental set tried at Toft Grange K site in late June, where fires had been made from simple combinations of creosote and roofing felt. Four 'production' types were developed by Sound City technicians to serve the operational programme, each using rather similar apparatus to produce subtly different effects. The original creosote and roofing felt equipment was standardised as the *large spluttering*

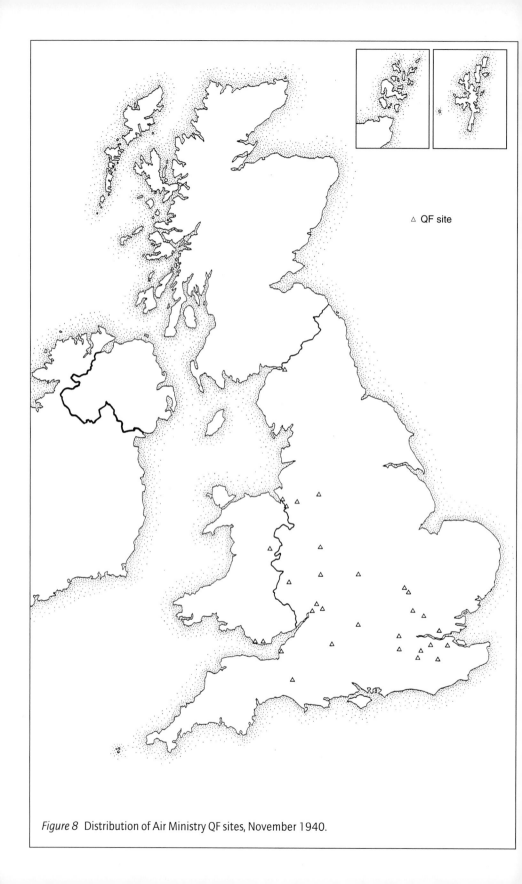

Figure 8 Distribution of Air Ministry QF sites, November 1940.

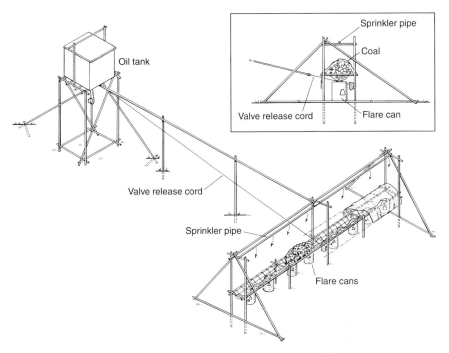

Figure 9 The coal drip fire, designed first for the QF site and later used widely in the Starfish decoys of 1941–42. Around 36 feet in length, the apparatus worked by sprinkling fuel over burning coal, itself ignited by the flare cans beneath (see inset).

fire, a term which adequately captures its effect. To this was added the *coal drip fire* (Fig 9), which was a long coal brazier, ignited by creosote in tins, onto which further creosote was gravity-fed from a header tank: the effect was spluttering and much smoke. A similar principle underlay the soberly-named *dull basic fire*, which simply lacked the tank and pipework feeding additional fuel, while the *heavy initial smoke fire* again used creosote, this time in large drums, with rolls of roofing felt placed end-on above the flames. These produced the smoke – heavily for five minutes after ignition, and less so for the next five – before the creosote settled down to a steady two-hour burn. The variety in effects from these devices was intended to mimic building fires, characteristically punctuated by bursts of flame as collapsing roofs were consumed and contents ignited. To add realism, at least some of the early fires were immured in the basic shells of dummy buildings, made from asbestos sheets, to reflect the flames and suggest their containment within non-combustible walls. Some of the devices themselves were subsequently modified in the light of further research, or came to be known by different names, but these were the archetypes around which the 1940 QFs were built.

The tactical aim of all decoy fires used by the British in World War Two was to draw the attack of the second and subsequent waves of aircraft bombing a specific target. For this reason they were sometimes known as *second-degree* decoys, in contrast to *first-degree* types (such as K and Q sites) which drew an opening attack. The key to successful operation was precision in timing, the fire being lit after the first wave of aircraft had bombed, but before any subsequent wave came into view. Judiciously-timed ignition meant that the following aircraft would, with luck, misread the burning QF site as the successful outcome from the first wave's attack, and drop its bombs there. As always, the trick was to play on what the attacking aircrew was hoping to see, and in this sense whether or not the first wave *had* started fires at the target was immaterial. If any were burning, however, prompt and vigorous fire-fighting was essential, since thorough dousing of any 'real' fires better deflected attention to the blazing decoy. A cardinal rule, however, was that lighting should never take place while bombers were actually in the vicinity. Lighting a decoy of any sort directly under the eyes of enemy aircrew was guaranteed to advertise its falsity, as Bomber Command crews were by now discovering in their operations over Germany. To ensure careful control in timing the decision to ignite the QF rested at the target, not at the decoy, where on the model of Q sites there were only two airmen, a telephone, and a shelter. Two, or at most three, hours was the maximum life of these fires, which were designed to meet raids of limited duration.

In time, as we shall see, the technology of fire decoys was elaborated, site crews enlarged and tactics refined, but already by autumn 1940 the basic site was spawning the specialised variant designed by the Petroleum Board to protect oil installations. Development of this 'oil QF' apparatus was hampered from the start by trouble in finding a suitable trials site. Though work was in hand at Leamington during August 1940, it was soon uncomfortably evident that tests with copious quantities of blazing fuel oil needed a more isolated venue.[44] This was found at Greystoke Park, to the south of Carlisle, where trials began in September with sunken channels in various shapes which, it was hoped, would resemble the appearance of burning fuel tanks seen from the air at night. Circular channels and tanks in crescent and polygonal forms were tried, with linings variously of clay, ferroconcrete and brick.[45] None was very much use, and within a few weeks 'considerable difficulty' was reported in discovering the best means of building receptacles for the oil. This, after all, was pioneering work, as the trials team explained:

> All technical experience has, hitherto, naturally been concentrated upon measures to avoid oil fires and no definite knowledge was available on the subject of how to *make* them. All the experts in fact had different opinions regarding the type of fire, the type of oil to be used, whether or not it should float on water, and what form the container to take the fire should take. Hasty experiments had, therefore, to be made [. . .]. It appears that the consumption of oil is very high which not only means an expensive fire but adds considerably to the task of transporting the oil to the sites which are almost invariably very difficult of access.[46]

Reference to 'the sites' here reflects the progress made by the end of September in selecting operational positions for oil QFs. Though experiments were incomplete, eight had been found, covering widely-spread installations at Grangemouth, Stanlow, Preston, Saltend, and Killingholme, together with Thames Haven, Shell Haven, and the Isle of Grain in the Thames Estuary (the eventual number of decoys built in 1941 was twelve, for eleven parent sites). Plans for these first oil QFs were drawn up in the autumn of 1940, and costings prepared, but before they could go ahead oil consumption had to be cut to economic levels.

By mid November, as the Luftwaffe were poised to open a new phase of the Blitz in attacks against provincial cities, 23 sites were awaiting development as civil QFs. Chosen by the MoHS representatives working on the national programme, these were intended for the cities of Bristol (five sites), Middlesbrough, and Birmingham (nine each), where their role was less to protect discrete targets than to safeguard the urban area generally. As things stood in November these sites were expected to be built gradually in the following weeks; but by the end of the month it was clear that some would need to be occupied a great deal sooner than expected.

CHAPTER 4

Starfish

NOVEMBER 1940 – JUNE 1941

On the night of 14/15 November 1940 the Luftwaffe visited Coventry. Bombing started at twenty minutes past seven, when Heinkel 111s of Kampfgruppe 100, the Luftwaffe's specialist target-marking force, began to discharge their cargoes over the eastern part of the city centre.[1] Containing a high proportion of incendiaries, KGr 100's bomb loads started a cluster of fires around Coventry's fourteenth-century cathedral, which now became the centre of the target area. Drawn by the fires, as if to a beacon, successive waves of bombers from Luftflotten 2 and 3 piled more than 500 tons of bombs into central Coventry in the ten hours that followed. Years of civil defence planning could not entirely prepare a city for raiding such as this. The telephone system essential to co-ordinate fire and rescue services broke down. Gas and electricity mains were severed, and water for fire-fighting ran short. By the morning 100 acres of central Coventry were laid waste, the cathedral was a shattered ruin, two hospitals were destroyed, and much of the city's car and aircraft plant was wrecked. Daybreak exposed the faintly surreal scenes typical of bombed townscapes. Water mains sprayed into debris-strewn streets. Lamp-posts were twisted into grotesque forms. A sight which lodged in one memory was an earthen bank 'alive with tiny blue flames, like crocuses'.[2] That was a ruptured gas main, as seen by the nineteen-year-old Philip Larkin. Like many natives of Coventry, Larkin made an anxious trip home in the days after the raid, seeking his family.

The raid of mid November was not Coventry's first – the city had been bombed on no fewer than seventeen occasions since

18 August[3] – but its weight and severity marked a sharp departure from previous operations. That said, it is perhaps as well to remember that by the standards of the later war years the loss of life was comparatively small. Each of the 554 dead and 865 seriously injured was an individual tragedy, but these figures gain perspective when set against the 40,000 killed in Hamburg during July 1943, or the 87,000 estimated to have perished in one USAAF raid on Tokyo in March 1945[4] – bombing was an art only gradually perfected in war. At the time, however, the Coventry raid seemed a grave disaster, and was celebrated by the Luftwaffe as a famous victory. It gave the wartime German language a new verb in *Coventrieren*, to 'Coventrate', meaning to terrorise by force of bombs. In fact the technique could just as well have been named after Rotterdam, victim of a similar raid six months earlier, but for Britain its use at Coventry heralded a new phase of the Blitz.

At the heart of the Luftwaffe's success in the Coventry raid was the accuracy of their bombing, achieved with electronic navigation technology which enabled the leading aircraft to pinpoint the target and so mark it for succeeding waves by fires started with incendiaries. Two rather different variants of this 'blind bombing' equipment were used early in the Blitz, both ultimately derived from the Lorenz blind landing technology in use on airfields since the mid 1930s.[5] The first – the predecessor of the system used on 14 November – was *Knickebein* ('crooked leg'), a system using two radio beams broadcast from ground stations across the Channel to intercept over the target. Using *Knickebein* the pilot simply flew along the main beam – the *Leitstrahl* – attending to tones in his headset which indicated deviations from course. An audible signal from the second, intercepting beam then announced that the target had been reached. The British first learned of *Knickebein* – or at least came across the word – in March 1940, though it was June before anyone was certain that it referred to a bombing aid. Much of the achievement in the interim was to the credit of Dr (later Professor) R V Jones, and the codebreakers at Bletchley Park, whose decrypts of Enigma signals mentioning *Knickebein* pinpointed the locations of transmitter stations and finally confirmed the nature of the apparatus. On 18 June 1940 the RAF formed 80 (Signals) Wing, under Group Captain E B Addison, especially to monitor and study the beam transmissions.[6] Working from a headquarters at Radlett, a few miles north of London, by August 80 Wing was able regularly to jam *Knickebein* and did so severely during the London Blitz.

Jamming aside, *Knickebein* had the advantage that it could be used by any aircraft carrying the Lorenz blind landing system, which by 1940 was standard fit in Luftwaffe bombers. This was not true of its more sophisticated successor, known as *X-Gerät*, the apparatus which was actually used in the Coventry raid. Like *Knickebein*, *X-Gerät* was a beam system, but operated to finer tolerances and used three beams rather than two. As in a *Knickebein* operation, the aircraft was guided to the target by a director beam – narrower and more precise than *Knickebein*'s – until it intercepted the first of two transverse beams, at which point a 'bombing clock' (the *X-Uhr*) would be started. The clock ran until the second beam was reached, fifteen miles further on and five miles from the target itself, when the elapsed time between the two intersections showed the aircraft's precise speed over the ground. The clock then used this discovered ground-speed to release the bombs automatically after a further five miles, exactly on target. When properly functioning and unjammed, *X-Gerät* was foolproof; but it did require specialised apparatus, which could not be fitted to all aircraft, and thorough training for its crews.

Like *Knickebein*, the term *X-Gerät* was first heard by British intelligence in the spring of 1940, when it was unclear whether it referred to a second system, or a component of the first. Clues to the answer began to emerge in August, with the detection of cross-Channel transmissions differing subtly from the *Knickebein* beams, and were built upon early in September by Enigma decrypts referring to beam settings and other technicalities of what was clearly a separate device. These messages also associated *X-Gerät* with a single Luftwaffe unit: Kampfgruppe 100. This was a late finding. That the British discovered the existence of a Luftwaffe gruppe specially trained to bomb on *X-Gerät* only in autumn 1940 reflects the poor state of the Air Ministry's scientific intelligence in the 1930s, and indeed in the first year of the war. For *X-Gerät* had been under development in Germany since 1934, and had seen its first airborne service trials by 1938, in the hands of a unit first known as Luftnachrichten-Abteilung 100, the direct ancestor of KGr 100. Initially flying adapted Junkers 52 transport aircraft, this unit had by early 1939 begun to re-equip with Heinkel 111 bombers, in which they used *X-Gerät* in raids against Poland. The apparatus was first used operationally over Britain on the night of *Adlertag* – 13 August – in attacks on factories at Castle Bromwich and Birmingham. By this time KGr 100 was established at the airfield at Vannes, overlooking the Bay of Biscay, and six beam transmitters, with code-names drawn from German rivers, were in place on the northern French coast.

Though *X-Gerät* gave the Luftwaffe a huge advantage in bombing accuracy, the system as it came to be used in the autumn of 1940 was eventually compromised by a weakness in the communications system serving its ground organisation. Because the beam alignments demanded adjustment for each target, and plans generally had to be co-ordinated between KGr 100, higher command and the beam stations, much signals traffic flashed between the units involved in each operation. And these signals were sent, not by a relatively secure land-line, but by wireless telegraphy, encrypted using Luftwaffe *Enigma* keys. It was one of these keys which, on its breaking at Bletchley Park in September, suddenly opened the door on a wealth of information about beam alignments, targets, and *X-Gerät* as a whole. Although the key used to pass settings to the beam stations was not broken until 14 November – the day of the Coventry raid itself – from September the Air Ministry began to accumulate vital information about the system, and some measure of warning about the alignments of beams on specific occasions.

One recipient of this information was Professor Frederick Lindemann, Churchill's scientific advisor, who on Thursday, 24 October minuted the Prime Minister with a suggestion on how the new German tactics might be countered.

On many occasions recently [wrote Lindemann] it has been possible to inform Fighter Command in advance what targets were going to be attacked and approximately what course the first raiders would take. EG [*sic*] last night it was known that Coventry would be attacked by KG [*sic*] 100, using one of the beams in the four metre region [ie by *X-Gerät*]. It must be assumed that everything was done to warn the AA batteries so that they could concentrate a barrage in the right place and that it was really impossible to lay mines in the path of the advancing aircraft.

There is some reason to believe that the method adopted is to send a few KG [sic] 100 machines fitted with special devices to assist in blind dropping on these expeditions in order to start fires on the target which any subsequent machines without special apparatus can use. If this be so the possibility of laying numerous decoy fires round such targets becomes important; especially if a few hours' warning were given, this should not be difficult provided the targets are not situated too near the centre of large inhabited areas.

The counter measures in this wave-length region do not seem to be progressing as fast as might be hoped. In my view they should take precedence of any other radio work.[7]

Churchill passed this note to the CAS (coincidentally, Sir Charles Portal took over from Newall on 25 October, the day after Lindemann's note was written) who in turn dutifully raised its various points with the officers concerned. On Lindemann's observation about the slow development of countermeasures to the *X-Gerät* – the point of his final paragraph – Portal was assured that 80 Wing would have jamming devices operable in the Midlands by about the middle of November.[8] The question about decoys passed down the line to Turner, who on 30 October was asked what could be done to divert the *X-Gerät* attacks with fires.

As you know [wrote Whitworth Jones, Director of Fighter Operations] the enemy have special methods of navigating and bombing without seeing the ground or the target. The most highly developed of these systems calls for special aircraft equipment and specially trained crews. We know that at the moment the enemy have not many of either. It is probable, therefore, that in night attacks in bad weather conditions on places such as Coventry the first few sorties are these special aircraft and crews whose aim is to start fires as a guide to following aircraft. Dummy fires on the track of the beam short of the objective might well in these circumstances attract bombs away from the vital area.[9]

The repeated mention of Coventry in this correspondence is merely an ironic coincidence. Although there was much controversy after the war over the extent to which Air Intelligence had warning of the fateful operation, with the best intelligence in the world neither Lindemann nor anyone else could have known about the especially heavy raid a fortnight in advance. And in fact Turner was already studying how decoy fires might be used to meet the tactics of KGr 100 in just the way proposed. By the end of October he had devised a scheme whereby QFs would be placed in the line of approach and ignited in *advance* of bombing – in other words as first-degree decoys – on the basis of beams for that night's operation passing nearby.

> As usual [wrote Turner on 1 November] it took me two or three weeks to get the approval of Fighter Command which was neces-sary as I wanted No 11 [Fighter] Group to run these decoys direct from its own Headquarters. I have selected five sites and expect to select a good many more round London as close in as possible with the idea of using them under the control of No 11 Group as direct decoys. This means that when No 11 Group know the lines of attack on any particular night having passed over or near one of the decoys, the decoy will be lit irrespective of whether any bomb-ing has occurred and it is hoped that bombs will be dropped on the decoys instead of in London, especially by those pilots who view with some distaste the Anti-aircraft barrage in front of them.[. . .][10]

We have no evidence, however, that these fires were ever built or operated in the way described. Certainly – and regrettably – none was prepared for Coventry in advance of the heavy raid on 14 November.

It was early in November that the *Enigma* intelligence con-verged with that from other sources to suggest that the major shift in German strategy which would lead to the Coventry raid was imminent. Hints that something new was afoot had been accumu-lating for some weeks: reports that airfields in northern France were being extended and that fresh bomber units were arriving were clear portents in themselves. Building upon this evidence, the new discovery of early November, which came from both *Enigma* and a prisoner's report, was that the Luftwaffe were soon to begin an especially heavy campaign against industrial centres, using lead aircraft from KGr 100 guided by *X-Gerät* to mark the tar-gets with incendiaries. One such operation, it was learned, went by the name of *Moonlight Sonata*, while other intelligence pointed to

three numbered targets – 51, 52 and 53 – identified by beam alignments as Wolverhampton, Birmingham and Coventry. *Moonlight
Sonata*, in fact, was the Coventry raid, though this identification
was not immediately made by intelligence analysts who from 11
November onwards were presented with a large volume of data on
the forthcoming operation, only some of which could be read as
pointing towards Coventry. As it was, Addison's staff at 80 Wing
were able to confirm that the *X-Gerät* beams were aligned on
Coventry at three o'clock on the afternoon of the 14th, four hours
before bombing would start.

So Coventry was bombed, and a new phase of the Blitz began.
For the German high command this latest change of tack was justified by the need not only to diminish Britain's capacity to wage
war through disrupting centres of production, but increasingly to
wear down the populace at large. Over the next three months, until
late February, the Luftwaffe visited fourteen major cities in 48 separate raids (three quarters of them heavy), paying particular attention to industrial centres and major ports.[11] The British soon
recognised the Coventry raid as the start of the new campaign
threatened over the preceding weeks, and saw in its mechanics the
tactics which now needed to be countered by every means available. The *X-Gerät* beams could of course be jammed by 80 Wing,
and with some forewarning of targets anti-aircraft defences might
be marshalled accordingly. And Turner's provisional scheme to
provide fire decoys for the vulnerable cities now needed to be executed urgently.

So it was that around ten o'clock on the morning of Saturday, 23
November, a message arrived in Turner's office from Air Chief
Marshal Sir Wilfred Freeman, the Vice Chief of the Air Staff,
instructing that decoy fires must be arranged that night for towns
liable to attack by KGr 100. Practically nothing had been prepared
for this work. Some sites, as we have seen, had been found for QFs
in the hinterlands of major cities, and Turner had his plans for a
London scheme, but nowhere had building begun. Seven and a
half hours of daylight remained in which to commission the sites,
and to make matters worse Turner himself was in the Hebrides

(where he seems to have been advising the navy on its decoy schemes for the national plan) and was not expected to return until the next day. It fell to one of his staff, Wing Commander J H Harris, to do what he could.[12]

Later that morning a meeting was held at the Air Ministry to study what might realistically be achieved in the following hours.[13] The thirteen officers present – among them J H Harris and Air Commodore Board – soon decided that work for that night must be confined to just two cities: these were Birmingham and Coventry, where three decoys each would be built, some of them at sites already reconnoitred for QFs. There was no possibility, however, of using standard QF equipment, which could not be installed in time and in any case would not yield fires of sufficient size and duration. For that night, therefore, it was decided to use a fuel oil mixture – 400 gallons crude oil and 100 gallons petrol – ignited by whatever means could be improvised. Three officers were selected to supervise installation at each city, mostly drawn from Turner's staff but also including Lieutenant-Colonel E H L Jacobs-Larkcom, the War Office's decoy liaison officer, who was given charge of the Coventry party. General supervision lay with the Deputy Director of Operations (Home), who managed to round up extra hands from a group of officers who happened to be awaiting posting at the RAF Depot at Uxbridge. With no experience of decoy work nor, at the time when they were summoned to the Air Ministry, any idea what they were about to do, these men in Harris's later account 'had only the clothes they stood up in, and most [. . .] did not even have razors or toothbrushes'. Cars were found to take the party across north London to RAF Hendon, where aircraft of 24 Squadron were waiting to fly them to Elmdon and Ansty airfields.

As this scratch party was dispatched on its mission, Whitworth Jones set about tackling those arrangements which could be handled from London. Attempts to raise the mayor of Coventry through the city's still-crippled telephone system got only as far a desk sergeant at the central police station, who promised to pass on the request for a fleet of vehicles and 90 men to be made available to the task force on arrival at Ansty. The Lord Mayor of Birmingham, who was contactable personally, agreed to provide the same at Elmdon. Another call was to the distribution manager of Shellmex in London, whose Birmingham and Coventry depots would issue the drums of crude oil and petrol. These arrangements did much to smooth the paths of the installation teams, but to be doubly sure Jacobs-Larkcom and Squadron Leader W Ridley, who was in charge of the Birmingham party, carried letters giving them *carte blanche*, on Air Ministry authority, to do whatever was necessary.

What followed on that Saturday afternoon was one of the Second World War's minor miracles of improvisation, not to say one of its most improbable. Officers who had dressed that morning for desk jobs in Whitehall found themselves, by late afternoon, in the fields of the West Midlands supervising gangs of local authority workmen. Trenches were dug to hold the oil and petrol mix and, in the gathering late November gloom, the filthy job of pouring 500 gallons of the stuff was begun. The sites where these scenes were enacted at Coventry lay around four to five miles from the city centre (or what remained of it) at Brinklow to the east, Princethorpe to the south-east, and Stoneleigh on the southern side; this last was a few miles south of the Armstrong-Whitworth factory at Baginton, itself shadowed by the dummy buildings and QF at Leamington Hastings. Headquarters for the Coventry detachment were at Priory Farm, Princethorpe (whose family was later commended for giving hospitality to the oil-smeared strangers who had come to persuade the Germans to bomb them).[14] Birmingham's sites were at Illey, to the south-west of the city, Overgreen, to the north, and Bickenhill, to the south-east, all but the last of which had earlier been earmarked for a QF in the national programme. Each site was intended to be linked by telephone – somehow – to its local headquarters, where raid warnings would be received from 80 Wing at Radlett. It is unclear how much of this network was in place on the first night, however, and in the absence of telephones the site officers had discretion to ignite when they believed their target cities to be under attack. But otherwise the job was completed, and by the evening of 23 November Birmingham and Coventry were protected by six huge decoy fires, poised for lighting when the bombs began to fall. And bombs did indeed fall that night, when at ten minutes to seven KGr 100 opened the evening's proceedings; but they fell 150 miles away, on Southampton.[15]

That the frantic efforts of 23 November were spent on decoying the wrong targets was nobody's fault. Birmingham and Coventry had been the focus of the Luftwaffe's attentions in the previous week or so, and if any two cities were to be given emergency decoys on that day, these were the obvious ones to choose. In any case, already by the afternoon of the 23rd Wing Commander Harris was planning extensions of cover to meet the requirements of the original orders. The first job, in Harris's judgement, was to consolidate the improvised work done that day; and beyond that he proposed to build fire decoys for seven cities – Sheffield first, then Manchester, Derby, Crewe, Bristol, London and Middlesbrough – initially as emergency schemes and later in permanent form.[16] This was the state of affairs awaiting Turner on his return from the Hebrides on Sunday, 24 November.

Turner found little to quibble with in these ideas, and though the order of priority among cities was soon rearranged, the job was now set to develop along straightforward lines. It was clear to Turner, however, that the programme for what he soon dubbed 'Special Fires' – or 'SF sites' – must be conceived as an addition to the embryonic plan for urban QFs, and not merely as a modification to it: fires of this size demanded increases in safety distances, as well as good links to well-made roads for supplying fuel. On the model of the first emergency layouts at Birmingham and Coventry, Turner at this stage was thinking of building three sites for each town to be protected, these distributed at convenient points south of an east–west line through the city centre; this is how most were begun, though many towns would eventually gain more sites and the largest number eventually given to any one was fourteen. Reconnaissance officers sent out in early December were instructed to find positions between five and ten miles from city centres, and at least two miles from the built-up area. An 800-yard safety distance from buildings was imposed.

With the special facilities awarded him in the summer Turner was able to give the contract for building the fires directly to Sound City, whose technicians were already preparing materials for the QF programme and had, by now, added expertise in fires to their talents. One potential delay was thereby avoided, while Treasury authority was known to be merely a formality, since by the end of November Churchill – always a friend to decoy work – had personally endorsed the scheme.[17] The plan was for Sound City to build the initial fire before handing over to a local contractor to multiply it by a factor of three or four. On this basis Turner reckoned that one site could be prepared daily, as Loudon's men made their way around the country completing what, to begin with, was expected to be about 100 installations, serving perhaps 30 cities. This became the regular arrangement, though the sites opened in the first extensions to the scheme do appear to have used a crude fuel oil principle similar to that employed at Birmingham and Coventry. This was a pity, since as things turned out the fuel oil method was far from satisfactory: most of the fuel soon percolated into nearby rivers.

Turner lost no time in getting the first sites of the main programme into operation, and by 27 November additional fires of some sort were in place at Bristol, Sheffield, Derby and Crewe. Rewards came almost immediately. Though one of the Bristol sites was lit without result on 26 November,[18] the night of 2/3 December saw another, at Stockwood, draw a moderate attack.[19] Next night one of the original Coventry sites was lit, a few bombs falling sufficiently close to suggest that the decoy had again done its work.[20] Both of the decoyed raids had been led by KGr 100, bombing on *X-Gerät*, though the Coventry fire appears to have been lit in response to an operation actually directed at Birmingham. Exactly how many SFs were provided for each town in these early days is uncertain, though the evidence suggests that Derby and Crewe were each covered by only two fires, and that spreading cover among probable targets took priority over multiplying sites at individual cities. It was on this basis that approval was given, on 3 December, to push the work on to Wolverhampton, Middlesbrough, Manchester, Cardiff, Liverpool and Belfast. Turner, however, queried whether Belfast should be included at so early a stage, given the number of vulnerable towns in England, Scotland and Wales, and doubts over whether the *X-Gerät* beams could reliably reach Northern Ireland.[21] Belfast was shelved for later attention.

That is not to say, however, that the evolution of policy always ran smoothly in these early days. Given that the Air Ministry was occasionally receiving notice of beam alignments from *Enigma* traffic there was an argument for closely harmonising the sequence of decoy provision with what was known of enemy intentions. This question was raised early in December with reference to what appeared to be the Germans' unfinished business at Wolverhampton. Early in November, as we have seen, Bletchley had decoded the instructions sent to the X-beam stations ordering them to prepare for operations against three numbered targets – 51, 52 and 53 – identified as Wolverhampton, Birmingham and Coventry. Coventry had been bombed under *Moonlight Sonata*, while codenames for the sister operations had by now also come to light. Birmingham (Target 52) had been bombed on 19 and 20 November under the flag of Operation *Regenschirm* – a term meaning 'umbrella' – which with surprising ease had been associated with the umbrella-carrying Neville Chamberlain, at that time Birmingham's most famous son. But what of Target 51, at Wolverhampton? In confident expectation of attack, Dr Jones had urged that Wolverhampton's anti-aircraft gun defences must be strengthened, and this had been done. But much to Jones's embarrassment Wolverhampton was left alone: as we have seen, KGr 100's attentions after Coventry and Birmingham had turned to Southampton.

The solution to the problem of the missing raid was not long in coming, when an overheard conversation between two Luftwaffe prisoners revealed that the Wolverhampton operation had indeed been planned, but then cancelled. This raid, the prisoners conveniently disclosed, had gone under the code-name *Einheitspreis*, whose translation to 'unit price' suggested a train of thought to Woolworth's (where goods were priced at sixpence), which in turn approximated to the name of the target city.[22] This appeared to settle the problem, but in the first week of December, Lindemann began to agitate for Wolverhampton's defences to be intensified urgently, particularly with SF sites (which were then gaining the name, soon to be dropped, of 'Crashdecs'). Lindemann made his case in a paper to Churchill; this was in turn referred to Portal, and thence to the DCAS, who since 25 November had been Air Marshal Arthur Harris.[23]

As is well known, Lindemann's opinions on air defence, while sometimes well-founded, were seldom wholly welcomed by the Air Staff. So it was now, as Harris made clear to Portal on 4 December.

We are already aware of all the information available to Lindemann [wrote Harris] which consists solely of a report from a prisoner of war that a Wolverhampton crash concentration scheme
had been prepared by the Boche *and had a code name equivalent to
'Woolworths'*.

We are now engaged in preparing the crashdec fires as fast as
possible, and have still got Sheffield, Birmingham, Derby, Wolverhampton, Crewe, Coventry, Middlesbrough and Manchester to
deal with in that order.

By upsetting the working plans already made, Colonel Turner
might be able to lay the Wolverhampton crashdec fire on in four
days as opposed to seven, but I personally think that the order
above represents as near as possible the order of importance of
the various towns to us, taking into consideration that the Boche
probably thinks that Coventry has already been dealt with sufficiently for the present. [. . .][24]

In fact the prisoner's indiscretion was not the only information
available to Lindemann, who was in touch with Jones's work on
the beams; and though the captive had held the Wolverhampton
operation to be dead, he could have no way of knowing whether it
might be resurrected. Nonetheless, Harris was implacably
opposed to Lindemann's intervention, and his feelings toward
Churchill's advisor coloured his closing remarks.

Lindemann's note appears to be based entirely upon information
leaking out of D[irector] of I[ntelligence]'s Department through
Dr Jones [wrote Harris], but naturally, we get it all sooner than
he does. Our work is made none the easier by the continual
necessity of leaving it in order to write papers and answers to
meet the naive queries of outside busybodies who peddle sec-
ondhand information in the guise of esoteric knowledge until it
finally boomerangs back to us in the guise of a bogey or a new
discovery.

I would therefore suggest a reply to the effect that Lindemann's knowledge emanates from this Department, and that
action was taken in the matter long before he heard of it.[25]

So that was that; but Wolverhampton in any case was included in
the next batch of towns to be dealt with.

In the second week of December Turner visited 80 Wing's head-quarters to discuss means of controlling the growing layout of SF sites. It was decided that one of his officers would move permanently to Radlett to pass alerts to SFs covering particular target cities on the basis of 80 Wing's monitoring of beam alignments. Flight Lieutenant Dick (who had been in the Birmingham party for the emergency work a fortnight earlier), was duly appointed fire control officer. It was also around now that SF decoys gained the name by which they would be known for the rest of the war. 'Crashdec' had never caught on, so by a back-formation from the initials SF, large fire decoys were christened 'Starfish', becoming unique among Turner's decoys for being known by a name as well as an abbreviation. By the end of December eighteen Starfish were operational.

From December 1940 new Starfish continued to open at a rate averaging almost one site daily until June, when the end of the Blitz brought a hiatus in construction. Most were selected jointly by Turner's department and the MoHS, though from the beginning a few were surveyed and built by the Admiralty, making use of the apparatus for decoy work put in place when the national programme was authorised in July. Naval Starfish were in fact among the first to be approved, when sites were improvised at Plymouth in December 1940 and subsequently consolidated.[26] Nationally, by 23 January 1941 the number of civil sites had risen to 43, covering thirteen cities – Bristol, Birmingham, Sheffield, Derby, Crewe, Wolverhampton, Coventry, London, Manchester, Middlesbrough, Liverpool, Warrington and Glasgow – most of which had two, three or four decoys, though Glasgow's initial layout extended to nine sites, the last of which was approaching completion that week.[27] The next four towns on the list had their Starfish in place by the end of January: these were Gloucester, Newcastle, Portsmouth and Southampton;[28] after these came three targets in Wales, at Swansea, Cardiff and Newport, before attention turned back to England with work on layouts for Rugby, Leeds and Scunthorpe. So it continued, and by the end of April, 130 civil Starfish were in place, protecting 42 target towns.[29] This layout covered all the major cities in England, Wales and southern Scotland, but included many smaller English towns within reach of the beams. Thus in early spring 1941 Starfish were provided for major targets at

Leicester, Nottingham, Hull, Doncaster, Swindon and Edinburgh, but also for Slough, Stourport, Redditch, Reading, Stoke-on-Trent, Accrington, Cowley, Northwich, Ipswich, Darlington and Yeovil. To ease the burden on Turner's department, from the end of January 1941 administration and personnel responsibilities for the Starfish organisation were given to the RAF's Balloon Command.[30]

The order in which towns were handled in the main programme was reflected in the identification codes allocated them: the practice was to number towns and letter their sites, such that (for example) SF1(a) was Stockwood, protecting Bristol, SF9(d) was Chunal Moor, for Manchester, and so on. The end of June saw the civil sites reach SF48(b), which was Overton, for Lancaster, one of five towns covered in June 1941, the last month of the dwindling Blitz, when civil sites were also opened at Norwich, Luton, Northampton and Peterborough. By this time the original Portsmouth sites – Farlington and Sinah Common – had been transferred to the navy, while now or soon after (and certainly by the end of July) additional Starfish had been built under naval arrangements at Barrow (two sites), Greenock (two) and Hull, where a pair of naval Starfish defended Killingholme and Grimsby, as distinct from the civil sites covering the city itself.[31] In common with many naval Starfish, these sites were already provided with QL lighting by early summer of 1941, prefiguring an arrangement later extended to their civil counterparts. Most civil Starfish used newly-found positions, rather than adapting those already found for QFs or doubling-up with existing decoys, but there were exceptions. SF7(a) (for Coventry) was at Leamington Hastings, where it joined the dummy factory and QF covering the Armstrong Whitworth works at Baginton, while SF8(e), one of five London Starfish built in spring 1941, was sufficiently close to Biggin Hill's joint K/Q site at Lullingstone for the two to share personnel.

Figure 10 shows the Starfish layout as it stood in June 1941, when the Blitz ended and the rate of site-building began to slow. Even plotted at this scale, it will be obvious that the layouts for individual towns and cities varied widely in extent: some Starfish hugged their targets closely, lying no more than two or three miles from the edge of the built-up area, while others belonged to more expansive layouts spreading over vast areas. On the Humber, to take one sample area (Fig 11, page 92), Starfish on the

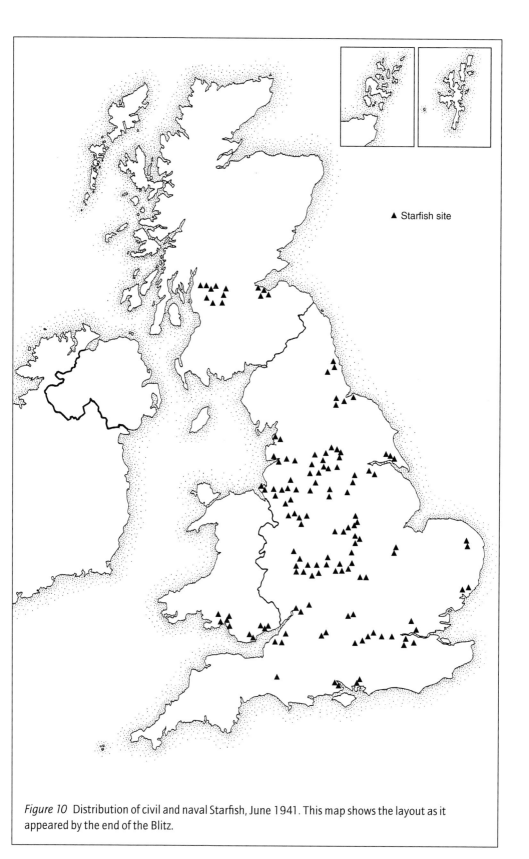

Figure 10 Distribution of civil and naval Starfish, June 1941. This map shows the layout as it appeared by the end of the Blitz.

▲ Starfish site

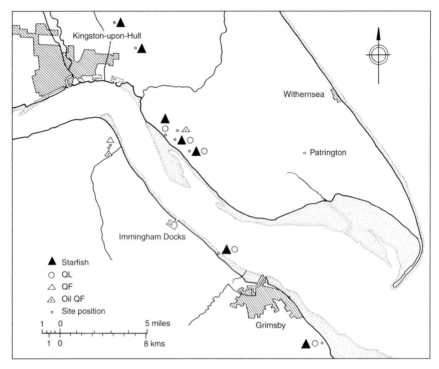

Kingston-upon-Hull

Withernsea

Patrington

Immingham Docks

▲ Starfish
○ QL
△ QF
⬠ Oil QF
∘ Site position

1   0   5 miles
1   0   8 kms

Grimsby

Figure 11 Decoys for Hull and targets on the Humber Estuary. In this and subsequent area maps small symbols shows the exact position of the sites, the larger symbols the types of decoys present.

northern bank covering Hull came to occupy two distinct areas, one immediately to the east of the city and the other further downriver, providing two clearly-defined alternative decoy zones to widen the range of potential responses to attack. Opposite these, to the south, Immingham and Grimsby were each covered by single Starfish which effectively displaced the two targets by two or three miles in the direction of attack. At Bristol, on the other hand (Fig 12), the sites formed a cordon across the southwestern approach such that raiders approaching up the Bristol Channel would pass within two or three miles of at least one decoy. Some Starfish layouts were more dispersed still. That for Leeds, for example, effectively covered not just the entire Leeds–Bradford conurbation, but reached westwards towards Huddersfield and the (separate) Manchester system.

In some cases these very scattered Starfish layouts were intentional, though other systems contained remote sites for want of better positions further in. Throughout the first half of 1941, as the Starfish layout steadily grew, Turner met outbreaks of vigorous local resistance to his sites, and sometimes from surprising sources. Decoys, understandably, were never popular with local people and landowners, and the strict siting rules introduced in summer 1940 for the national programme acknowledged as much. But the building of Starfish sites pushed complaints to epidemic levels – indeed, to the point where some officers whose duty it was to deal with them voiced concern that they had little time left for their real work. The grumbles began early, and already by 5 January, a month or so into Starfish work proper, had become sufficiently numerous to permit classification by an Air Ministry official. One type of complaint was from landowners who resented the risk to property and general inconvenience caused by decoy

Figure 12 Starfish protecting Bristol, spring 1941. Subsequent development of the Bristol decoys is shown in Figure 33.

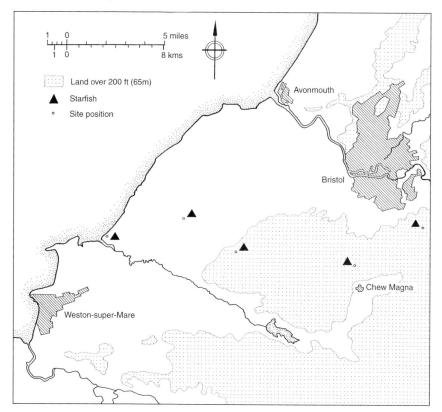

sites; another came from nearby residents anxious at the hazards which decoys brought on their heads – though to balance these it was noted that 'Tenants of land rarely complain and farmers generally have behaved splendidly.' But then there was a third category of complaint, from:

> Busybodies (mainly local property owners) whose mission in life is to criticise all actions of the Government and who think they have found golden opportunities in drawing attention to the heinous crime of placing [. . .] decoys near objects of local interest or in agricultural areas where invariably the finest crops in the country are grown.[32]

The military reacted more strongly still, particularly when local complaints began to be joined by others from MPs, and by claims from the Ministry of Agriculture that sites had been commandeered in a 'high-handed' manner. The latter accusation landed on Arthur Harris's desk in early February. Certainly, Harris agreed, the Air Ministry had moved quickly in bringing Starfish into operation, and had bypassed the usual channels to do so, but then in the process they had probably saved the city of Bristol (whose Starfish by now had been regularly raided). Starfish, like other decoys, simply could not be built with widespread consultation. 'The fact remains', he wrote, 'that the whole essence of the decoy fire racket is operational secrecy, and the very suggestion that these matters should be bandied about and discussed by such bodies as local Agricultural Committees, fills one with horror.'[33] Harris in fact saw the Starfish programme as a 'test case', in which the Air Ministry should seek a precedent by insisting on more or less complete freedom of action. In contrast:

> This case, as in others [continued Harris], savours strongly of a tendency to bureaucratic interference *in the actual course of battle.* If it is allowed to pass unchallenged, one can only say that hundreds more similar cases will occur, and, through force majeure, will have to be dealt with in the same 'high handed' manner; in the possible event of invasion, for instance.[34]

Just how badly some of those working on the decoy programme came to feel about interference – whether bureaucratic or based in self-interest – is reflected in some notes put together by Turner late in May 1941, ostensibly dealing with the problem of decoy secrecy. The risk of compromise, wrote Turner, 'is greater in the neighbourhood of towns than in the country.'

> In country districts the local inhabitants soon find out about a decoy, chatter about it amongst themselves and then forget about it. Few countrymen talk freely to those who are not their neighbours. The chief danger in the country is the pompous country house owner, male or female, who considers that any additional risk to his or her person must be due to muddling by the bureaucracy. They frequently protest through various channels including MP's and Ministers. They discuss the iniquity among the county families. Considerable information has to be given away in answering these egotists, and in consequence many sites obtain an undesirable degree of publicity.[35]

And this, it should be noted, was not a private letter, but a technical briefing written for wide circulation. Confidentially, Turner's invective was still more vigorous. In late January 1941 he complained to the Air Staff of the 'unceasing' obstacles put in his path by 'the numbers of individuals who in our democratic regime consider it their duty to raise objections.'

> Generally speaking those most affected object least. The attitude of farmers and tenants of land to decoys is generally beyond all praise. Some trouble can generally be anticipated from landowners and their agents, but it is the self-appointed local busybodies including Members of Parliament who provide the most virulent and inaccurate diatribes and demands for disciplinary action against officers who are only obeying orders. We live and learn – even from a fat female MP whose description of a stone's throw is 1,200 yards. [. . .][36]

Turner's description of MPs as 'self-appointed' shows that he was not immune from inaccurate diatribe himself; and one wonders whether it was the lady's size, sex or occupation which offended him the most. But these, surely, were justified reactions, even allowing for Turner's characteristically pugnacious language. Revisionists might seize upon these quotations as further evidence that Britain's experience of the Blitz was altogether less co-operative and communal than we like to think, and up to a point they would be justified to do so. But it is important to be clear where the trouble lay. Turner's complaints were chiefly about prominent figures who objected to intrusions which would bring the Blitz onto their doorsteps. He had seen it all before, as Director of Works from 1931–39, when just the same types of people (county families, MPs, 'egotists') had routinely put up strong objections to new airfields. Property interests were part of this, no doubt, but it is tempting to identify resistance to decoys as much with the gulf between urban and rural experiences of war as the simple instinct to preserve estates inviolate. The Blitz was twentieth-century aerial warfare at its most extreme: it was pre-eminently a mechanised war of the cities, and some at least in the country were happy for it to remain there.

On their commissioning in the first half of 1941 Starfish became the most technically sophisticated decoys in Turner's repertoire. They could not be otherwise. Imitating the effects of incendiaries dropped at the onset of a raid demanded large, fierce fires, with internal diversity. Precise timing in use added the requirement for instant ignition and rapid 'take', while the tendency for raids to last many hours demanded longevity of burn. Moreover, a need for still fiercer and larger fires arose a month or so into the programme, when KGr 100 refined its fire-raising tactics by sharply raising the proportion of incendiaries in its bomb loads. First used in a raid on Sheffield on the night of 15/16 December, the effect of this change was startling even to KGr 100's crews, who now began to speak of 'fire-ribbons' laid down across the target by igniting incendiaries, and of the *Brandbombfeld* ('fire-bomb field') which emerged as these fires coalesced.[37] It is possible – though we cannot be sure – that the growing technical sophistication of Starfish during 1941 was designed to match this fiercer form of incendiarism. However that may be, size and variety of blaze was achieved by a range of standardised fire types, and by multiplying these at each site. Instant lighting depended upon electrical igniters, while the all-night burn of a Starfish was achieved simply by prodigious quantities of fuel.

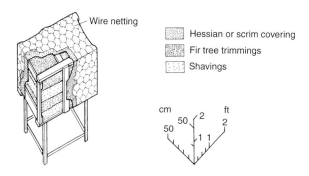

Figure 13 Construction of a basket fire, as used on Starfish and later on QF sites. Baskets were ignited by flare cans placed adjacent (see Plate 9).

Structural description of a Starfish site best begins with their fire equipment, four main varieties of which were produced by Turner's department and Sound City in 1941, some of them refinements of apparatus previously developed for the QF.[38]The simplest was the 'basket fire' (Fig 13), which was a small (approximately 3 feet square), roughly-made wooden crate, lined with wire netting and filled with a layercake of highly flammable but inexpensive materials – scrap wood, shavings, sawdust, pine clippings and other waste – with a gallon of creosote spread between each layer. Weighing about two and a half hundredweight, this package was covered in a top skin of wire netting and hessian or scrim, set on a wooden stand, and capped with roofing felt to keep it dry while dormant. Beside the basket and linked to it by a wick was set a 'flare can' to provide a catalyst for the initial blaze: these were four-gallon tins of creosote with vents cut in the side. Basket fires were always used in groups – usually clusters or rows of eight, sixteen, 24 or occasionally more (Fig 14, page 98) – in which the majority were fired by their own igniters, though closely adjacent baskets were sometimes left to catch the fire from their neighbours. Basket fires and flare cans together produced an impressive blaze within about two minutes, and for this reason were always fired first when a Starfish came into action. Their life, however, was short – no more than 50–70 minutes – so Starfish which were required to burn, typically, for four hours required multiple basket groups, lit in relays.

More sophisticated and longer-burning than the basket fires were the 'coal fires' and 'coal drip fires' adapted from the types used

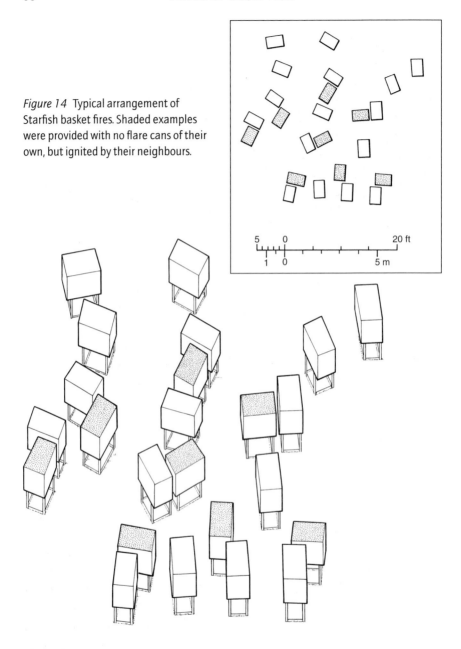

Figure 14 Typical arrangement of Starfish basket fires. Shaded examples were provided with no flare cans of their own, but ignited by their neighbours.

on the early QFs of 1940 (Fig 9, page 73). In their Starfish application these devices used a single or double metal brazier, 20ft long, built from a frame of tubular scaffolding carrying a coal tray of expanded metal, onto which the electric igniters were fitted. A variant of the coal type using a wire-mesh container and flare cans

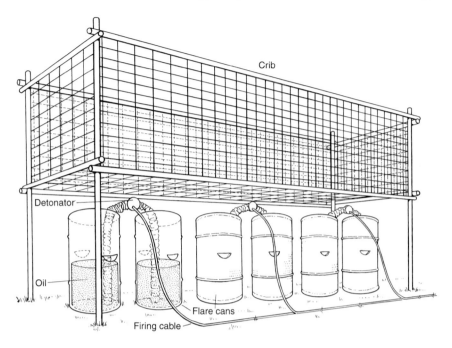

Figure 15 The crib fire. Fuel was contained in the wire mesh crib and ignited from flare cans, which in turn were lit from detonators linked by a firing wire to the site's control shelter.

was called the 'crib fire' (Fig 15). The double brazier type held about four hundredweight of firewood to kindle the fire, which consisted of three tons of lump coal. The main difference between the normal Starfish coal fire and its predecessor was the absence of a sprinkler feeding liquid fuel – making it the coal drip fire proper – which was normally present on the QFs of 1940 but appears to have been present only on the early Starfish, where the fuel used was diesel oil rather than creosote. Though rather slow to get started, the dull red glow of established coal fires served as a steady background to the livelier effects produced by the other types.

Unquestionably the most dramatic of these was the 'boiling oil fire', one of two types to use liquid fuel. The fire was contained in a heavy steel trough containing ten hundredweight of coal mixed with creosoted waste, over which was set a steel tray. Fuel – diesel or gas oil – and water were fed from two separate tanks (Fig 16). Once lit by the electric igniters, the coal burned through a cord which, on snapping, opened a valve in the oil supply pipe; at this,

Plate 6 Starfish boiling oil fire.

Plate 7 Wartime view of SF29(c), Sulham (for Reading).

Plate 8 Starfish grid fire.

Plate 9 Starfish basket fires.

Figure 16 The boiling oil fire. Water flushes introduced to the burning fuel in the metal tray produced a violent and explosive effect. A typical apparatus measured 62 feet from the tanks to the furthest end of the fire tray.

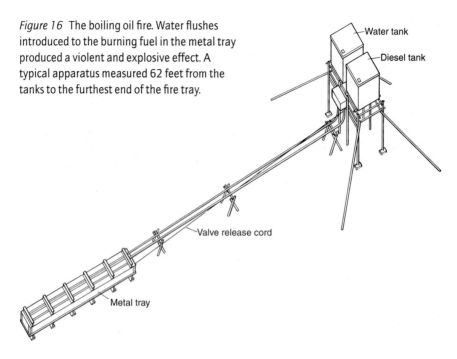

the first 66-gallon flush of oil flooded into the tray, which was still warming, and spilled over to nourish the coal fire. This was repeated for the first few flushes of oil, which were automatically released every three minutes or so. After about 20 minutes, however, the tray had become hot enough to boil and vaporise the oil, which thereafter burned with increasing vigour. Once this stage was reached the water tank came into operation, releasing two-gallon flushes into the tray alternately with those of oil. Cold water suddenly meeting boiling oil produced violent and explosive bursts of flame, reaching heights up to 40 feet. These fires burned for four hours on a supply of 480 gallons of oil and 200 of water, producing as they did so huge temperatures – the trays needed regular replacement – and dramatic effects. Twelve or fourteen boiling oil fires were provided on most Starfish.

Liquid fuel, in this case paraffin, was also used in the 'grid fire' (Fig 17). This was a framework of steel tubing – the grid itself – to which were attached wire waste and metal turnings towards the top and wicks and igniters below, protected from weather by roofing felt. Paraffin was fed over this framework from a sprinkler pipe, brought into operation when one of the igniters burnt

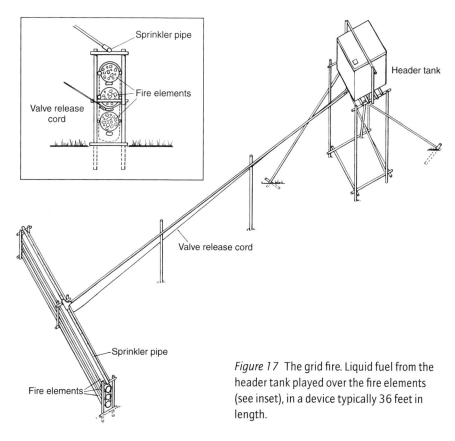

Sprinkler pipe

Header tank

Fire elements

Valve release
cord

Valve release cord

Sprinkler pipe

Fire elements

Figure 17 The grid fire. Liquid fuel from the header tank played over the fire elements (see inset), in a device typically 36 feet in length.

through a release cord. It was fed from a 180–200 gallon tank to sustain a four-hour burn. Producing a vivid yellow flame, the grid fire added variety rather than volume, and for this reason was the least common type used on Starfish, most of which had between three and five examples. In addition, some of the naval Starfish made use of a specialised fire type known as the 'cordite flash', which simply used pieces of electrically-ignited scrap cordite to suggest the crackling effect of a successful attack on an ammunition store.

These four basic fire types were arranged on a typical Starfish in groups, each separately controlled from a sunken shelter. In time, most Starfish came to be provided with two major fire groups, each of which would burn for four hours with 25 tons of combustible material, while a further 25 tons was kept on site to allow immediate rebuilding of one of the groups; a few, however, were double this size.[39] Over the duration of the war, as we shall see, sev-

Plate 10 Wartime view of an unidentified Starfish. The tanks for the fire apparatus were the main features visible from ground level.

eral variations were introduced in Starfish firing procedures, allowing isolated components of the sites to be let off individually to meet changing Luftwaffe bombing procedures. In the early days, however, the usual ignition pattern (later known as the 'Full Starfish') called for all of the fires in one group to be let off at the start of the operation – typically 120 baskets, two boilers, one grid and one coal drip and one plain coal fire – together with part of the second group, usually just one set of 24 baskets and all the other types. Hour by hour, the remaining baskets in the second group would be then ignited in sequence, to maintain body in the blaze and ultimately consume the full 50 tons of fuel.

With so much volatile material concentrated on the site, and little equipment available for *extinguishing* fires, an essential of Starfish design was to isolate the fire groups from one another, and from the nearby fuel reserves. This was the function of the shallow 'firebreak trenches' dug around each group of fire devices to prevent grass fires spreading to engulf the entire site in an uncontrolled blaze. Together with the looping access road for fuel deliveries (which was later camouflaged), these firebreak trenches were the most distinctive features of Starfish seen from the air, and

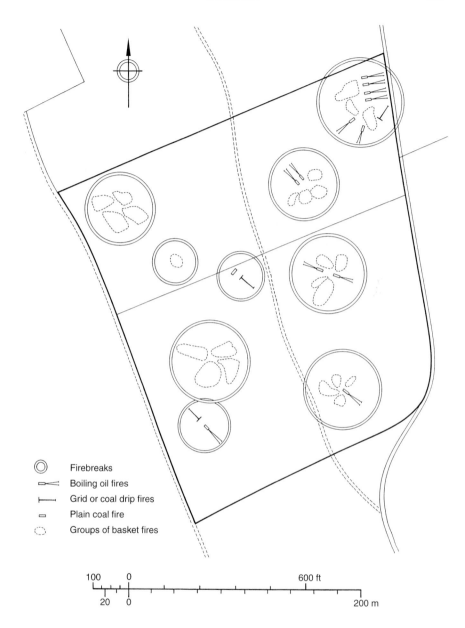

Firebreaks
Boiling oil fires
Grid or coal drip fires
Plain coal fire
Groups of basket fires

100   0   600 ft

20   0   200 m

Figure 18 Partly schematic layout plan of a Starfish, based upon SF2(g), the Strategic site at Halford, in the Birmingham layout, to Air Ministry Drawing CTD 272A/41. Combinations of fire types were arranged in discrete groups and separately fired from the sunken shelter several hundred yards distant (see Fig 20). Though shown diagrammatically in circular form, firebreak trenches were usually excavated in irregular polygons or curvilinear shapes.

were excavated in curvilinear shapes, irregular polygons, or occasionally crude circles. Some were subdivided further to separate
fire equipment (especially baskets) which were to be ignited
sequentially. Accidental fires were an ever-present danger on
Starfish sites, not only from uncontrolled spread in operation, but
also from lightning, static electricity, and all too frequent electrical
faults. Lightning conductor poles were raised on some sites, while
all fire groups were bonded with copper wire and carefully
earthed. Cables to the shelter were interrupted by plugs, enabling
the fire groups to be isolated during the day.

The electrical engineering of Starfish was complex, requiring
constant maintenance from the two electricians included in the
sites' initial regular staff of 24 airmen. The wiring of the decoys
built in 1941 obviously grew in complexity as sites expanded in
size, and with refinements demanded by innovations in tactics.
But the basic principle was to run cables from the fire groups to the

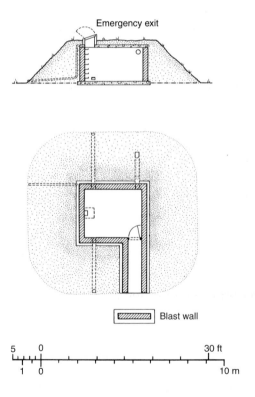

Figure 19 Starfish control shelter, to Air Ministry Drawing CTD 557/41.

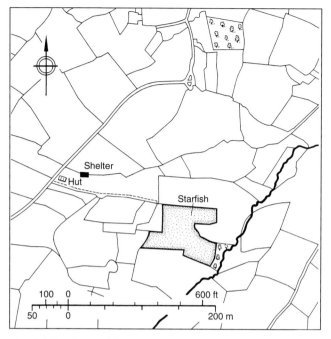

Figure 20 A Starfish locality. SF1(a) – Stockwood in the Bristol layout – showing the site boundary and retired shelter position.

shelter holding the telephone from which orders were issued to ignite, and the switchgear which brought the decoy to life. The shelter consisted of little more than a rectangular cell walled with brick or concrete blocks (Fig 19) capped by a reinforced concrete roof and banked with earth for blast protection (above-ground shelters were generally adopted in 1941 after the sunken types at early Q sites had been found to flood). With several hundred yards between site and shelter (Fig 20), Starfish needed a mass of wiring, all of which was prone to failure through breakage, deterioration in winter or attacks by animals (it was reported that 'sheep, particularly, were inclined to nibble the cables').[40] Keeping a Starfish primed for action was a full-time job.

★　★　★

There were a good many Starfish operations in the first half of 1941, each of which contributed to an accumulating fund of experience which could be drawn upon to refine tactics and equipment. But while Starfish could rightly be counted as a great success by the end of the war, their ability to divert raids in the Blitz – which they had been designed specifically to meet – was more limited. The greatest Starfish successes before June 1941 were at Bristol, Portsmouth and Cardiff, all of which drew massive attacks in these months. Elsewhere, however, the record was poorer. Many Starfish were lit during the Blitz, and many of those succeeded in drawing bombs; but these attacks were usually minor – not much heavier than the pepperings which continued to be given to Q sites over the same period.[41]

The success of the Bristol sites was the first to emerge. Following the raid drawn by the Stockwood decoy on 2/3 December 1940, when 61 HE bombs were recorded, another Bristol site drew 56 HEs four nights later.[42] Together with a large number of incendiaries – which were always difficult to count – the bombs of the second raid were estimated to represent some 40 per cent of the Luftwaffe's effort against Bristol that night.[43] Thereafter, Bristol Starfish were bombed on eight further occasions down to 11/12 April. Some of these attacks were small – nine HEs on 3/4 January, four the next night – and comparable to those hitting Starfish nationally, but the others collected at least a dozen high-explosive bombs and a major success came on 16/17 March, when no fewer than 152 HEs landed on and around SF1(c) at Downside, together with incendiaries.[44] March was the month in which Starfish began to score more highly elsewhere, a trend in part reflecting their steadily-growing numbers. Seventeen sites were lit (compared to only four in February), all but one of which drew an attack, though the numbers of bombs involved were generally small. Apart from the Bristol raid, the only big attack on a Starfish in March was at Cardiff, where on the night of the 4th, SF20(b) at Lavernock attracted 102 HEs and 'innumerable' incendiaries.[45] By coincidence seventeen Starfish were also lit in both April and May. Though April's ignitions brought bombs on eleven occasions, only one site managed a big haul. This was SF16(b) at Sinah Common, which drew practically the whole of a major attack aimed at Portsmouth on the night of the 17th/18th and achieved the most successful Starfish operation ever. May's seventeen firings attracted only 52 HEs and a few hundred incendiaries in total, before activity dwindled in June.

A closer look at two of the most successful Starfish operations during the Blitz illustrates what the organisation could achieve when communications and equipment worked as intended. The success at Bristol on the night of 16/17 March was an occasion when events at the target city and the decoys combined to the defenders' advantage. For the decoy system this raid began at 21.13, when Bristol local control contacted 80 Wing to report that enemy aircraft were overhead and had already dropped a stick of bombs outside the city – as it happened around a mile from the waiting Starfish site at Chew Magna. Aware that the Luftwaffe's main force was approaching from the south, and could thus be heading as much for Avonmouth as for Bristol itself, at 21.30 Addison at 80 Wing ordered SF1(c) (Downside) to be ignited. The baskets came to life instantly, but although conditions were good – ground haze suffusing the light from the decoy and masking its tell-tale rural surroundings – no bombs were drawn. Soon after, incendiaries falling on Bristol opened a two-hour raid, though effective firefighting prevented a serious blaze. Consequently a further bombing wave which arrived at 02.00 expecting to find Bristol burning was promptly diverted to the still-flaming Starfish at Downside. Ringing to check on the situation, Addison found the telephone link to Downside severed, but a runner soon reported that the site was being 'plastered with HE'. At 02.28 Addison accordingly ordered SF1(b) at Chew Magna into action, in the hope of diverting further bombers. By 03.00 the site was well alight, though it drew no attack and, by 04.00, raiding had ceased. Downside's success was therefore won by a combination of energetic fire-fighting in Bristol itself – which prevented the target attracting the second wave of bombers – ground haze, which masked the exact detail of the decoy from the attacking aircraft, and the Starfish's capacity for sustained burning, which enabled it to draw bombs at least two and a half hours after ignition.

The success at Portsmouth on the night of 17/18 April 1941 was also aided by misty weather, and probably owed a good deal in addition to a particularly well-sited decoy layout. As Figure 21 shows (page 110), Portsmouth's sites lay unusually near to their parent, an arrangement made possible by the compact built-up area of the city and its position on a spit of land flanked by water and mudflats. Most were laid out on the islands in Langstone Harbour, only five or

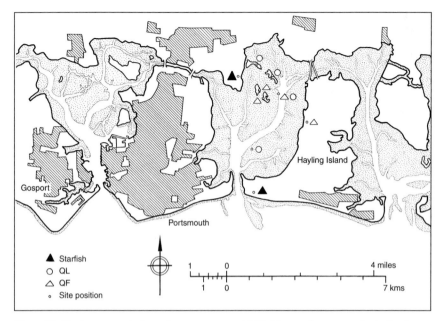

Figure 21 The Portsmouth decoy layout, summer 1941. The southernmost site is Sinah Common – SF16(b) – which on 17/18 April 1941 took part in the most successful Starfish operation of the war.

six miles from the city limit, where many diverted bombs would fall harmlessly into the water. The decoy which drew the bombs on this night was the most southerly of the group, sited on the western tip of Hayling Island at Sinah Common, a former golf links. Ignited early in the raid, the decoy was immediately spotted by the incoming aircraft of the main force, one of whose radio transmissions was heard to report 'Portsmouth obscured by mist, but can see fires.' Thereafter, only two of the 144 aircraft which attacked appeared to have bombed Portsmouth rather than the decoy site – at any rate only eight bombs fell on the city from 576 calculated to have been dropped. Around 200 of those fell on land, and some casualties ensued. Eight people died – most of them gunners at an anti-aircraft battery, whose domestic camp was flattened – while 30 people were injured and heavy damage was caused to housing on Hayling Island. The remaining bombs were swallowed by the water around Langstone Harbour and the sea off Portsmouth, so preventing an exact count of the number diverted by the decoy, though some of the aiming was accurate enough to wreck the boiler fires of the Starfish itself.[46]

These were the Starfish triumphs of 1941, but what of the failures? By early May 1941 Turner was becoming troubled by the sharp contrast between the operations at Cardiff, Bristol and Portsmouth and the near absence of success elsewhere.[47] Several reasons were possible. Clear nights were always unfavourable to Starfish operations, and there had been a good many of those. Equally, some decoys sited many miles from their target cities were too far out to be effective, both through their remoteness, and because anti-aircraft batteries and searchlights lying closer to the target themselves tended to mark it: this problem would later be addressed by closer co-operation between the two organisations. But a greater difficulty lay in failures of communication. The Starfish control system during the Blitz relied upon 80 Wing to alert towns and, if possible, individual Starfish to the likelihood of bombing on the basis of the *X-Gerät* beam alignments. Local controls were then expected to report developing raids back to Radlett where the fire control officer would give the order to fire a Starfish. Communications often broke down for technical reasons or through enemy action, and on these occasions authority to light fell back upon the local controls, but even when the telephone lines were intact reports often reached Radlett far too late to allow ignition to be judiciously timed. Two such failures occurred on the night of 8/9 May, when KGr 100 had set off to bomb Derby, had been thwarted by 80 Wing's beam jamming, and had then prowled around the Midlands and the north of England in search of alternative targets. But, as Addison explained to Turner the following morning, the Starfish organisation had largely failed to meet any of the attacks that ensued.

> As you know [wrote Addison], last night the Germans attacked the Midlands in very great force indeed – nevertheless, we were successful in keeping them off their main target, which was Derby. We could see from the plots [. . .] that although aircraft were not reaching their target some were returning to their bases. This meant that they had dropped their bombs somewhere, but from the plots on the table it was impossible to tell who was getting the punishment. We made a happy guess and rang Nottingham whom we found had already been attacked, and had a large fire blazing in the middle of the city. We therefore lit one of the Nottingham Starfish but I am afraid it was too late. The weather was very fine,

so perhaps the Starfish would not have been successful in any event, but the fact remains that had conditions been such that [the] Starfish might have drawn off the attack, the fire still would not have been lit in time, merely because we were unaware of the attack that had developed in the city.[48]

As KGr 100's unit records revealed after the war, four of the aircraft which had been unable to find Derby had diverted to Hull, where they began to assist in a major attack. And here, the Starfish organisation's failure was, in Addison's words, 'even more blatant.'

Hull got very badly knocked about last night. The whole place was on fire, yet our plotting table showed no signs of an enemy concentration in that area. We heard the news quite accidentally from Sheffield. We immediately got on to Hull and the Local Control officer then told us that the town had been on fire for at least an hour. It apparently had not occurred to him to tell us this. We then decided to set off one of the Hull sites but by this time all communications between the two banks of the Humber had gone. We

Plate 11 SF29(b), Arborfield (for Reading), 8 March 1944. The clusters of basket fires are particularly evident.

were then informed that it would take at least 35 minutes to signal instructions via Grimsby for the fire to be set off. By that time the Starfish would have been useless as the attack was already then drawing to its close. Here again weather conditions were such that Starfish may not have been successful in attracting a lot of attention, but by reason of the fact that Site 'C' is situated very near the river and not far from the town, we might possibly have got something.[49]

In Addison's view the underlying problem in these and similar incidents was the often 'lackadaisical' attitude of local controllers, who either did not properly digest their orders, or simply ignored them. He admitted, however, that equipment failures must bear part of the blame, particularly in cases where local controllers tried to raise 80 Wing, failed to do so, and then hesitated to light the Starfish on their own initiative in case Radlett could be reached on a subsequent attempt. Delays of this sort usually ensured that the Starfish, if it was lit at all, came into action much too late. Addison's

Plate 12 SF3(c), Ringinglow (for Sheffield), seen on 20 December 1945 after the removal of fire apparatus.

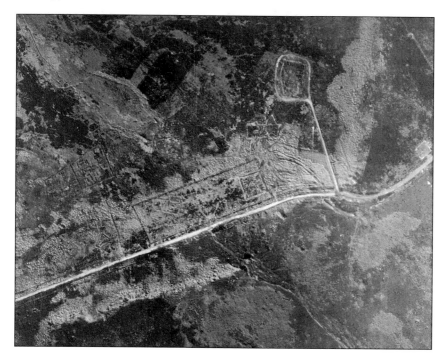

Plate 13 The defence of London: Richmond Park, 22 April 1944. The Starfish site occupies the top right of the picture, while a heavy anti-aircraft battery lies on the left. The earliest military feature is a series of ditches dug in 1940 to prevent troop-carrying aircraft from using the park as an airfield. The large building at the very top of the picture is White Lodge, home of the Royal Ballet School.

solution to this problem, recommended to Turner on 9 May, was for local controllers to be given authority to light *part* of a Starfish – say the first group of baskets – if Radlett could not be raised on the telephone within twenty minutes of an attack beginning.

Should the Starfish then begin to draw bombs while Radlett remained uncontactable, the local control could go ahead and light the entire site. 'The advantage of this scheme, as I see it,' explained Addison, 'is that the Local Control on their own initiative does do something, and having done it, he then has an appreciably longer time in which to get through to us.'[50] Addison's idea was adopted, and in early June become known as the 'Short Starfish' procedure. Capitalising upon this new flexibility, Turner arranged for the Short Starfish element at some sites to double as a QF – under entirely local control – so allowing the site to act as a large or small fire as events required.[51]

Although hardly diminishing the force of Addison's point about communications, subsequent analysis of the events on the night of 8/9 May showed that the ignited Nottingham Starfish (actually SF30(c) at Cropwell Butler) probably had influenced that night's bombing, if in a novel way. For some time after the raid no one could readily explain why 64 bombs had fallen on the village of Plungar, to the east of Nottingham (killing two cows and four hens), and a further 404 HEs in the surrounding fields of the Vale of Belvoir. Addison hit upon the answer towards the end of May.[52] On the ground, he realised, the Plungar area bore much the same relationship to the Starfish at Cropwell Butler as did Nottingham to north-east Derby, where KGr 100 were probably attempting to mark the Rolls-Royce works. The obvious implication, argued Addison, was that a late wave of bombers heading for a subsidiary target at Nottingham had mistaken the burning Starfish for a fire in Derby, which they then used as a reference point to manoeuvre themselves over what they thought was Nottingham, but was in fact Plungar. The whole raid had consequently been displaced. It was never established whether this reading was correct, though it does seem credible. And, if true, the interpretation illustrated the ability of the Starfish system to influence events in unexpected ways, as well as showing that clear nights – as this was – need not compromise individual Starfish if their fires were big enough, and seen from a distance.

Another reason for the rather indifferent performance of many Starfish during the first half of 1941 was undoubtedly that some were identified as decoys and simply ignored. The compromising effect of moonlight aside, Starfish could easily be spotted by day-

Plate 14 SF30(a), Clipston (for Nottingham), seen on 27 September 1942. Starfish were never easy to conceal from daylight reconnaissance cameras, to which the long, looping access road for supplying fuel was particularly obvious. Clipston also accommodated the QL site C18(c).

light reconnaissance photography – as the plates in this book show – and many were probably unmasked as a result. Certainly, later attempts to camouflage them were less than successful. Identifying a decoy by day, of course, was still a very different matter from doing so in the course of a night raid, since even if every site *was* mapped, a crew operating over England in darkness could seldom be so sure of their position as to know where, exactly, their aircraft was in relation to known decoys. This was very much the experience of their British counterparts, who were themselves often misled by the increasingly sophisticated layout of decoys accumulating across the North Sea.

Plate 15 SF30(c), Cropwell Butler (for Nottingham), 27 September 1942. It was this site which probably displaced the raid on 8/9 May 1941, when it was mistaken for a fire in Derby and misled the Luftwaffe into bombing the Vale of Belvoir, believing they were over Nottingham. The QL site C18(b) shared this position.

A brief look at some German decoys, and particularly the fire types in place by 1941, illustrates these tactical points and shows how technicians in the Reich handled similar problems to those confronting Turner and Sound City during the Blitz. The Air Ministry began to gather information on German decoys at an early stage of the war, and by June 1940 Bomber Command crews had identified 25 sites as decoy airfields (night and day) and twelve as dummy factories.[53] The security of these identifications, however, was often tenuous and at this stage there was clearly a tendency to suspect anything unusual as a decoy, sometimes on the flimsiest of grounds (much as interrogated Luftwaffe pilots had been found to do). As far as contemporary British intelligence was aware, attempts to decoy towns in Germany – rather than airfields and factories – came rather later, just as they did in Britain, though by December 1940 evidence pointed to the construction of six sites covering major cities such as Berlin and Stuttgart.[54] These appear to have been light displays (comparable to British QLs) though by the summer of 1941, as Britain was gaining a thickening layout of Starfish, Germany too was building night fire decoys in some numbers.

A study of these sites by the RAF's Central Interpretation Unit at Medmenham, produced in August 1941, collated clues which tended to betray fire decoys as such, and classified the known types.[55] The tell-tale operating habits which gave decoys away to

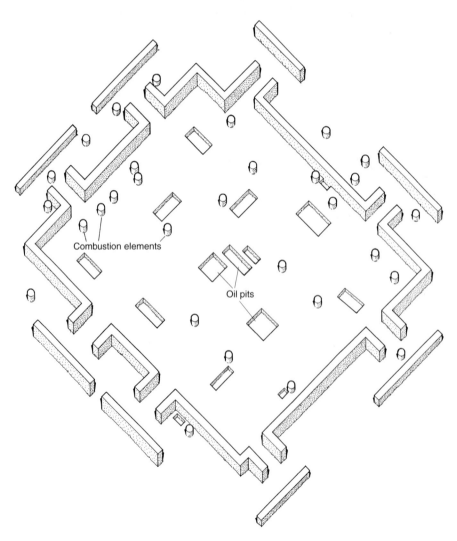

Combustion elements

Oil pits

RAF pilots were remarkably close to those which Turner had warned against over the previous year. German fire decoys were frequently ignited directly under the eyes of the attacking aircraft – some, indeed, had been lit before bombing had even started – while in general the fire types were betrayed by a lack of diversity and over-regularity (a few appeared to be powered somehow by electricity). German lighting decoys were, however, more cunning, and one near Berlin was known to be masked from day observation by being disguised as a village. The Germans, by summer 1941, had also grasped the potential for anti-aircraft and searchlight batteries to advertise the true targets, and had begun to use both – as the British later would – in close association with decoys.

Thanks to the work at Medmenham by the high summer of 1941 the Air Ministry had established that German fire decoys were built

Figure 22 Two types of German fire decoy, as reconstructed from reconnaissance photographs in the summer of 1941. Plate 16 (page 121) shows the lower type in place.

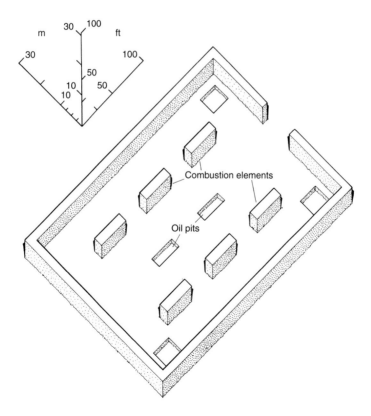

in more or less uniform types, and although at this time they could be studied only through reconnaissance photographs, inspections on the ground by officers from Turner's department immediately after the war confirmed much of what was surmised from this evidence.[56] Of the three varieties classified by mid 1941, the Type A and C decoys, as they were termed by the Air Ministry, were directly analogous to Starfish in using fires of various types (the Type B, a specialist oil decoy, is discussed later in the context of the British oil QF). The Type A presented itself to the camera as a rectangular enclosure, measuring about 230 feet by 170 feet, containing piles of what was evidently combustible material, while the Type C was essentially a larger and more complex variation on the same theme (Fig 22). One of the best early wartime pictures of a Type A was secured in mid July 1941 at a site eight and a half miles north-west of Hamm (Plate 16), where one complete and one unfinished example were present together. The absence of any track activity around the completed decoy in this and comparable photographs suggested to wartime interpreters that the piles were probably ignited remotely by electrical power, in the manner of Starfish. This judgement was confirmed by post-war inspections, which also showed that the enclosures were actually screens formed from reeds: these were probably intended to reflect the fires as if from the walls of burning buildings, much as asbestos sheets did on early QF sites. Site inspections of abandoned decoys also discovered that the piles were made from highly-combustible and cheap materials such as brushwood, shavings, celluloid film, paper, bitumen, and so on, very much along the lines of Starfish baskets. Indeed, a single enclosure with its combustible piles was more or less equivalent to a group of basket fires on a Starfish, surrounded by its firebreak trench; later sites could have as many as five separate Type A enclosures which, in combination, would produce fires broadly comparable to a complete Starfish, though without the variety added by boiling oil and other fires. Later in the war diversity was introduced among Type A sites with surplus 250kg 'Flam' oil-based incendiary bombs – the type actually used by KGr 100 on British cities until December 1940, when they were exchanged for newer variants[57] – punctured to yield oil-based fires. Oil fires on a smaller scale also seem to have been used in the Type A and C decoys from an early stage in their development: this

Plate 16 German fire decoy, eight and a half miles north-west of Hamm, in an RAF reconnaissance photograph of 14 July 1941. The two fire groups are central to the picture (annotated 'DUMMY'), with the lower example still under construction. Arrowed craters show that this site had already drawn British bombs, in quantities shown by the numerals.

appears to have been the function of the shallow rectangular pits visible in the floors of both, and particularly in the Type C, which in an example recorded at Dinslaken was also associated with a variety of smaller fire contrivances and dummy walls, again for reflections. These decoys were certainly successful. Scattered craters around the Type A decoy at Hamm (counted and enumerated on Plate 16) testified to several British attacks by mid July 1941.

The unexpected commitment to building Starfish sites which arose in November 1940 brought the number of separate strands of decoy work active in the first half of 1941 to nine. Starfish, of course, claimed the first priority in these months, but that is not to say that nothing was achieved elsewhere. Army and naval QFs and QLs were built in some numbers, while limited work was done on the oil QFs tested in late 1940. In addition, the layout of airfield Qs and QFs saw modest, continuing growth. In fact the only strand of decoy work to be seriously retarded in these months was the urban QL programme (though the staff at Leamington pressed for the Sheffield site to be reinstated), since among the sites for the national programme this, uniquely, lay jointly in the hands of Turner's department and the MoHS, whose energies were diverted to Starfish. And for the staff of Colonel Turner's Department the start of the Starfish programme brought another important change, for it was in late November 1940 that the department moved its headquarters from Aerial House in the Strand to join Sound City at Shepperton.[58]

By the last week in January 1940 there were about 100 Q sites in operation, a total which rose to 121 by the middle of July (Fig 23).[59] Although Qs continued to be parented by specific RAF stations, by now their value as simply a generalised array of spoof targets had been fully recognised, and the distribution as it appeared in the summer of 1941 was planned with this in mind. Turner's continuing commitment to Q sites rested on their repeated successes throughout the bombing of winter 1940–41 which, despite its focus upon provincial cities, had also included many night attacks on airfields. Though the number of Q site incidents dropped to eleven during December 1940 and only six in January 1941 – their worst month of the war so far – the figure leapt upwards again in February to reach no fewer than 36 attacks (against 24 on parent stations with Qs). Thereafter Q sites continued to earn their keep for the remainder of the Blitz, drawing 21 attacks in March and 46 in April before dropping back in May and June to 26 and thirteen respectively. Many of these raids were far from minor: three separate attacks in February, for example, drew as many as 300 bombs on Qs in East Anglia and Lincolnshire. We cannot be entirely sure what

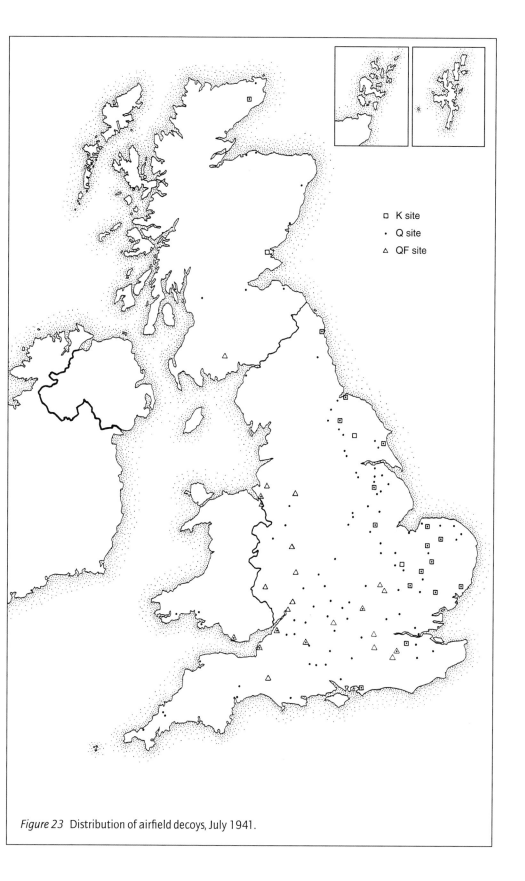

K site

Q site

QF site

Figure 23 Distribution of airfield decoys, July 1941.

lay behind this sudden upturn in Q site attacks, which from March to May was paralleled by a corresponding rise in attacks on parent stations. Some no doubt reflected the intense and widespread night activity over Britain – which exposed a larger number of sites to Luftwaffe target routings – and the tendency for lost crews or those with faulty or damaged aircraft to bomb Qs opportunistically as they turned for home. The February figures, however, cannot readily be explained in this way since it was in this month that raiding against cities eased to its lowest point, before growing again in March. One clue to the upturn may, however, be found in a strategic ruse which British intelligence attempted to foist upon the Germans at this time. Faced with a worsening onslaught against the cities over the winter, early in 1941 the espionage system was used, at Portal's suggestion, to attempt to divert attacks from urban targets to airfields. This was done through the network of double agents overseen by the Twenty Committee – Twenty deriving from the Roman numeral XX: a double cross – who were briefed that RAF stations held unusual concentrations of aircraft and were only weakly defended with anti-aircraft guns. In the official historian's account this policy was discontinued in July 1941 following 'no identifiable effect' on the pattern of German bombing;[60] yet this interpretation is not easily reconciled with the 326 raids on parent stations and their Q sites recorded in the four months from February to May inclusive. The weight of attacks over this period, it is true, was still directed at the cities, but then we have no way of gauging how much heavier they might have been without these airfield attacks. It seems possible that the ruse was more successful than previously thought.

The effectiveness of Q sites in the first half of 1941 also owed something to their continuing refinement. Some sites were given additional lamps in imitation of hangar lights, 'bad ground' lights, and so on, multiplying diversity and keeping the system in a state of continuous flux. By the end of the Blitz plans were in hand to introduce a new form of Q display imitating the 'Drem' configuration in widening use on real airfields, though these modifications did not reach the sites until the autumn. Station commanders were repeatedly urged to light their Qs more often, and with more sensitivity to Luftwaffe tactics, though the frequent changes of command at some airfields fostered large discontinuities in practice.

New men arriving in station headquarters often brought different ideas from those of their predecessors or – through inexperience in what was still a novel field – no ideas at all. Turner was obliged to keep up with this shifting population, continually bombarding stations and their chiefs with news of decoy incidents and tactical bulletins. Before long he began to circulate statistics showing unequivocally that the more Qs were lit, the more they were attacked. High-scoring stations were named in this league table, bad ones not: even Turner could play the diplomat at times.

K sites, on the other hand, fared less well in the Blitz. The preponderance of night operations undoubtedly worked against them, but this only partly explained why only two attacks were recorded in the first four months of 1941, bringing the total launched against K sites by the end of April to just 36.[61] The larger reason was that many had by now been compromised. A map recovered from a crashed enemy bomber at this time annotated practically all of the K sites in southern England as dummies, though three in this area were still marked as targets and the northern sites in general remained secure. Turner's suspicions were roused by these findings. Efficient reconnaissance photography, he thought, could not wholly explain why so many decoys had been exposed, since some of those breached – such as Lakenheath – were practically indistinguishable from true satellites, while others which had never looked well were still marked as targets: West Wittering came into this category, and despite its shortcomings in Turner's eyes was one of the most frequently attacked K sites of all. Nor could photographic reconnaissance explain why several genuine airfields, only recently selected and yet undeveloped, were already marked as stations. Spies were a possibility, Turner thought, as indeed they were. Equally, however, the wide network of consultees which the Air Ministry by now had to respect before siting decoys also opened numerous loopholes for leaks. Indeed, with the local War Agricultural Committees in this circuit Turner suspected that 'the only further publication the Germans would like [. . .] is the exact latitude and longitude and description from the BBC.'[62]

It was in January 1941 that Turner finally decided that no more K sites should be built.[63] Together with their indifferent operational record and evident susceptibility to disclosure (however achieved), K sites made demands on land and manpower which,

by this stage of the war, could no longer be justified (the maintenance difficulties of the Gateshead-built Whitleys had by now put
the crews of their K sites up to 30). And, in any case, since satellite
airfields were themselves becoming more heavily built, any new K
sites would need to match them. Once this decision was taken, closures among existing sites could not be far behind. One was
already being dismantled by late January, when Donna Nook, parented by North Coates, became a satellite airfield in its own right.
Three months later Turner circulated proposals to abandon fifteen
more.[64] Various factors condemned these sites. Menthorpe (for
Church Fenton), Lakenheath (Feltwell) and Hagnaby (Manby)
were all hemmed by new operational airfields. Nazeing (North
Weald), Bulphan (Hornchurch) and Lenham (Detling) had all been
spotted as decoys by the previous December. The remaining nine
were simply 'not convincing'. Owston Ferry (Finningley), Gautby
(Waddington), Fulmodestone (West Raynham), Swayfield (Cottesmore), Alwalton (Wittering) and Barnet (Northolt) all came into
this category, along with Grendon Underwood (Bicester), Pyrton
(Benson) and Gumber (Tangmere). These fifteen sites were closed
between the last week of June 1941 and the first week of July, leaving only 20 Ks in place to meet whatever the second half of 1941
might bring.

Cuts in the K site layout were, however, balanced by expansion
in decoy numbers elsewhere, particularly among the army and
navy sites of the national system. The first army decoys appear to
have opened in mid January 1941, when a joint QF/QL was commissioned for the Thingley marshalling yards and a QF for the
mechanical transport depot at Ashchurch, near Tewksbury. Other
sites opened through the spring and early summer protected
installations as diverse as the supply depot at Norton Fitzwarren,
near Taunton, the Royal Ordnance Factories at Glascoed, Brid-
gend, Pembrey, Chorley and Blackburn, the Central Ammunition
Depot at Longtown, Cumberland, and several railway marshalling
yards of particular importance in the army's supply systems, such
as Crewe and York.[65] By mid July 1941 the periodic schedule of
decoys issued by Turner's department listed 40 sites in the army
layout – now termed the 'A' Series – though some in this total were
probably not yet operational, and a few may have existed merely
as marks on Turner's master map at this time (Fig 24).[66] However

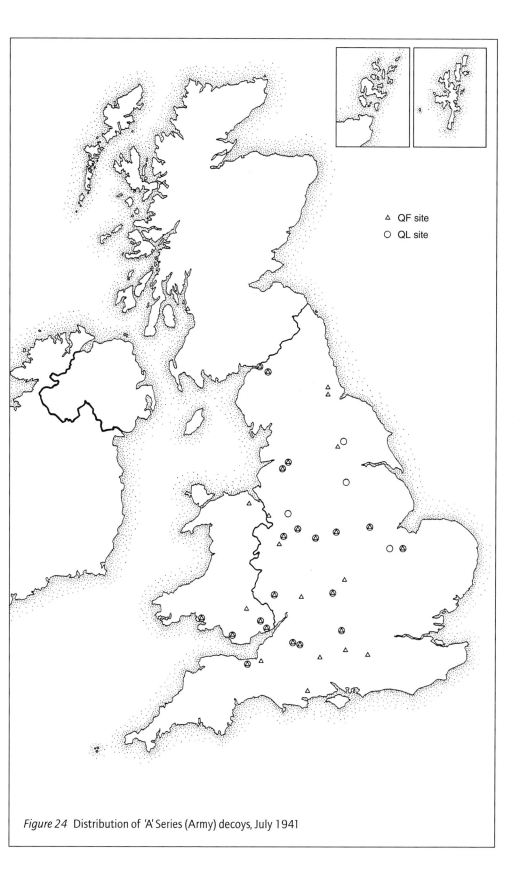

△ QF site
○ QL site

Figure 24 Distribution of 'A' Series (Army) decoys, July 1941

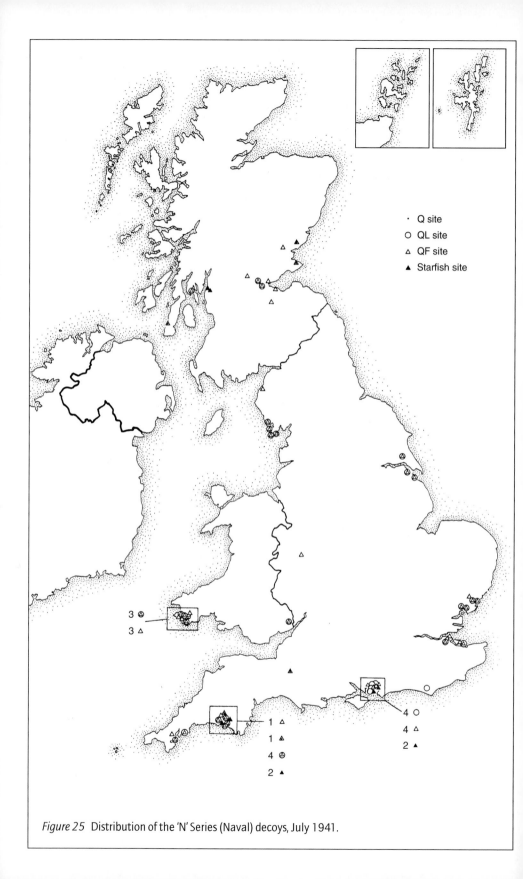

- · Q site
- ○ QL site
- △ QF site
- ▲ Starfish site

3 ⊛
3 △

1 △
1 ▲
4 ⊛
2 ▲

1 △
1 ▲

4 ○
4 △
2 ▲

Figure 25 Distribution of the 'N' Series (Naval) decoys, July 1941.

many were operating by early summer 1941, the 'A' Series was soon sharply truncated when those of essentially civil character, such as marshalling yards, were transferred to the roster of civil decoys – now the 'C' Series – whose period of most active growth came in the second half of 1941.

Although the navy's work on sites for the national scheme was disrupted over the winter of 1940–41 by their commitment to building the Starfish required at major port cities, a good deal was accomplished on these 'N' Series QLs and QFs during the spring and early summer (Fig 25). By the end of the Blitz extensive schemes were in place in Orkney and Rosyth in Scotland, together with Harwich, Chatham, Portsmouth, Plymouth, Falmouth, Milford Haven and Barrow. Most of these places could call upon at least half a dozen QLs or QFs (many were joint sites), while decoy positions in ones and twos had by now been selected for targets such as Invergordon, Dundee, Leadburn, Portland and Poole. A system of lights had also been laid out along Cuckmere Haven in Sussex, whose topography closely shadowed that of Newhaven, a few miles along the coast to the west, with individual lamps sited to displace specific features of Newhaven town and harbour. Q sites protecting naval airfields, too, were in place by this time, for Crail, Arbroath, Yeovilton and Worthy Down, among others. Though some locally-originated schemes were amended before reaching the final 'approved' list – and Turner's master map – sources show that the basis of most of the naval layouts extant by the summer had been reconnoitred by siting parties working between January and March.[67]

As the Blitz dwindled to its close in June 1941 Britain's decoy layout emerged from what would be its most active year of the war. There were certainly many more battles to come, and some fierce action, but never again such a period of sustained activity. In the thirteen months from June to June inclusive, Q sites had drawn 322 attacks, almost three-quarters of the 443 confirmed operations against them over the duration of the war. K sites had seen 36 attacks – their final wartime total, reached in the month of June itself – while dummy aircraft sited temporarily on real airfields had been attacked eleven times and nine day raids had been recorded on dummy factories. At just 25 raids drawn in this period, QFs and QLs (of all types) had yet to show their worth; but their numbers remained small and the fact that most of these raids had been drawn by the early sites giving night protection to the aircraft factories boded well. Starfish had done reasonably, drawing 44 recorded raids in the seven months between December and June, though this simple figure tended both to exaggerate the sites' general effectiveness – since many attacks were minor – while at the same time masking their major successes. The point about Starfish was that their 'draw' had to be large: one fully diverted raid, like the Sinah Common operation, was worth any number of ignitions pulling in ten or twenty bombs. When luck was with them, Starfish were magnificent.[68]

The figures for attacks just quoted were those collated by Colonel Turner's Department as they came in from day to day: they reflect what the department and the Air Ministry believed the decoy system was achieving over the period of the Battle of Britain and the Blitz. Closer analysis later in the war and subsequently, however, showed that these figures probably underestimated the true number of night attacks by as much as 15–25 per cent. Among the reasons for under-reporting was Turner's cautious ruling of June 1940 that, for all sites except Starfish, a bomb had to fall within half a mile to count or, exceptionally, within a mile if no other target could have been possible (the Starfish threshold was three-quarters of a mile). Surprisingly, Turner clung to this limit even when the Air Warfare Analysis Section had conclusively shown that bombs aimed at an isolated target routinely fell up to two miles away: officers whose job it was to deceive the enemy were admirably rigorous in not deceiving themselves. Experience had also taught that under-reporting could occur for many other reasons, such as laxity among decoy crews and station commanders (though the frequent changes of the latter did not help) and, strange to discover, occasional uncertainty among decoy personnel over whether they had actually been attacked. Odd as this may sound, it was a genuine problem, particularly on Q sites, where shelters could be as much as half a mile from the centre point of the decoy and a small attack missing the site by as much in the opposite direction might easily be overlooked, especially in poor weather. Another difficulty discovered on early Q sites was that the headlamp operator often could not hear the approach of an enemy aircraft, which was drowned by the noise of the generator, and at one Q 'the first indication he had was when a bomb fell near to the night shelter and blew him down the stairs'.[69] Come daybreak, decoy crews did not routinely scour the countryside for evidence of an attack unless they had good reason to suspect one. Taken together, these factors suggested that the recorded figures for Q site and Starfish attacks probably represented only about 85 per cent of the true total. Turner's decoys were not decisive in the Battle of Britain and the Blitz – their overall contribution to the war is weighed in Chapter 7 – but they were more potent than Turner himself was prepared to acknowledge.

CHAPTER 5

City lights and Baedecker raids

JULY 1941 – DECEMBER 1942

Towards the end of September 1940, as Londoners were facing the third week of the Luftwaffe's Blitz on their city, the Oberkommando der Wehrmacht – the German high command of the armed forces – issued a directive calling for plans to be made for an assault upon the Soviet Union. Formalised and put in motion by Hitler's War Directive 21 of 18 December, this operation was intended to provide Nazi Germany with *Lebensraum* in the east, initially by rapidly occupying an area reaching 1000 miles across the German–Soviet border to a line between Volga and Archangel. Launched in the early hours of Sunday 22 June 1941, Operation *Barbarossa* mobilised 3.6 million troops, 3600 tanks and 3915 aircraft – the mightiest force ever committed to a military operation in Europe – against a thousand-mile front between the Baltic and the Black Sea. The Luftwaffe's initial role in this massive operation was to support the ground troops in their push across the border, by mounting an intensive three-day campaign against the Soviet Air Force. It was *Adlertag* over again, with the significant difference that the air war against the Soviets ran firmly in the Germans' favour. Many crews operating over Russia were veterans of the Battle of Britain and the Blitz, and had arrived with their aircraft from bases occupied in the war against Britain in the three weeks prior to the campaign. Now, with Germany committed to its ultimately futile war against the Soviets, those bases mostly lay empty. From the British perspective the opening of *Barbarossa* signalled that the dwindling Blitz must be at an end.[1]

For the most part this was so, but the invasion of the Soviet Union did not entirely deplete German air power in the west, and nor did it mark the complete cessation of operations against the United Kingdom. One unit which remained was KGr 100 which, together with the remnants of Luftflotte 3 which had not been sent east, in the following months continued a limited campaign against British land targets. Infrequent and seldom heavy, these raids were of minor strategic importance compared to the continuing operations against Britain's shipping lanes. But the fact that raiding would continue despite Germany's turn eastwards was announced on the very night that *Barbarossa* began. At 01.41 hours on the morning of 22 June – an hour and a half before bombs fell on Soviet airfields – KGr 100's aircraft began to attack Southampton. Explosions and small fires were seen by the departing crews.[2]

For Turner's department the continuing raids between late June 1941 and the winter gave rise to what might be considered the third phase of Starfish building, taking the first as the improvised measures of November–December 1940 and the second as the main programme during the Blitz itself. July brought five Starfish operations, most of them minor. A Short Starfish lit under the new procedure managed to draw ten HEs on 7 July at Southampton, while full burns at two Birmingham sites on the following night drew one attack, though at an estimated 70 per cent of the enemy's effort the thirteen bombs recorded on SF2(c) at Maxstoke shows how light this raid was. A larger operation on 28 July saw 60 bombers dispatched against London in retaliation for a minor raid on Berlin, though the single Starfish lit drew only three bombs. Similar small victories were won by the naval Starfish at Hull, which drew a few HEs on the nights of 17/18 and 22/23 July, the second occasion through the Short Starfish procedure.[3] Hull saw action again on the night of 31 August, when SF31(b) at Bilton was brought to life and drew 40 or so HE, estimated as about 60 per cent of the bombs delivered. Although one Starfish was lit in September (SF15(d) at Sunderland) and four in October, none produced any result and the Hull lighting of 31 August emerged as the last major Starfish operation of 1941.[4]

It is possible that this lighting may have drawn still more bombs, were it not for an arrangement introduced in August 1941 which, paradoxically, was aimed at improving the effectiveness of

Starfish. Early in August Sir John Turner (as he had become in June) arranged with Anti-Aircraft Command that gunfire from their batteries would be concentrated directly over lit Starfish in the hope of overcoming the guns' worrying tendency to advertise the position of the true target.[5] Special studies were made to determine how easily this could be achieved at each Starfish in the country and, as it happens, Bilton for these purposes was rated 'good'.[6] According to 80 Wing's records, however, on the night of the 31st August the concentration of fire actually served to drive many bombers away from the Starfish: in some cases aircraft were seen to begin their bomb runs, only to be deflected by bursting shells. Apart from its role in physically destroying aircraft, anti-aircraft gunfire was in fact designed to have precisely this deterrent effect, though no-one seems to have anticipated such a result when the co-operation scheme was first mooted. Worse, once deflected from the Starfish several raiders discharged bombs on the nearby village of Bilton – the very outcome which so much effort had been taken to avoid in the siting of decoys generally. Surprisingly, the co-operation of AA guns and Starfish at Bilton was still written down as a success – at least by Turner and his officers in a conference on 19 September – since despite the 'unfortunate' fall of bombs on Bilton village, there was apparently no doubt that the gunfire 'upset the enemy's intentions, broke up the attack on Hull and put the enemy off the main target.'[7] So the policy remained. Later, special dummy AA flashes were introduced at some Starfish sites to enhance their realism, and by the early summer of 1942 a few sites had been provided with anti-aircraft rocket batteries of their own.

The high summer of 1941 also saw some important changes in the overall shape of the Starfish system. A few new sites continued to join the main layout, as they would into the winter and following spring, but in June a new type of Starfish was introduced with the aim of protecting general *areas* rather than specific cities, with lighting under the direct authority of 80 Wing at Radlett, with no tier of local control. Though they were usually somewhat larger than the conventional type, these so-called 'Strategic' Starfish differed largely in the criteria used for their siting, and in their operational role – despite its name, the Strategic Starfish played no part in any truly 'strategic' deception scheme. Though positioned with an eye to covering areas – which in practice meant serving any one of a number of cities – for convenience Strategic Starfish were brought within the established runs of number and lettercodes of nearby groups. The first three to open appear to have been those in the Middlesbrough system, at Osmotherley, Guisborough and Sneaton Moor, respectively SF10(c)–(e), while six more were commissioned in September 1941, at Cheddar, which became Bristol site SF1(e), Elkstone (Manchester SF9(i)), Llandegla, Llanasa and Fenn's Moss (Liverpool SF11(i)–(k)) and Lee, designated Southampton SF17(c). (Lee was joined by two more conventional Starfish in this group, at Nutburn and Chilworth, in October.) Further Strategic Starfish were added by March 1942 at Aldbrough (SF31(d) in the Hull group) and Peopleton and Halford (Birmingham SF2(f) and (g)),[8] while on the Lincolnshire coast Huttoft, site SF51(a), opened in March. Silvington became almost the last of the Strategics when it opened as SF2(h) in the Birmingham layout during June.[9]

Progress with the QL and QF decoys for civil targets took a brisk step forward in summer 1941. Unlike their naval and army equivalents, these sites had been practically in abeyance since the first weeks of 1941 thanks to the Starfish programme, with the result that much work had to be taken up where it had been left six months earlier. It is difficult to be certain how much was achieved in the first few months of the civil programme, though we do know that by 21 November, when the diversion toward Starfish lay only a couple of days away, positions for civil QFs had been reconnoitred in some numbers at Bristol, Middlesbrough and Birmingham – 23 sites in all – as well as several of those for oil QFs to be built by the Petroleum Department.[10] Two months later, towards the end of January, Turner reported that the Middlesbrough scheme was complete, that Bristol's was nearly so, and that sites had been found for Slough and Liverpool. But there came the pause; the *floruit* of the 'C' Series sites had to wait for the latter half of 1941.

Groups of civil QL and QF sites were given general numbers codes which, on a similar principle to those for Starfish, were allocated to the target towns roughly in the order in which schemes were approved (though for a variety of reasons this sequence did not always translate into the order of building). It is important to note, however, that since towns and sites were handled in different sequences for the QL/QF and Starfish programmes, their code numbers under the two systems – C and SF – were usually independent of one another. Thus Bristol and Middlesbrough, the first towns surveyed for QL and QF layouts in the winter of 1940–41, had decoys with the prefixes C1 and C2, and since Bristol was also the first target in the main Starfish programme (discounting the emergency work), its Starfish had the prefix SF1. But Middlesbrough, coming later in the Starfish list, used the prefix SF10: in fact, over the course of the war, only Bristol (C1/SF1), Coventry (C7/SF7) and Cowley (C36/SF36) coincidentally had SF and C prefixes in sympathy. Similar rules governed the lettercodes allocated to decoys within each town's system. Like Starfish, each QL, QF, or joint QL/QF decoy was lettered in accordance with its place in the order of *building*, with the result that when co-located with Starfish – as many were – these sites almost invariably had different lettercodes from the Starfish themselves. To give an example, the joint QF and QL workings at Shrawley, in the Birmingham layout, were known as C4(m), while the Starfish on the same site was SF26(b): the numbers came to apply to decoy *functions* rather than *sites*. Had the need for the Starfish programme been anticipated it is unlikely that the system would have been planned in quite this way; but KGr 100 were not so obliging, and the result was that civil QFs/QLs and Starfish were coded using independent formulae.

Early in the summer of 1941 some 39 targets were scheduled to receive decoys in the 'C' Series, though by mid July two had been deleted: the Severn Junction Tunnel had been switched to the army roster and – a faintly Betjemanesque touch – the officers planning this part of the system decided to forsake Slough. The 37 towns remaining called for twelve QFs, 23 joint QF/QLs, and no fewer than 96 single-function QLs (Fig 26). Of these, Bristol and Middlesbrough had been dealt with earlier in the year and reconnaissance, at least, had been completed at Liverpool, but otherwise a weighty volume of work remained. Coventry appears to have been dealt with early in this programme, together it seems with Leeds, whose nine QLs (there were no QFs) were all overlain on Starfish. 'C' Series decoys sharing fields with Starfish were naturally easier to commission than those on new sites, and perhaps for this reason

Glasgow was next to be finished, with eight QLs, four of them at existing Starfish, operational early in the second week of July. By now work was also under way at Birmingham, Newport, Swansea, Sheffield, Cardiff, Tyneside, Basingstoke, Gloucester and Scunthorpe, while preparations were in hand at Bedford, Peterborough, Leicester, Kettering, Corby, Ipswich, Norwich, Preston and Lancaster. Most of these layouts were finished in August and September, to be followed by those for Accrington, Luton, Yeovil, Doncaster, Stoke, Cowley, Workington, Ravenglass and Northwich. Work on the first 37 towns appears to have been completed in October – when 47 QFs were in operation, and 111 QLs[11] – by which time the programme had already turned to the lower-priority targets, most of which required only one or two decoys apiece.

As we shall see, new QFs and QLs in the 'C' series continued to open throughout the following year, the civil QF layout peaking at 83 positions in August 1942 and the QLs reaching 212 sites three months later.[12] It was a heavy programme of work, though from Turner's point of view commissioning QL and QF sites was made easier by personnel in many cases being provided by the departments responsible for them. Army and naval sites were staffed by soldiers and sailors, while the civil decoys on non-Starfish sites were usually manned by civilians, often supplied by the specific industrial or railway targets which the decoys were emplaced to protect. Control, too, was handled locally. In time many civil QLs and QFs came to be attached to the RAF's barrage balloon squadrons, though diversity was the rule and many sites were parented by bodies as varied as anti-aircraft operations rooms, local civil defence controllers, and even the police.

The QL sites built to replicate urban areas and, under the army and naval programmes, the wide range of military targets were in some ways the most ingenious decoys of the war. They were also the most varied. Sizes ranged from tight four- to five-acre plots to sprawling displays extending exceptionally up to 30 acres. Internally, no two were quite alike, though in 1941–42 the majority of the civil types imitated factories and heavy industrial plants, marshalling yards, docks, or combinations of these. Lights replicating common features of townscapes – streets, houses, vehicles and so on – were usually incorporated in displays of all types. These effects were achieved by drawing upon a palette of standard light-

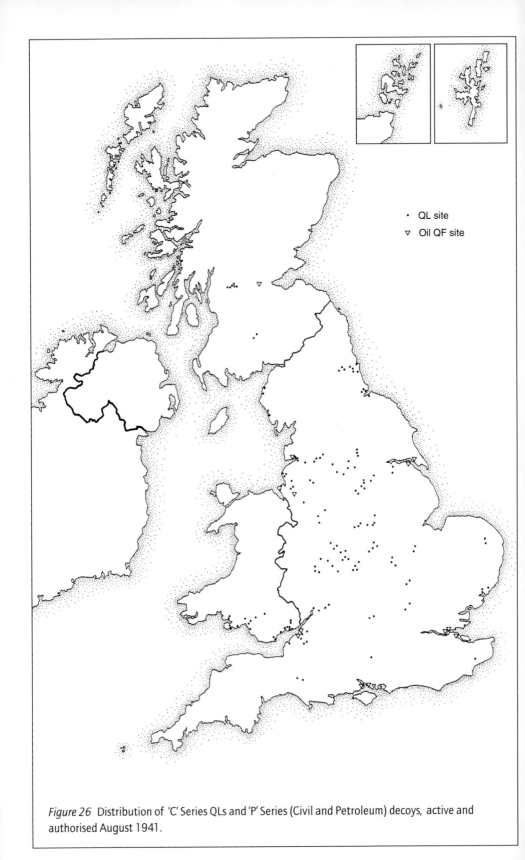

Figure 26 Distribution of 'C' Series QLs and 'P' Series (Civil and Petroleum) decoys, active and authorised August 1941.

ing devices, with elements positioned to replicate the specific target to be decoyed with more or less precision depending upon how clearly its lighting 'signature' appeared from the air.

Some of the lighting devices were simply the genuine article, somewhat incongruously emplaced in open fields. Thus railway signal lights on poles were often included in marshalling yard decoys, while sets of vehicle lamps contributed to the displays for poorly blacked-out residential or industrial areas. Many devices, however, were specially designed. General lighting for marshalling yards used shielded lights raised on poles around ten feet high (Fig 27), arranged in lines to suggest the working illumination permitted in railway sidings. Coking furnaces in industrial area decoys were imitated by 'furnace glows', using a tray of sand or soil, a few yards across, with a canopy fitted with red and yellow electric lights suspended above it. Shining downward on the tray, the lights when seen from the air resembled the dim glow of a coking fur-

Figure 27 Marshalling light devices used on QL sites. Both mimicked the working lights used in railway complexes.

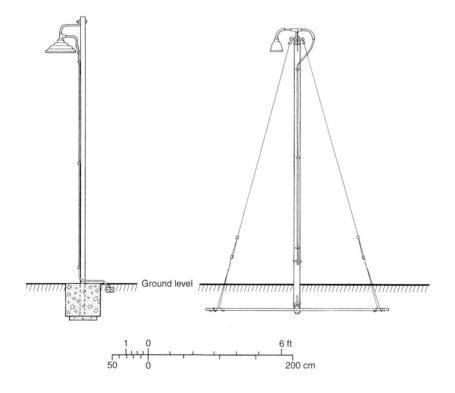

nace at work. 'Loco glows' used a similar principle, in this case replicating the faint firelight produced by the open firebox door on the footplate of a steam locomotive. Reflective principles were also incorporated in some of the dock lighting, which used lights on poles (similar to the marshalling yard types) positioned to reflect downward onto small pools of water, built just large enough to capture the reflections of the lights and arranged in patterns to suggest the edges of dock basins.

More generalised lighting suggesting poor blackout – 'leaky lighting' – often relied upon the principle that dim, steady lights appear to flicker when viewed from altitude. Thus 'hurdle lights' and 'reed lights' used screens of wicker placed over domestic light bulbs, producing a wavering effect when seen from a moving air-

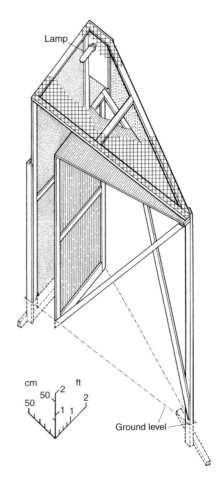

Figure 28 The open door. One of the 'leaky lighting' devices used on QL sites, this timber-framed and hessian and plaster-covered construction allowed light to show through the frontal aperture, so suggesting a door left ajar.

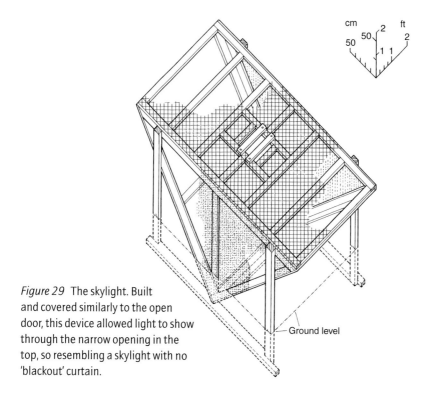

cm   ft
              50   2
         50   2
                   1   1

Figure 29 The skylight. Built
and covered similarly to the open
door, this device allowed light to show
through the narrow opening in the
top, so resembling a skylight with no
'blackout' curtain.

— Ground level

craft. 'Jinx lights' achieved a similar effect by a lamp, hooded from
above, suspended over a tray of water from a cord attached to a
cane rod: as it swung gently in the breeze the light was seen to
flicker. Cheap and readily made, these were the simplest lighting
devices. Rather more elaborate were the 'open doors' and 'skylights' intended to mimic poor blackout, both of which used a light
fitting enclosed within a wooden frame covered with chicken wire
and scrim. For the open door (Fig 28) the frame was so constructed
as to allow the light to show through a right-angled crack, suggesting a street door left ajar. The skylight (Fig 29) worked on a similar
principle, in this case suggesting light escaping through a slightly
open fixture. Most elaborate of all were the electrical 'tram flashes'
and 'rivetting fires', one for townscape displays, the other for ship-
yards. Both relied upon sudden bursts of vivid light from powerful
carbon arc lamps controlled by a randomly-closing switch. The
tram flashes had blue glass housings to replicate the electrical
arcing made by the glancing contact between a tram's pickup and
its power supply.

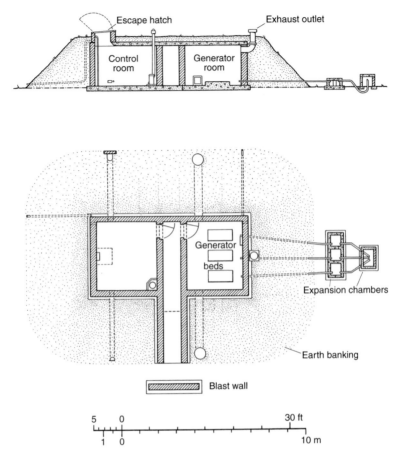

Figure 30 Control shelter for a QL site, to Air Ministry Drawing CTD 151/41.

On Starfish sites the QL lights and wiring were carefully threaded around the fire groups, and controlled from a separate shelter resembling that used on later Q sites (Fig 30) with switches, three generators and a telephone.[13] The plan of Swarkestone, QL site C17(a) in the Derby system, shows a typical example (Fig 31). Imposed upon SF4(c), this lighting display combined marshalling yard and factory lighting to 'displace' the area around the Qualcast works in Derby city. As the plan shows, the six marshalling yard lights were arranged in two straight rows to represent railway tracks, while a single loco glow towards the middle of the site suggested a locomotive at rest. Open door lights and skylights were dotted around the display, together with a few 60 watt bulbs (prob-

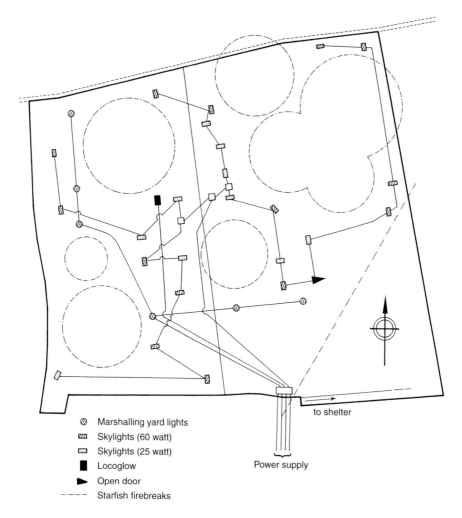

Marshalling yard lights
Skylights (60 watt)
Skylights (25 watt)
Locoglow
Open door
Starfish firebreaks

to shelter

Power supply

Figure 31 Partly schematic layout plan of a QL decoy, based upon site C17(a), Swarkestone (for Derby). Using a combination of marshalling yard lights, loco glows, skylights, open doors, this site was intended to suggest the area around the Qualcast works in Derby city. It shared a site with SF4(c), whose firebreak trenches are shown in outline.

ably reed or hurdle lights) to give the general impression of a poor blackout. Much the same principles underlay the design of Nare Point, one of the combined SFs and QLs operated by the navy at Falmouth, where it was known as site N20 FA1 (Fig 32). Here, the general scatter of 'leaky lighting' simulated the buildings of the nearby dock area, while a row of signal lights suggested the nearby railway.

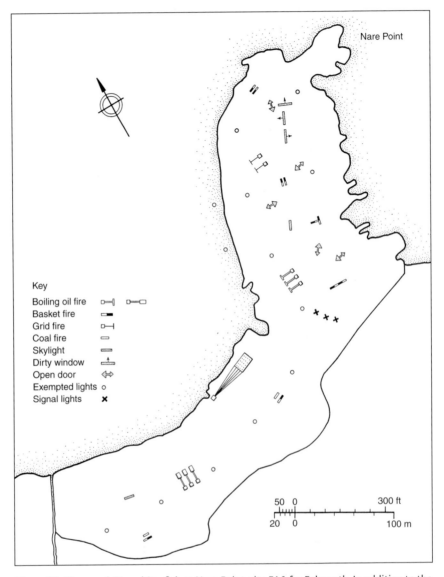

Nare Point

Key

Boiling oil fire	⊐⊣	⊐–⊐
Basket fire	▬	
Grid fire	⊐⊣	
Coal fire	⊐	
Skylight	⊏⊐	
Dirty window	⊏⊐	
Open door	⇔	
Exempted lights	o	
Signal lights	✕	

50 0   300 ft

20 0   100 m

Figure 32 The naval QL and Starfish at Nare Point, site FA1 for Falmouth. In addition to the stardard range of fires and lights used on civil sites, this layout also included a cordite flash – the single large device – to mimic the effect of a burning ammunition store.

In order to replicate not only the appearance, but the behaviour, of a true target from the air, QL lights were divided between those which would normally be visible in moderate blackout, and others which would be doused – or were supposed to be doused – when an air-raid warning was in force. Sites were therefore wired in *primary* and *residual* circuits, the first controlling lamps which would be extinguished with the warning – such as marshalling yard lights – and the second, effects which were permitted under blackout or impossible to control. Normally both were left on, the primary circuit being switched off when the enemy was close enough to see the target – this is why the signal lights, loco glow, and the remaining lights at the Swarkestone site (Fig 31, page 143) were each wired on separate circuits. The residual would remain to form the aiming point for the enemy bombs. When QL sites were first introduced, the lighting configuration and intensity to be used on any one occasion was left to the discretion of the local controller, but with experience it was discovered that local changes in moonlight and cloud cover, together with the effect of friendly searchlights, could produce rapid and marked variations in the background lighting against which the site was operating. This problem was eventually solved when, in February 1943, control of QL displays was given to the site crew, who in addition to manipulating the primary and residual circuits under orders from the local control, would make subtle adjustments through a dimmer switch to match their decoy's intensity to the changing ambient conditions.[14]

Deception was also heightened at QL sites by manipulating the intensity and duration of some of the lights, so giving the display the all-important 'living' quality. This technique was applied particularly to loco and furnace glows, which were operated on a continuous cycle of rising and falling intensity.[15] From the shelter, one of the site crew would gradually brighten a furnace glow over a period of about 30 seconds, leave it at full strength for two minutes, dim again in about 30 seconds, and then leave the lights at their lowest for two or three minutes before repeating the cycle. Loco glows were handled similarly, except that their brightening was much faster and the dimming slower. When QLs were ordered to be lit for long periods these routines were continued in half-hour stretches with fifteen minute intervals, when the glows were switched off – doubtless to the relief of the crewmen crouched over the controls – though when enemy aircraft were around there were no breaks. Loco and furnace glows were among the main lights to be left on when the QL had been switched over to the residual circuit, though orders were to douse them if enemy aircraft approached low, when they might be compromised. Imagination is needed to read the night-time appearance of these decoys simply from their plans, but the picture was a scattered field of lights – some steady, others twinkling faintly – given life by gently pulsating glows. On the fall of bombs the whole site, if overlain on a Starfish, would suddenly turn into a firefield, as the igniter switch was thrown and the primary basket fires burst into flames.

The addition of QLs and QFs to the existing array of Starfish added new life and complexity to the decoy systems for specific areas and cities. Though Bristol's QL layout in its primary form was one of the few put in place before the distraction imposed by the Starfish programme, the city's lighting layout continued to grow in late 1941 and 1942 to become one of the most complex in the country. As the plan shows (Fig 33), Bristol's QL pattern by 1942 consisted of two distinct sets of decoys, one broadly shadowing the city's Starfish layout, and the second, coded C82, forming a tight group on Black Down, near Burrington, to the south-west of the city. This second group was an unusual attempt to replicate practically the entire of the target city with displaced lighting – rather than simply isolated features within it – and made much use of marshalling yard lights to imitate the variety of railway facilities in Bristol itself. Thus site C82(a) used railway, factory and dock lighting to replicate the Canons Marsh marshalling yard and docks; C82(b) used marshalling yard lights to displace Bristol West railway depot, while 82(c) and (d) used more marshalling yards lights with loco glows collectively to replicate the Temple Meads station and Pyle Hill goods depot. Sites 82(e) and (f) were respectively the Kingsland Road sidings and the Bristol East railway yard and depot, which were again mimicked with marshalling yard lights. In the midst of this ambitious complex of six related sites lay the Strategic Starfish at Cheddar, which would come into action, under the direct control of 80 Wing, in the event of an attack.

The QF sites built from the latter half of 1941 onwards, in parallel with the urban QLs, were able to draw upon the great advances in decoy fire technology made during the Starfish programme, and were both technically different from their predecessors of 1940 and usually more standardised. Many QFs of the national programme resembled miniature Starfish, using groups of electrically-lit basket fires to produce the small blazes necessary to decoy localised targets: three basket groups were often used, to be

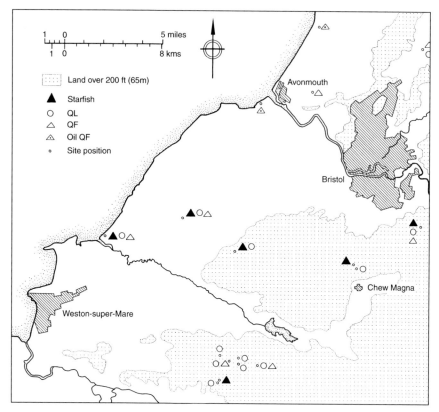

Figure 33 Decoys in the Bristol area, summer 1942. Comparison with Figure 12 shows the development of the layout since spring 1941: all of the Starfish had gained QL layouts, two Oil QFs were in place for Sheepway and Severn Beach, and a large cluster of QLs, some with QFs, had been installed in the Burrington area to replicate the whole of Bristol city.

fired in sequence to give a rather longer burn than had been normal for the QF of 1940.

Different again were the oil QFs which, after more than a year of development became operational in numbers during the second half of 1941. Classified as the 'P' Series decoys, these Petroleum Board sites were developed from the prototypes tested at Greystoke Park in the autumn of 1940, and used fuel oil in quantity burning in specially-shaped pools and channels which, from the air, resembled the structures typically seen on oil tank farms (Fig 34, page 148).[16] The standard site was provided with three fuel receptacles, lined with brick or pipeclay, comprising an annular channel or 'ring' – which was also provided with two boiling oil fires of the Starfish variety – a 'crescent', and an irregular 'pool',

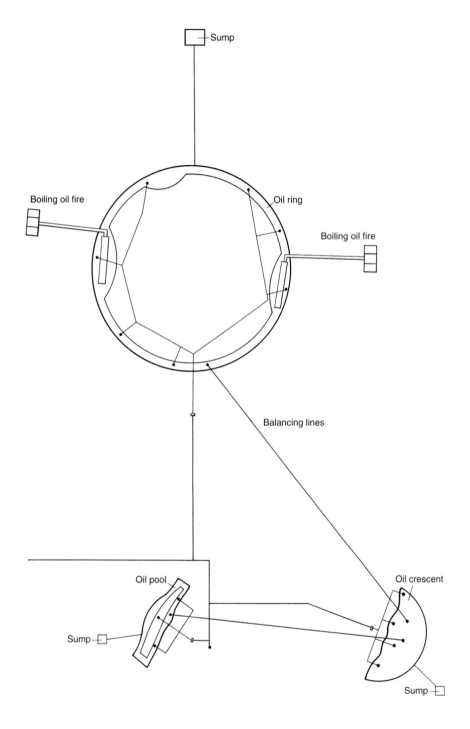

Figure 34 Typical layout of an oil QF.

all electrically ignited from a remote shelter. Oil was supplied through a system of buried pipework, and maintained at a uniform level within the receptacles by balancing pipes passing between.

The basic principles of the oil QFs were sound enough – indeed, by summer 1941 at least one site designed on very similar lines existed in Germany – but their commissioning ran into many difficulties, chiefly because they were built and manned by the oil companies rather than Turner's staff. Land was requisitioned for the first during October 1940,[17] when the whole group was expected to be ready within a few months, but the project was stalled when the oil companies first became nervous of the decoys' alleged potential to draw attack – by this time a discredited fear among the initiated – and then proved reluctant to release men to operate them. Five sites were built by May 1941, and ten were ready by mid August, though by this time the Petroleum Board's requirement had risen to twelve (Fig 26, page 138).[18] Even those which were structurally complete were usually unserviceable through faulty construction or lack of staff. An inspection in mid August revealed that two of the three sites in the Thames Estuary – covering Shell Haven and Thames Haven – were redundant for want of crews, while the third, covering the Isle of Grain, had deep cracks in its clay lining. Polmont, covering Grangemouth, was also breaking up, while the decoys at Ince, for Stanlow, and at Paull for the Salt End installation on the Humber were being manned by local Starfish detachments – Turner's men, rather than the oil companies'. Killingholme, also on the Humber, was complete and occupied but, ludicrously, was short of oil. The only really satisfactory sites were the two protecting Avonmouth, at Sheepway and Severn Beach, where six-man crews were in place and everything was apparently ready to go. Sites covering the Fawley and Hamble oil installations were unfinished, while P6 at Clifton Marsh, covering Preston, was operable but, so far, only with Starfish-type oil fires.[19]

Turner, of course, had a view on all of this. 'For a year's work it is a shocking result', he wrote on 22 August, 'the steady opposition of the oil companies in doing nothing to help themselves, their demand that personnel [. . .] should be provided by the Army or the Air Force so that they should have no trouble, and the failure of the Petroleum Department to bring pressure on to these companies

through the Petroleum Board are the root causes of this really dis-
graceful progress.' Describing the oil QF programme as a 'calamity'
Turner was no doubt justified in claiming that 'had they been
mine, they could have been finished 9 months ago.'[20] In time they
were finished, but in truth they emerged as the decoy system's
only unqualified failure.

The Q site system took a new direction late in the summer of 1941.
In this year RAF airfields began to be equipped with a new system
of approach and landing lights known generally as 'Drem' lighting,
after the Scottish station where it was first installed. Hard on its
heels came the Drem Q, the first of which was lit at Houghton,
Q68(a) for Middle Wallop, on 15 September.[21] The Drem was a Q *de
luxe*. Much larger than the old T-type, the lighting configuration
closely resembled the true Drem system, with a long flarepath and
a V-shaped approach funnel, though the decoy had only one line of
lights where the real thing usually had two, to allow operation in
either direction (pilots using a true system would take off and land
with the active row of lights on their left), and lacked an outer
circle of lights common to real airfields. This meant that unless the
lights were dismantled and moved around, the Drem Q's align-
ment was limited to one direction only, which was usually north-
east–south-west, with the approach funnel to the north-east.
Though a little shorter than the real thing, at 2300 yards in length
– almost one and a half miles – the Drem Q's flarepath (Fig 35)
occupied more a tract of landscape rather than a site.

The main flarepath lights of the Drem Q were Glim lamps – the
standard type of RAF runway lighting, dimmer than those used on
the T-type – mounted on poles above the crops, while the inde-
pendently-controlled funnel lights were somewhat larger and
brighter (Fig 5, page 44). Obstruction and other hazard warning
lights of the usual type were also included in the Drem. So too was
the motor headlamp designed to catch the eye of hostile pilots,
though as a concession to the safety of the operator in the Drem Q
this was mounted on a platform atop a newly-designed shelter,
now adapted for surface construction and protected by heavy
banking with earth (Fig 36, page 152). Apart from switches and a

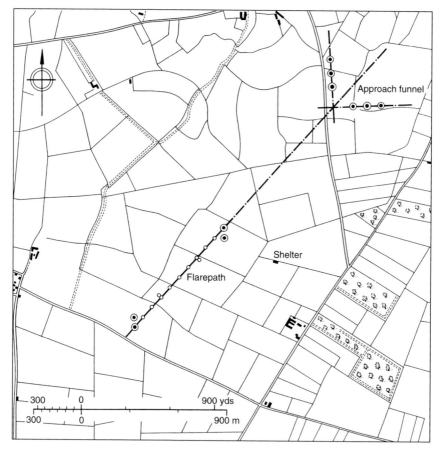

Figure 35 The Drem Q at Somersham, site Q36(b) for Wyton.

rest room for the crew, the shelter housed two generators, giving separate power sources for the main lights and the approach funnel. The Drem Q's shelter lay no more than 400 yards from the flarepath, owing to the high current needed to power the lights and the danger of power loss – 'voltage drop' – in the cables over a longer distance.

The Drem Q was operated similarly to the T-type, though its less intense lighting gave the headlamp a more important role in drawing attack. Again, one of the two crewmen worked the lamp while his companion kept watch. The instructions to these men were exacting, showing that successful operation of a Drem Q depended as much upon conscientious personnel as technical ingenuity in design.

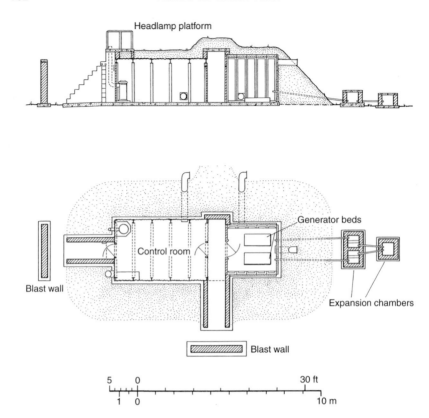

Figure 36 Control shelter for a Drem Q site, to Air Ministry Drawing CTD 367/41.

When the lamp is to be used [ran the instructions] both men must leave the shelter but one of them must be within earshot of the telephone. One man operates the lamp as follows. He switches it on, using the outside switch, and rotates it through an arc of 90 degrees very slowly taking some 5 seconds to finish the movement. As he swings the lamp he should use the vertical play sufficiently but not excessively to give the rough ground movement required. After 5 seconds the lamp should be switched off for at least one minute and in conditions of good visibility at least two minutes or even longer. He then moves the lamp to another arc, switches it on and repeats the performance [. . .] for the period of time he is instructed by the Station Commander to work the light. Meanwhile the other man moves to the nearest place where the noise of the engine does not interfere with his hearing and listens for aircraft. When he hears one he waits until it approaches to about three miles away and then tells his friend to switch off the headlamp. By that time the oncoming aircraft crew should be able to see the flarepath and other lights, and the further working of the headlamp will do much more harm than good. Untrained men are inclined to swing the light much too quickly and too jerkily and it consequently fails to represent what is intended.[22]

The only significant modification to the Drem Q was introduced soon after the first were built, for the rather gratifying reason that they proved rather *too* convincing. Friendly aircraft attempting landings on night decoys – or, worse, succeeding in doing so – had always been a danger, but the stepping-up of Bomber Command's night operations in autumn 1941 brought a new rash of incidents as homecoming bombers, often in difficulty, tried to put down on the first visible airfield, which often turned out to be something startlingly different from what was expected. Site crews had long been briefed to douse their Q if a friendly aircraft attempted to land, but even before the Drem was introduced it was plain that this procedure was failing. It was John Slessor, then serving as chief of 5 Group, who warned Turner of this in mid September. The trouble with simply shutting off the lights when an aircraft approached, explained Slessor, 'is that quite often the Q site personnel won't see or hear it coming into land [. . .] we had a case the other night on Waddington's Q where a Whitley came in on a long low approach from the opposite end to where the dugout was, and was indignantly surprised to find himself sitting in a potato field; the Q personnel meanwhile had not the faintest idea he was there.'[23] Stories of hapless aircrew who found themselves in this predicament naturally circulated in RAF messes, and were no doubt more richly embroidered with each telling. But the problem could have grave implications, particularly for bomber captains who landed injured crews on Q sites miles from anywhere. A conference was called at Bomber Command headquarters on 4 October, when Slessor proposed that a red 'bar' of lights, hooded to be visible only on a landing approach, should be installed across the funnels of Drem Qs.[24] This was done – the first appeared at Drem Qs for Waddington and Coltishall in mid October[25] – and with some result, though the problem was never entirely solved. As late as December 1943, Turner's department was obliged to spread the word through an illustrated booklet, ominously entitled *Beware Q Sites*.

Over the following year the conversion of existing T-type Qs and the building of wholly new sites for Drem equipment dominated work on night decoy airfields. By now, some older Qs had been closed, some at least because their sites could not accommodate Drems without violating safety distances. Late 1941 also brought a second contraction among the K sites: reduced to nineteen positions earlier in the year, the layout was now pruned again to just three. Turner in fact opposed this move, which originated with the Air Ministry's Director of Plans, arguing that several sites should be retained in case they again became profitable, and could meanwhile be used to store dummy aircraft.[26] But the facts spoke for themselves: by late October 1941, when the closures were proposed, no K site had drawn bombs for four months and only six attacks had been registered in the first half of the year.[27] Moreover, land was urgently needed for cultivation. So, for once, Turner lost the argument. Lullingstone, site Q/K48(a) (for Biggin Hill), was retained largely because its personnel were shared with SF8(e), one of the London Starfish, while West Wittering (for Thorney Island) and Skipsea (now parented by Catfoss) survived on the strength of their unusually strong records, which at West Wittering – despite Turner's scepticism, the most successful K site of all – probably arose from its being one of the few 'tracked' grounds.[28] These three sites remained until 11 June 1942, when in the absence of any further attacks they, too, were closed.[29]

As the autumn of 1941 turned to winter the decoy system entered its quietest period of the war so far. Though Starfish operations continued at a low level during the summer and Q sites drew 36 attacks from July to September, October was quiet all round and the last two months of the year were practically silent, bringing only one recorded attack in November and two in December, all on QFs or QLs. Despite the steady growth in the 'C' Series layout in the latter half of 1941, they had appeared too late to play a part in the Blitz and their scores so far were almost negligible, reaching three attacks in August, two in September and ten in October before the general slump set in. The trend continued into 1942. January brought just one attack and February claimed distinction as the first month since June 1940 in which no activity was registered against any decoy, anywhere in the UK.[30]

The *longueur* over the winter of 1941–42, of course, reflected the sharp fall in Luftwaffe operations during these months, rather than any sudden failure in the decoy system, which in many ways was at its strongest yet. Though the Luftwaffe flew some night intruder operations against bomber stations and their returning aircraft in the second half of 1941, as Turner's department passed its second anniversary in September the Luftwaffe in Europe remained heavily committed to the Soviet war which, originally expected to last for only a few months, would eventually stagnate into the bloodiest and most futile campaign of the Second World War. For the German High Command, 1942 was supposed to have been the year in which the Luftwaffe returned to Britain in force. They did return, as we shall see, if not in the numbers originally expected, and by May some of Turner's decoys were again immersed in front-line operations. But the winter of 1941–42 offered the first real respite since June 1940.

Among other things the lull allowed room for housekeeping. Since its foundation in October 1939 Colonel Turner's Department had steadily grown: first at Aerial House and later at Shepperton, staff were added as the department's remit widened and success fuelled demands for decoys in ever greater numbers, both at home and, increasingly, through the supply of mobile decoy lighting sets for use overseas. In result, by autumn 1941 there were four numbered sections in Turner's organisation at Shepperton. Section I dealt with operational intelligence, collating action reports from the sites and also, by this stage in the war, from the Air Warfare Analysis Section – who supplied data from investigation of bombing patterns – and the staff at the Central Interpretation Unit at Medmenham, who kept Turner's staff abreast of German decoy strategy. Section I also issued instructions on decoy tactics, as well as liaising with government departments over new sites. In this they were aided by the officers responsible for the K Areas, whose pattern had been thrice subdivided since the early days, first to seven areas in July 1940, next to thirteen in January 1941, and most recently to seventeen. Section II was Turner's administrative arm, dealing with the internal running of the department itself, as well as personnel services for the 3000 or so men who were by now serving on Starfish and the dwindling number of K sites. Equipment and land matters were handled by Section III, whose staff worked closely with Sound City for designs and experimental work, while in addition to their administrative duties the secretariat and financial staff constituting Section IV also (in Turner's words) fielded 'the more important criticisms and objections continually raised by local busybodies and others.'[31] It was a big team, and an efficient structure, reflecting Turner's genius for organisation.

But it had always been unorthodox. In the early days, when Turner operated almost alone to mastermind the commissioning of K and Q sites, his aptitude for working informally, outside service bureaucracy and the normal channels of command, had been one of the decoy programme's greatest strengths. One of the surviving oddities in this system was Turner's freedom to deal directly with station commanders over Q and K sites, largely circumventing the RAF's complex structure of commands and groups. For the most part this had worked well – not least because Turner was careful to keep these august formations acquainted with what was going on – though the exchanges with Dowding in the first six months of his work illustrated what could happen when an AOC-in-C felt his domain being encroached upon (if indeed that was the root of the problem). Two years on, however, with hundreds of decoys serviced by a sizeable staff, it was clear that the old ways must change.

It was in these circumstances that in the winter of 1941–42, the decoy service was reorganised with the twin objectives of bringing the RAF's commands and groups more formally into the picture and, at the same time, giving Turner responsibility for a wider range of matters cognate with decoy work. The first was achieved by establishing a Concealment and Decoy (C&D) Service within the RAF, to which were appointed full-time C&D officers on the staffs of every command and most groups, and part-time officers to each station. These arrangements, which officially came into force on 1 March 1942, replaced the old pattern of K Areas and Area Officers (though Turner continued to use the old terms informally). Colonel Turner's Department retained responsibility for decoy policy, which within the RAF was now implemented through this new structure. The addition of 'concealment' to this title reflected the second major change ushered in by the restructuring, for as well as decoy measures, Turner and the C&D Service were now given responsibility for monitoring camouflage at RAF stations. Under this new arrangement the *construction* of camouflage remained with the Air Ministry's Director of Works, but the new service was given the job of scrutinising the result from the air, a duty previously handled by No 1 Camouflage Unit, a small flight of aircraft currently based at Hendon and destined to move in June 1942 to Stapleford Tawney.[32] This unit was now transferred to Colonel Turner's Department, where it was known as the Special Flying Unit (though the original title remained in use externally). A new branch was formed within Turner's department – Section V – to shoulder the added responsibilities of airfield concealment. Uniquely in Turner's organisation, Section V had no decoy duties.

If the winter of 1941–42 saw Turner's empire expand and consolidate, it also brought its threats. The first emerged in early October, when Turner's 1A Priority to obtain essential supplies of decoy materials for construction and maintenance was withdrawn by the Central Priority Committee. Turner fought this, of course, and so on behalf of the Air Staff did Sir Wilfrid Freeman, who took the question to the Chiefs of Staff Committee on 10 October.[33] Freeman argued that the decoy organisation must retain its privileged claim upon resources because it was often called upon to respond urgently – the Starfish experience was demonstration enough of this. As well as pointing out how sparingly he had actually used his 1A Priority hitherto, Turner urged that decoys must be treated as operational weapons, not merely as incidental components of the passive defence system.[34] It was a point he began to make with increasing frequency at this time, and rightly so. Once their worth had been proven, decoys could be judged to have more in common with anti-aircraft guns than they did with, say, air-raid shelters (and, though Turner did not say as much, they were actually far more effective than AA gunnery in the first year or so of the war). By the end of 1941 the decoy organisation was coming to be recognised as an arm of the fighting services; it would have been more widely so, had it not been so novel, and still so secret.

Turner was obliged to marshal very similar arguments for a second time when, shortly after the priority question was settled, his organisation came under further scrutiny, this time from an old adversary. In the autumn of 1941 Sir Hugh Dowding was personally appointed by Churchill to undertake an inspection of manning levels – 'establishments', in the technical term – across the different branches of the RAF 'and to report to what extent and in what particulars they can be reduced without prejudice to operational efficiency.'[35] It was a job Dowding neither wanted nor relished, suspecting that his duties would be seen throughout the air force as a 'witch hunt' which would restore his position (as he wryly characterised it after the war) as 'Public Enemy No 1'. He was right. To scrutinise establishments was to threaten empires, and Dowding's spell in this unhappy position was marked by a series of border skirmishes, few of which added much to the efficiency of the RAF. One of these, perhaps inevitably, was with Turner.

Dowding's tour of inspection reached Turner's headquarters on 4 December 1941, when he was shown around the workshops and studios at Shepperton to satisfy himself that manpower was not being squandered. Since Turner was by now handling decoy and concealment work for all three services, and the MoHS, Dowding deferred judgement on whether Shepperton's staffing was reasonable. But once his inspection of Littleton Park House and the Sound City lots was complete, Dowding travelled out to look at a Starfish and a Q site, with Turner as his guide. Dowding was generous enough to grade the Q site as 'the last word in economy and efficiency', and was particularly impressed by its employing only two men. But the Starfish arrangements gave him pause for thought: could things not be done as efficiently, he asked, with simpler technology and fewer personnel?

Dowding's specific criticism was not that Starfish were overmanned for the sites as currently designed – staff had in fact already been reduced to seventeen from the original 24 – but rather that the electrical firing apparatus was unnecessarily elaborate and so required too large and specialised a crew. Electrical firing, explained Dowding in his report to the Secretary of State on 12 December, required continual testing of the circuits and, moreover, demanded that each of the 170 Starfish currently in place had a trained electrician on its strength.[36] By substituting a system of hand ignition for the fires, he argued, each site could relinquish the electrician and around half of the men, especially if less emphasis was placed on recharging a site on the morning after a lighting. To test this idea Dowding had actually asked for the Starfish inspected on 4 December to be partially ignited with the torches kept on site as a stand-by in the event of the electrical system failing. Presumably to Turner's satisfaction the results had been feeble, one fire taking ten minutes to get going and another nearly half an hour to take hold. But this delay, explained Dowding, could be overcome by drenching the fire with petrol or paraffin immediately before ignition; and as to the argument (evidently put by Turner at the time) that men could not reasonably be asked to venture forth into a blazing Starfish to light the second and subsequent groups of fires, Dowding thought that some sort of slow-burning fuse between groups could be fitted to allow the whole layout to go up in sequence. Dowding accepted that hand lighting would be less efficient than electrical ignition, but pointed out – reasonably enough – that the infrequent use of Starfish in recent months did diminish their claim on resources and that the present arrangements could remain at some of the 'most important' sites. The bottom line, in Dowding's calculations, was that hand-ignition, and a more relaxed attitude to replenishing fires, could save 1500 men nationally.

These arguments, it will be clear, threatened the two fundamental principles – instant ignition and rapid rebuilding – upon which Starfish tactics had depended over the previous year. Turner of course was vigorously opposed to any scheme which might jeopardise either. Dowding's ideas were discussed for almost a month before the DCAS, Air Vice-Marshal Norman Bottomley, came out in support of Turner's case, which depended chiefly on the delays attending hand ignition, but also invoked an estimate that hand-firing would actually increase the staff needed at each site by as much as 50 per cent. Unfortunately for Turner this decision, in the form communicated to Dowding, was claimed to result from 'experiment' in hand-firing, a word on which Dowding immediately pounced. Dowding's request to know the dates of the experiments, and to see copies of the reports, could not be answered, since in fact no special trials had been carried out. It appeared, as Dowding explained on 21 January 1942, 'that the word "experience" should be substituted for "experiments" in DCAS's report, and that DCAS had reached his decision on Colonel Turner's arguments without discussing them with me.' Continuing, Dowding suggested that Turner was 'prejudiced against any system of hand-lighting' and had avoided practical trials for fear of the results. Dowding asked for facilities to hold some tests himself.[37]

So it was that on two days in early February 1942 the austere figure of Sir Hugh Dowding was seen at SF25(b) – Stanwell Moor, one of two Starfish protecting Slough – supervising a party of airmen who, in a blustery wind, intermittent rain and eventually snow, tried in various ways to light the basket fires manually. With officers from Shepperton looking on (Turner stayed away) the Marshal of the Royal Air Force first gave the order to light a basket saturated with two gallons of petrol. The rather violent ignition which resulted when a match was applied persuaded Dowding to reduce the volume of fuel, and a satisfactory result was eventually achieved with a petrol-filled beer bottle which was laid on top of the basket, shattered with a hammer blow, and then lit. Next, Dowding tried burying a thermite bomb in the side of a basket and firing this with a pull on a lanyard connected to the detonator; again, the basket sprang immediately to life. The next test used a Molotov cocktail – a small bottle filled with a benzine, rubber and liquid phosphorous mix – which was laid under the basket, smashed with a hammer and lit. Dowding liked this method best of all, though he did try one last test, with a small incendiary bomb. For this adventurous procedure an airman was required to unscrew the bomb's casing and strike the percussion cap with a hammer, after which in the period available before ignition – 'about 30 seconds' – he would shove the bomb into the basket's superstructure and scurry away. Using the Molotov cocktail method Dowding found that he could get the basket fires of a Starfish alight in about five minutes or so with a small team of men communicating with megaphones and torches, and on this basis considered his case proven. The method would, of course, only work with the baskets, but then Dowding argued that the other types of fire should be scrapped at all but a few sites. The boiling oil and grid fires, he said, 'appear to require a good deal of maintenance and, even then, seem to be somewhat uncertain in their operation.'[38]

Once this report began to make its way around the Air Ministry it was clear that Turner had a fight on his hands. His response was a long and detailed letter of mitigation to the DCAS and a private letter to General Ismay, Churchill's personal representative on the Chiefs of Staff Committee who was himself receiving Dowding's papers on the case. The letter to Bottomley was technical and measured, while that to Ismay ('Dear Pug') more personal and written in the hope of enlisting Ismay's support should the matter reach his 'level' (this was evidently an attempt to prepare the ground for an appeal to Churchill). Turner was blunt with Ismay, saying that 'Dowding's proposals will ruin the Starfish scheme as a protection for the country', that Dowding was 'biassed', and that he had 'made up his mind before he saw one of my sites or made any investigations.'[39] But Ismay was reluctant to be drawn. Replying to Turner ('My dear Conky') on 12 February, Ismay advised that the decision would probably rest with the Air Council rather than the Chiefs of Staff or the Defence Committee, 'so that I am unlikely to have any say, much as I sympathise with your feelings in having the good show which you have put up spoilt or even curtailed.' So Turner's defence would rest on technical arguments alone.

These were carefully marshalled. With his engineer's eye for detail, Turner soon exposed some of the implications of Dowding's ideas. Firing baskets from Molotov cocktails might be all very well in isolated trials, argued Turner, but a simple calculation showed that the 200 Starfish which would eventually be built yielded a requirement for 160,314 bottles nationally; petrol amounted to 40,179 gallons permanently on site, with 65 gallons needed to replenish stocks every time a site was fired. And these devices, explained Turner, were stores of a very special kind.

> The Molotov Cocktail or SIP grenade [he continued] is highly inflammable and has to be handled with great care. War Office Order BMW 88/805 of 16th October, 1941, states that these grenades must be moved by special train with two empty trucks between the engine and the leading vehicle containing grenades and two empty trucks between the last vehicle with grenades and the brake van. Rail transport under these conditions cannot be arranged quickly, especially for small quantities for replacements. Road transport, except for short distances, is discouraged. In both cases a trained conductor must be provided, service personnel have to be used, and special fire fighting, medical, and protective equipment has to be carried.[40]

It is not clear whether Dowding had thought of any of this. And nor perhaps had he considered the extra guards which would be necessary on each site to secure such a large stock of petrol, which in 1942 was a precious commodity, ripe for pilfering. Turner picked over many more of Dowding's points and added several of his own – including the news that he had in any case been training Starfish crews in electrical maintenance, expressly to release specialist electricians for other work. In summary, argued Turner, Dowding's proposals would save only 40 men and weaken the tactical value of Starfish in so doing. But, at the same time, he conceded that the present lull in operations might justify some economies. In these circumstances, he suggested, it was better to mothball a proportion of the sites and leave the others fully equipped than impose a blanket reduction all round.

In the end the matter went to the Vice Chief of the Air Staff, Sir Wilfrid Freeman, who had the difficult task of arbitrating between Turner and Dowding.[41] Freeman came out in favour of Dowding's case for reducing the number of men allocated to Starfish but, in a rather perplexing judgement, declared this to be a quite separate issue from how the sites were fired. Freeman's verdict in fact betrayed a misunderstanding of both protagonists' cases, as Turner was quick to point out;[42] but there the matter rested. Rather bizarrely, electrical ignition was retained – so Dowding lost there – but manning was cut to the Dowding level at a proportion of Turner's sites, where assistance in reloading was arranged from nearby RAF stations. This decision was taken at the end of February, nearly three months after Dowding first raised the question. It was an odd episode, with an odd outcome.

Close checks on the labour absorbed by Starfish remained important in the winter of 1941–42 partly because the layout was still growing. Liverpool, Birmingham, Bristol and Hull all received additional sites in ones and twos in the first three months of 1942, while March saw the first open in Northern Ireland, with the commissioning of six sites for the protection of Belfast.[43] Belfast, it will be recalled, was originally scheduled to be ringed by Starfish as early as spring 1941, but had been deferred at Turner's request largely because of the practical difficulties of extending the organ-isation into Ulster. Work had later been postponed further because of the special problems of security in Northern Ireland where, it was believed, the sites – and perhaps the character of Starfish more generally – might by compromised by IRA agents passing infor-mation to the German Embassy in neutral Dublin.[44] Exposing Starfish to prying eyes in the rural fringes of Belfast was therefore something of a risk. It was offset by design modifications intended to conceal the purpose of the sites, at least until such time as they were set off.

This was done by disguising the Starfish as RAF bomb dumps.[45] Each of the six Belfast sites, and the two for Londonderry opened later in the year, was surrounded by a double circuit of barbed and Dannert wire and heavily guarded by a detachment which, here alone, was increased to 20 men. The fires, too, were differently constructed from those on the mainland. Most were formed from bales of compacted greaseproof paper soaked in a mixture of diesel and gas oil, though a few longer-burning peat fires were included to add variety. Each cluster of bales – usually 20 or 30 together – was concealed from view by a dummy hut made from plasterboard on a tubular steel frame, with each Starfish having twelve or 24 huts. The false impression of their function was planted by run-ning open lorries laden with bombs into the sites while they were under construction, while inflammable Starfish materials arrived discreetly hidden in covered vehicles. The ruse seems to have worked. It was believed that none of the sites was compromised, though even if their true function had been discovered their designs differed sufficiently from those of mainland Starfish to give the Germans no clues on what to look for elsewhere. The Ulster sites were thus unique in practising deception on two sepa-rate parties, one in the air and the other on the ground.

The Belfast Starfish of March 1942 had codes prefixed by SF49 – the serial for Belfast itself – while another site opened in March 1942 was SF51(a), the Strategic Starfish on the Lincolnshire coast at Huttoft. Londonderry's two sites, at Glebetown and Lisglass, were coded as SF50(a) and (b) and it seems likely that they were origi-nally intended to open *seriatim* after those of Belfast in the spring of 1942. In the event, however, Londonderry had to wait until November for its Starfish, since in the early summer work on the programme, by now running at a very gentle rate, was suddenly diverted to meet a new phase of Luftwaffe operations. These were the Baedecker raids on Britain's historic cities, the first of which hit Exeter on the night of 23 April.

The sequence of events which culminated in the Baedeker operations is well known. In February 1942 Air Chief Marshal Arthur Harris was appointed AOC-in-C Bomber Command, with a brief to expand operations and particularly to target the morale of Germany's industrial workers. Within six weeks of taking up his post, Harris, who had been DCAS at the time of the Coventry raid in November 1940 and was involved in the early work on Starfish, turned the tables on Germany by mounting two raids using tactics similar to those of KGr 100. Harris's objective here was to test whether incendiaries dropped at the onset of a raid could provide as effective a marker for subsequent waves as they had for the Germans.[46] Harris at this stage of the war had no electronic gadgets to guide his crews – no *Knickebein* or *X-Gerät* – so was forced to select targets which could reliably be found by conventional means and, for the purposes of these raids, could easily be set alight. The first chosen was Lübeck, a medieval city full of timber buildings which was signposted from the air by its position on the Baltic. Lübeck did indeed burn under Bomber Command's attack on the night of 28/29 March, when 234 aircraft dropped more than 300 tons of bombs, almost half of this weight being incendiaries. Half the city was destroyed. Next was Rostock, another Baltic port, which was bombed on four nights between 23 and 26 April, with similar cumulative results to those achieved at Lübeck. Neither of these towns was a prime military or industrial objective, though Rostock did accommodate a Heinkel factory on its outskirts which was targeted by a subsidiary precision force during the 25 April raid. But the point of these operations was more to show that Bomber Command – whose performance earlier in the war had been famously indifferent – could inflict serious harm upon targets of some value, if not yet the more challenging cities of the Ruhr and elsewhere. Harris was disarmingly frank over the considerations which condemned both towns. Lübeck, he wrote, 'was not a vital target, but it seemed to me better to destroy an industrial town of moderate importance than to fail to destroy a large industrial city.'[47]

The Baedecker raids were Germany's answer to these attacks. Hitler was reportedly much affected by the Lübeck operation and already by 14 April, before the Rostock raids had begun, had authorised retaliatory strikes against British targets chosen to have 'the greatest possible effect on civilian life.'[48] These were terror-attacks – Hitler actually used the word *Terrorangriffe* – whose targets would be lightly defended historic cities not dissimilar in fabric to Lübeck itself.[49] Hence Exeter, target of the first raid on 23 April, the night on which Bomber Command were operating over Rostock; and hence 'Baedecker': the pre-war guide to places of historical and cultural interest.

The first Exeter raid of 23 April was a minor affair, mounted by crews diverted from mine-laying duties, and it was some days before it was clear that a new phase of German operations had begun. But a return to Exeter on the next night, then far heavier raids on Bath during the nights of 25 and 26 April (the second of which took a side-swipe at the Q for Exeter airport[50]), and then successive attacks on Norwich, York and Norwich again on the three nights following revealed an unmistakable trend. By the end of the month, in anticipation of widening attacks, anti-aircraft guns were moving into position at 24 English towns of more or less historic character, from Penzance and Truro in the south-west to as far north as Lincoln. Turner received this list of targets on 30 April, along with a request to do what he could to supplement the guns with improvised decoys. It was rather as if the events of late November 1940 were replaying themselves, with the significant difference that this time the decoy tactics to meet the operations – which were led by pathfinder units using similar technology to KGr 100 – had been tried and tested. Plainly, this was a Starfish job.

Three of the towns on the target list – Ipswich, Norwich and Peterborough – had already gained Starfish earlier in the programme, while a further fourteen had Qs, QFs or QLs somewhere nearby, any of whose sites might be pressed into service as homes to new Starfish: these were Basingstoke, Andover, Taunton, Maidstone, Tonbridge, Ashford, Bath, Colchester, Chelmsford and Lincoln, together with Aldershot/Guildford and Reigate/Redhill, both of which pairs shared decoys between them. Towns from the original list without suitable existing sites nearby were Penzance, Truro, Hayle, Salisbury, Winchester, Canterbury and Cambridge.

To this list Turner added several more towns which, given the emerging pattern of attack, would probably become Baedecker targets. Of these, Oxford was covered by two existing Starfish, while York – which had already been bombed – and Durham as yet had no suitable sites in place. These towns brought the targets on Turner's list to 27, of which all but four required new Starfish. By 1 May Turner's reconnaissance staff were already active around Salisbury, Winchester and Cambridge.[51]

Turner no doubt shared the widespread public distaste at the Baedecker raids, which unlike the attacks of 1940–41 seemed essentially cynical and vandalistic. But he could have been forgiven for a measure of satisfaction at the way in which this new turn of events vindicated his arguments in defence of the decoy organisation over the previous six months: for here was an urgent demand of the very kind that, as Turner had insisted, he must always be poised to meet. 'The personnel question', he explained drily to Whitworth Jones on 1 May, 'will be a little difficult owing to the recent cuts, but I have written to Records to hold up any men trained to Starfish who have not yet been removed.'[52] The demand was met on this occasion by what Turner dubbed the 'Temporary Starfish', which resembled its permanent cousin in all respects except the range of fire types, which was confined to baskets. Electrical ignition was used.

The first Temporary Starfish came into operation on 9 May 1942, covering Salisbury, Cambridge, Basingstoke, Lincoln, Bath, Canterbury and Winchester, each of which had a single site.[53] Though several of these towns did have existing decoys of one sort or another nearby, in the event most of the new Starfish occupied newly-found positions, only that for Basingstoke in this group – TSF57(a) – being grafted onto an existing QL. Nine further towns were protected in the following few days, namely Colchester, Reigate/Redhill (with a single TSF at South Godstone), Chelmsford, Andover, Ashford – an addition to the original list – and Hayle, together with Guildford/Aldershot, which shared a decoy at Wanborough. Again, most of these were new sites, though Colchester, Chelmsford and Ashford's TSFs exploited civil QL positions for their respective target towns. And so it continued: by the end of May the list of historic towns joining the Starfish layout for the first time had lengthened to include Andover, Taunton, Maidstone (which exploited an existing QF), Tonbridge, Penzance, Truro, York, Durham, Glastonbury/Wells – another addition – and Exeter. In the following month cover was extended to Chichester and Tunbridge Wells, while secondary TSFs were introduced at a few of the more vulnerable Baedecker targets, such as Cambridge and Canterbury. Rye joined the layout in July, when a second TSF was also built for Bath, bringing the total of new sites built to 33, protecting 26 towns (Fig 37, page 168).

Although Temporary Starfish did draw some attacks, the emergency programme began too late to play a part in some of the heaviest raids. Thus Exeter, one of the most vulnerable urban areas in Britain to fire attacks, was still without a Starfish on the night of 3rd May, when 50 tons of high explosive and thousands of incendiaries shattered the city centre.[54] Norwich was bombed in a Baedecker operation on the night of 8 May, again before any Temporary Starfish were in place, though by chance this city was one of the few historic cities already decoyed. The existing SF43(a) accordingly collected ten HE bombs and SF43(b) just four, though these seem to have been aimed at the QL on the site – C33(b) – rather than the Starfish itself. Otherwise, May brought more successes for existing Starfish, usually covering non-Baedecker targets. Naval Starfish won two minor successes on the Humber on 19 and 29 May, and fought a major battle at site PE1, for Poole, which was estimated to have drawn 60–100 HE bombs on the night of the 24th.[55]

Canterbury saw June's most sustained action against a Baedecker target, suffering three raids in the first week of the month, and claimed the only Temporary Starfish actually to be lit in this phase of operations. The first raid, on the night of 31 May/1 June, was mounted in reprisal for a British attack on Cologne on the previous night.[56] Though comparatively light – no more than 80 or 90 aircraft were involved – the operation did material damage to central Canterbury and was not deflected by lighting TSF61(a) at Bridge. Better results were achieved against the tiny force which returned the next night. The fall of incendiaries in Sturry Road at 03.10 led to an instant order to light TSF61(a), whose baskets were ablaze within two minutes.[57] The first bombs struck the Starfish at 03.20, and although only four HEs were collected – killing some livestock and damaging farm buildings – the force operating over

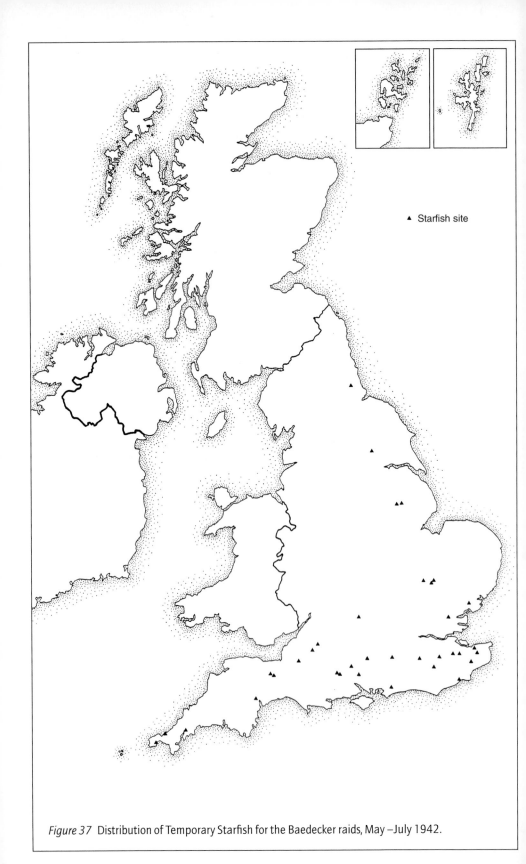

▲ Starfish site

Figure 37 Distribution of Temporary Starfish for the Baedecker raids, May –July 1942.

Canterbury had amounted to just six aircraft. The lighting of this single Starfish on two successive nights of course drove home Turner's point over the need for immediate recharging. Bridge was accordingly rebuilt for a second time, and five days later was again in action against another light raid. The first flares were seen over Canterbury at 01.05 on the night of 6/7 June, and the Starfish ignited five minutes later. Four or five HEs were collected before 01.30, though on this occasion a moderate weight of bombs also hit the city.[58]

Although the partial diversion of the two minor Canterbury raids vindicated the decision to provide Starfish for Baedecker targets, in truth the raids were all but over by the time cover was reasonably complete at the end of May. The Canterbury operations were among the last Baedecker raids, and Bridge the only TSF to see action in the campaign which brought these sites into being. Once operations over mainland Britain had been re-established in the Baedecker raids, the Luftwaffe soon switched to more profitable industrial targets. Some of these raids brought established Starfish into action, though a minor surge in the frequency of lighting between June and August 1942 was also caused in part by orders from Turner that Starfish should be used more boldly.[59] On 3 June the naval Starfish PE1, for Poole, was lit again, this time unsuccessfully, while a Starfish for Southampton, the Strategic Starfish at Cheddar, and the existing sites covering Ipswich, Peterborough and Norwich were all in action during the month. Of these, however, only SF38(b) at Ipswich and SF43(a) at Norwich drew bombs, and these in very small numbers.

Raiding followed a similar pattern in July. A short Starfish was fired at site PT1 for Portland on the night of 1st/2nd – when bombs aimed at the decoy fell into the sea – and site MH2 at Milford Haven four nights later, before raiding turned to the Middlesbrough area at the end of the week. Two Starfish were lit in these operations, though only SF15(d) saw any action, when it was machine-gunned by a passing bomber. Birmingham became the target at the end of the month, seeing Starfish operations on three nights between 27 and 30 June, on the last of which three sites were ignited at Bickenhill, Leamington – respectively Birmingham SF2(e) and Coventry 7(a) – and Silvington, Strategic Starfish for the Midlands. A second 'Strategic' at Aldbrough, on the Yorkshire coast, was lit on the next night, drawing six HEs, but otherwise July's total 'bag' of diverted bombs was meagre. August brought another series of minor raids in which a tendency seen during the Blitz showed signs of reappearing, certain Starfish coming into action repeatedly while others remained inert. Thus SF43(a) for Norwich was lit on three occasions in August, and its partner, SF43(b), twice. These sites operating together brought the largest Starfish success for over a year, diverting around 2000 incendiary bombs between them on the night of 13/14 August. Ipswich Starfish, too, were burning on three nights during this month, SF38(b) drawing a few incendiaries on the 10th/11th and SF38(b) a similar haul four nights later. But these were the only successes. Starfish lit at Hull, Leeds and Sunderland on odd occasions during August achieved nothing, and nor did TSF54(b) for Cambridge when it became the second Temporary site to be ignited, on the 6th/7th. Thereafter, the early autumn brought another lull. The single operation in September was on 19th/20th, when a short Starfish lit at SF15(c), Bolden Colliery for Newcastle, drew a few bombs meant for Tyneside, while another north-eastern site – 15(d) at Ryhope – was one of three Starfish in action during October, none of which drew any bombs. The other two were the Canterbury sites, both of which were lit in the early hours of 31 October; with four ignitions since 31 May, TSF61(a) at Bridge claimed the record as the most active Temporary Starfish of the war.

In the years after the Second World War the decoy programme of 1939–45 came to be recognised as an important element of Britain's air defences, but one whose overall value was weakened by a late start and a tendency to follow, rather than anticipate, developments in the German air offensive. The soundness of this judgement is reflected, *inter alia*, by the fact that the number of operational decoys reached its peak only in the closing months of 1942, at the end of a year in which attacks had sharply diminished. Though the spread of decoy cover in the first three years of war was never purely cumulative – a few sites were abandoned as others were commissioned – most types of sites continued to grow in number until the autumn of that year, before beginning a gradual decline in the first months of 1943. Thus the Starfish layout was still expanding in November 1942, with the commissioning of the two sites for Londonderry, one for Grantham and the final Strategic Starfish, at Alciston on the Sussex coast.[60] Apart from a single site protecting Hartlepool, which opened as late as November 1943 when many Starfish elsewhere had closed, these were the last Starfish of the war, and brought the number of civil sites operational to its all-time high of 209 in December (Fig 38, page 172). The number of civil QLs also peaked at this time, reaching 212 in November 1942, the same month in which Q sites reached their most populous at 171 and RAF QFs their more modest total of 22. The maximum number of QFs in other categories was achieved rather earlier, in August 1942, when 83 were operating, and by the end of the year their numbers were already slipping away. But altogether, November 1942 was the peak month for decoys, when no fewer than 695 functions were in place across the country. The number of *sites*, of course, was significantly smaller, since many of the QLs, QFs and Starfish were co-located; but the defensive value of the decoy system was measured in functions, not in positions, and by this criterion the UK was never more comprehensively decoyed than in November 1942.[61]

It will be clear that by the end of 1942 the decoy layout had become an almost exclusively nocturnal system. While the two dummy wireless stations were kept in commission almost until the end of the war; three of the four dummy factories built by Sound City in the summer of 1940 were closed along with the last K sites, in June 1942. With few day attacks and annual maintenance costs running at £7000–8000, Holwellhyde, Coven and Leamington Hastings had simply become uneconomic. Lying in a more vulnerable area on the borders of the Thames Estuary, the Chatham factory survived this round of cuts, only to be abandoned in April 1943.[62] Closure of the day decoys, however, was balanced by continuing refinements to the night sites. The conversion of Q sites to Drems continued steadily throughout 1942, and by autumn 1942 – when precise figures happen to be available – 105 Q sites (more than 60 per cent of the total operating) had been brought up to this standard (Fig 39, page 173).[63]

The late summer of 1942 brought experiments with new apparatus intended to lure pilots on intruder operations to attack Q sites

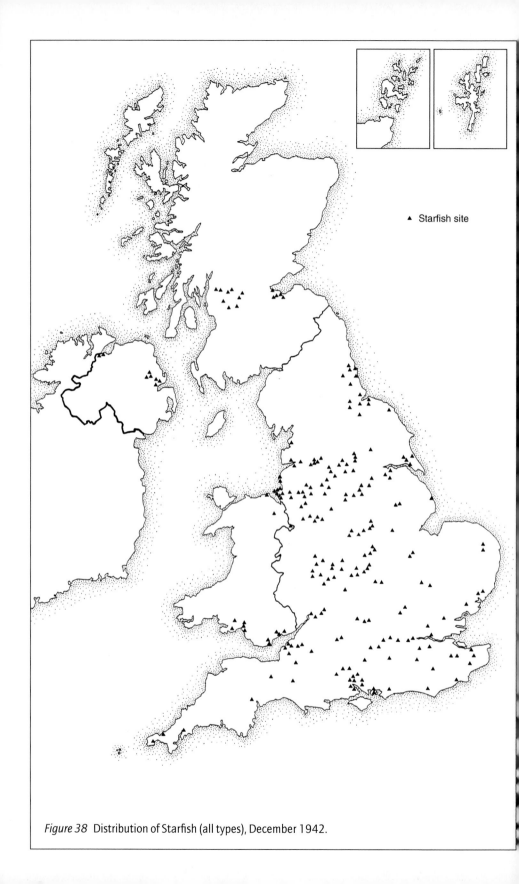

Figure 38 Distribution of Starfish (all types), December 1942.

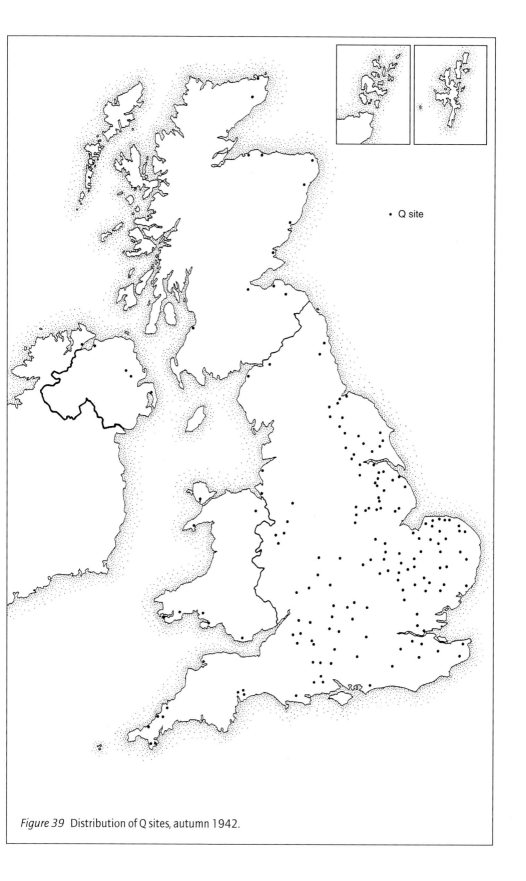

Q site

Figure 39 Distribution of Q sites, autumn 1942.

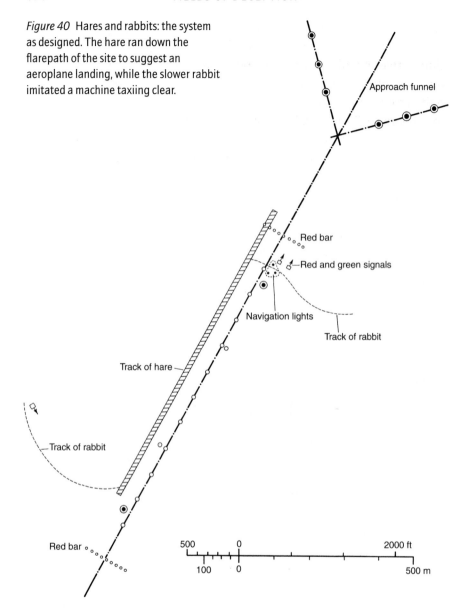

Figure 40 Hares and rabbits: the system as designed. The hare ran down the flarepath of the site to suggest an aeroplane landing, while the slower rabbit imitated a machine taxiing clear.

Approach funnel

Red bar

Red and green signals

Navigation lights

Track of rabbit

Track of hare

Track of rabbit

Red bar

500   0   2000 ft

100   0   500 m

more often. Known to Turner and his staff as 'hares and rabbits', these unlikely gadgets were intended to represent aircraft landing and taxiing on the (dummy) airfield. The 'hare', or landing aircraft, was simply a trolley carrying a collection of aircraft lights suspended from a pair of steel cables which ran down the flarepath on scaffold trestles (Fig 40). A cordite cartridge would hurtle the trolley down the cable run, initially at about 60 miles per hour but with gradually diminishing speed as the charge expired and friction between trolley and cable began to bite. Seen from the air, this did look remarkably like an aircraft landing and then coming to a halt. To complete the illusion, the 'rabbit' played the part of a taxiing machine. This consisted of a continuous wire loop, with an aircraft's head and tail lamp suspended, run over pulleys mounted on trestles and driven slowly by a small electric motor. A satisfying wobble imparted to the lights by the moving cable was generally agreed to resemble an aircraft traversing uneven ground.[64] These devices were first tried on 12 August 1942 at Houghton Q site (where Drem lighting had its first trials in 1941 and which had become something of a test-bed for Q site equipment), to the satisfaction of most of the commands' representatives present. Accordingly, in late October hares and rabbits were approved for limited use on more vulnerable Q sites, initially on twelve Drem Qs parented by Bomber and Coastal Commands.[65]

Innovations such as the Drem system may have done something to improve the performance of Q sites but, taking stock at the end of the year, there was no escaping the fact that attack rates had diminished sharply in 1942. Intruder operations, the Baedecker raids and the small campaign of generalised bombing which followed contributed to a modest rise in Q site incidents between April and August, these five months contributing 31 of the 37 attacks drawn in the whole of 1942 – but this annual total equalled that achieved in 1940 during the month of September alone.[66] Nor did the QF and QL sites achieve much in 1942. Though the QL's ability to confuse navigators was always an asset of indeterminate value, these sites between them drew just 35 attacks in the whole of the year, with a sharp peak in July when thirteen raids were recorded. Some of these operations, it is true, were significant in themselves. An attack on 3/4 June evidently intended for the RN cordite factory at Holton Heath was diverted almost completely by the naval QF, which drew at least 112 HE bombs and more than 5000 incendiaries and in doing so probably achieved the greatest QF success of the war.[67] Odd triumphs such as this, however, were widely remarked precisely because of their rarity. In all, Colonel Turner's Department placed attacks on decoys at no more than 93 for the whole of 1942, and while the more liberal criteria used by other analysts yielded higher figures (the Key Points Intelligence Directorate were prepared to recognise 160), a relative decline was evident whichever set of rules was used, and was of course emphasised by the larger number of decoys in place. No immediate cuts followed – for no one could be sure what the Luftwaffe might do next – but nor was the steady expansion in sites maintained. Christmas 1942 saw the number of decoys reach a plateau, before beginning a gentle downward trend in the spring of 1943. But by then, new tasks were in hand.

CHAPTER 6

Cockade and *Fortitude*

JANUARY 1943 – MAY 1944

In mid January 1943 Churchill, Roosevelt and their Combined Chiefs of Staff assembled at a hotel in the suburbs of Casablanca for *Symbol*, one of a series of conferences whose conclusions governed the Allies' grand strategy in the Second World War. It was at *Symbol* that the leaders settled two policies whose execution came to characterise the latter war years in Britain. One was the Combined Bomber Offensive – the campaign by RAF Bomber Command and the USAAF against Germany's military, industrial and economic system, and the morale of her people – and the other the commitment to planning for *Overlord*, as the invasion of occupied Europe was eventually known. The head of the planning staff for this operation was known as COSSAC (the Chief of Staff to the Supreme Allied Commander), who in the person of Lieutenant General Frederick Morgan set up a London headquarters at Norfolk House, St James's Square, in March 1943. Morgan's task was to plan for an invasion which, contrary to earlier Soviet and US expectations, was now scheduled to take place no earlier than summer 1944. But to keep the Germans guessing as to the timing and site of the real invasion, Morgan's 'Ops B' section was to plan a series of deception schemes for implementation over the following year.

In the fifteen months between March 1943 and the Normandy landings of June 1944, Colonel Turner's Department became closely involved in the deception operations which, with varying degrees of success, laid the ground for *Overlord*. In doing so, however, Turner's staff were cast in a new and sometimes uncomfortable role. The deceptive preliminaries to *Overlord* – first an enterprise known as *Cockade*, and later Operation *Fortitude* – were *strategic* operations, planned by higher command and executed by a wide range of military formations, of which Turner's department was only one. In recent years *Cockade* and *Fortitude* have become the most intensively studied deceptions of the Second World War, and as strategic operations both embraced activities far outside the scope of this book.[1] But since both employed decoys and misleading displays furnished by Colonel Turner's Department, and since these have actually been the least studied aspects of both operations, they do claim an important place here.

Turner's contribution to *Overlord* began several months before *Symbol*'s decision to create a planning staff for the final operation, and at first served a preliminary programme of cross-Channel raiding. Though dedicated preparations for the Normandy landings commenced only in the spring of 1943, British studies of amphibious warfare had a history reaching back as far as summer 1940, when Lieutenant General Alan Bourne was appointed commander of raiding operations and advisor to the Chiefs of Staff. Bourne was soon replaced by Admiral of the Fleet Sir Roger Keyes, who formed a Combined Operations Headquarters at Richmond Terrace in London; and Keyes in his turn was succeeded in autumn 1941 by Lord Louis Mountbatten. Apart from mounting experimental work on amphibious landing techniques – which took place at the Combined Operations Experimental Establishment (COXE) in north Devon – Mountbatten came to his post with a brief to initiate a programme of raiding on the French coast. To serve these operations, in the summer of 1942 work began on a series of concrete aprons ('hards') for loading landing craft at points strung along the south coast. The first sites – around the Solent, Newhaven, Shoreham and Portland[2] – were first used in anger during Operation *Jubilee*, the near-disastrous raid on Dieppe in August 1942, while in late September work began on a second and larger group running from South Wales eastward to Felixstowe, with concentrations around Falmouth, Dartmouth, Plymouth, Portsmouth, Dover and the Thames.[3]

Toward the end of September 1942 Mountbatten's staff invited Turner to investigate the possibility of providing decoy lighting for the complete system of hards built under the first and second schemes.[4] There was no particular urgency – the full suite of hards was not due to be complete until the end of March 1943 – but by early February Turner had the basic plan clear and some of the decoys were already in place. Since the hards were an Admiralty responsibility, the decoys were organised into a series of numbered groups to respect the navy's own structure of geographical commands. The first to be commissioned were ten in Portsmouth Command, which were given three-digit numbers starting at 600. Nine were newly-built – three at Lymington, two at Southampton and four at Portsmouth – while site 605 used part of the existing QL layout in Cuckmere Haven, laid out in 1941 to displace Newhaven.[5] All the new sites in this first group were initially built as permanent QLs (as Cuckmere already was) with displays mimicking the fairly sparse lighting typical of real hards and their small clutches of buildings. But this policy was soon changed. Since the hards would not be used again until some uncertain date in the future, it was decided in the spring that the decoys installed on site should be restricted to a fixed skeleton – essentially the shelter and fittings for the lights – with electrical gear held in store until the sites were needed, when fitting-out and operation would be given to detachments from nearby Starfish. The permanent QLs already built were eventually converted to this specification.

By the end of February the full complement of 23 sites had been selected for these 'Mobile QL' (MQL) installations: beyond the original ten in Portsmouth Command, there were six decoys in Plymouth Command (serials 550–555), three in Dover Command (650–652) and four in Nore Command (700–703) around the Thames Estuary and the Essex coast. In addition, the permanent QL at Alciston (C91) was also brought into the layout.[6] With the completion of these sites in their skeleton form during April and May 1943 (when they entered the site rosters as Naval Coast decoys – the 'NC' Series), Turner's first contribution to the deceptive preparations which would ultimately play a part in *Overlord* was complete.

Though Turner was first drawn into combined operations work simply to provide tactical decoys for hards, already by early 1943 he was pressing for a large deception component to be assimilated to plans for the continental landings. He first raised these anxieties within the Air Ministry in February, before Morgan had set up his headquarters as COSSAC, and returned to them in early April, when he submitted a paper to the Air Staff urging that deceptive plans for the operation should be 'taken up on a high level' without delay. Turner's thinking at this time was that the area of the coast *not* used for embarking troops should be exploited to contrive some kind of cover plan to mislead the Germans over the true site of the landing, and that tactical deception with lights, fires and other devices should be included in the armoury of the invading force. By early April Turner had already been pressing these ideas widely, but 'All my attempts to get a move on', he protested to the Air Staff, 'have been met with the answer that as the main plan has not been settled, no instructions can be given with regard to the deception plan.' In Turner's view this missed the point, since:

> Up to date the three Services have made no attempt to get together to work out any large deception scheme. No one has any idea what they will be called upon to do, nor what equipment will be necessary. The problems of co-ordination and control have not been studied at all. What is wanted is a practice scheme. It does not matter in the least whether this practice scheme is in the same area or of the same type as the final one. It is in the attempt to solve any scheme that we shall get valuable experience to help us put through the final scheme reasonably quickly. Operational Staffs always like to postpone schemes until the last minute, leaving the organization and implementation of them to be muddled through in a time all too short for success. Unless something is done at an early date so that all our commitments can be defined, the final deception scheme will be a botched makeshift, and is unlikely seriously to deceive the enemy.[7]

There was no doubting the wisdom of all this, though it is unlikely that Turner, when he wrote it, knew that *Overlord* was not to be mounted for at least another year. But these views were also sent to the London Controlling Section – the War Cabinet's central planning staff for strategic deception generally – along with a series of more general complaints about the neglect of deception plans for Operation *Husky*, the forthcoming invasion of Sicily.[8] Responding for the LCS, Denis Wheatley explained that everyone's hands were tied until Morgan had settled his own plans as COSSAC; even the LCS had been told to hold fire on deception planning for UK-based operations.[9]

There is every reason to suppose that Turner would have been glad to take general charge of deception work for *Overlord*, both domestically and in the theatre of operations opened across the Channel. He did have some say in the preliminary stages, through being appointed to No 3 *Roundup* Sub-Committee, which agreed early in the year that his department would be responsible for lights and fire deception in the operation. Turner, however, wanted more, and in the absence of what he considered to be adequate preparations elsewhere, actually began to design tactical decoy equipment on his own initiative: by mid April Sound City were developing portable lighting sets to mimic disembarking troops, camps and ammunition dumps, and studying methods of improvising decoy fires from materials which could be scavenged on a battlefield.[10] This independent action paid off, and some of the equipment was used. But Turner was soon left in no doubt that his would not be an executive role. In the last week of April he was visited by Major Money-Coutts of Morgan's Norfolk House staff, who told him that COSSAC's deception activities would be handled by the army, and that an officer previously involved in the very successful deceptive preliminaries for Alamein had already been seconded. The No 3 *Roundup* Sub-Committee, moreover, was to be disbanded. For a time it appeared that Turner's staff might be written out of the *Overlord* deception plans altogether, and as a result pressure was brought to bear on General Morgan.[11] In the event, Turner did keep charge of lighting and fire decoys, as well as a number of ancillary services, for the deceptive operations which began in the summer of 1943. But higher control of these operations would lie elsewhere.

Apart from the preparatory work on the Naval Coast QLs, which added 23 sites to the decoy layout during the spring, the first half of 1943 was occupied with minor adjustments to equipment and procedures at existing sites, and the beginnings of contraction in national cover. In January Turner came under renewed pressure to find economies in the personnel allocated to decoys generally, which by now amounted to 3236 men nationally for the Air Ministry sites, excluding the naval and army decoys and the civilians who staffed many QLs. Some 2624 personnel (including 36 WAAFs) were tied up by Starfish alone, and it was among these sites that the main cuts were imposed. But hard choices were involved. Fully a year after his second skirmish with Dowding, Turner was still complaining that the 'Dowding cuts', as he called them, had compromised security at many sites through curtailing guard duties. For these and other reasons there was no scope for further reductions in crews, which by now stood at ten men for standard Starfish and just five for those sites – such as the TSFs of 1942 – using baskets alone. Nor would temporary closures meet the need, since that equipment which was not stolen would soon deteriorate if not maintained. The only remaining possibility was to close some sites altogether, and this option Turner reluctantly accepted. But he did warn of dangers. By now, Turner explained, the Luftwaffe would have mapped every Starfish in daylight photography, with the result that a lit decoy spotted as such in a raid might mark the real target. In Turner's thinking, it followed that the more decoys there were, the less likely it would be that a crew would know *which* they were seeing. Reasonable as this argument may have been, however, Turner chose not to press it too hard.[12]

The first block closure of Starfish accordingly came in February, when seventeen sites were given up for good.[13] These were drawn from a list assembled in the previous month, when sites for closure were divided into four groups ('A' to' D'), in priority for relinquishment.[14] February's closures – the 'A' list – were mostly odd Starfish from the largest layouts, those whose siting had proved less than ideal, and sites serving targets which were themselves remote. Thus Glasgow, Sheffield, Swansea, Stourport, Redditch and Gloucester lost one site each, while two were deleted at Leeds, Manchester, Accrington and Belfast – which now had only four Starfish – and at Londonderry. These two sites had been opened only three months earlier, and their removal marked Londonderry as the most briefly-protected Starfish city of the war.

The difficulty of matching Starfish numbers to the pattern of German air operations was brought home in the weeks following these closures. On the night of 17/18 January the Luftwaffe mounted their first substantial raid on London since 1941,[15] an operation of more than 100 sorties which, unfortunately, the lighting of SF8(e) at Lullingstone did nothing to deflect.[16] Several months of virtual inaction in the Starfish system was then abruptly ended by no fewer than five ignitions and three attacks during March, when the Luftwaffe again operated over Britain in some force, if with little precision. Two Short Starfish were fired on the night of 3/4 March at sites protecting London, SF8(c) at Rainham Marshes and SF8(d) at Lambourne End both drawing a scatter of bombs for their trouble and contributing to the defeat of a raid in which most of the German crews failed to find the capital.[17] Success came again on the night of 12/13 March, when another Short Starfish lit at SF15(c) – Boldon Colliery for Newcastle – drew about a dozen HEs and numerous incendiaries. Another Newcastle site was lit on the night of 22/23 March, again using the Short Starfish procedure, though neither this operation, nor the firing at 43(a), Little Plumstead for Norwich on the night of 28/29 March, drew an attack. This latter incident pushed Little Plumstead's record to no fewer than five lightings in the previous year, once again exemplifying the tendency for certain Starfish to see far more action than others.

The upturn in Starfish operations in March 1943 was matched by a brief surge in attacks on other decoy types. Six were recorded on Q sites – which otherwise had drawn only two raids since 1 October 1942 – and no fewer than twelve on civil QLs and QFs, the largest monthly total since July 1942 (when thirteen had been recorded) and a conspicuous jump from the recent monthly tally of incidents in ones and twos. March, in all, was a busy month thanks to a general intensification of Luftwaffe operations, though the ineffectiveness of these raids owed much to inexperience among Göring's crews. In recognition of this, towards the end of the month a new appointment was made in the Luftwaffe, when an officer called Dietrich Peltz became *Angriffsführer England*. Under Peltz's leadership, in mid April the Luftwaffe began to mount night raids with fast fighter-bomber aircraft (their normal range extended by supplementary fuel tanks), first using this tactic against London on the night of 16/17th. Decoys played no part in this operation, but they were hardly necessary since most of the Luftwaffe crews became hopelessly lost (three pilots actually mistook the Maidstone area for northern France, and ended their sorties – and their careers – by landing at RAF West Malling). Starfish were of little use against the fighter-bomber raids, but with enemy navigation as poor as this it was obvious that QLs had a part to play. On 12 May Turner arranged that MQL sets manufactured for the 'NC' Series hard decoys then nearing completion should be hurriedly overlaid on Starfish near Salisbury, Reading, Chelmsford, Colchester, Maidstone and Canterbury – the last at Bridge, TSF 61(a), the site so frequently attacked in the Baedecker raids just a year before.[18] None of these QLs seems to have drawn any bombs, however, and neither did the remaining Starfish lit in April and May. The Temporary Starfish at Little Baddow (TSF64(a) for Chelmsford) was lit on two occasions in these months, along with SF43(b) for Norwich, which on the night of 4/5 May reached its third ignition since August 1942. No more success was achieved by single Starfish lit at Newcastle and Southampton during May.

In June 1943, as this rather inconclusive series of operations was approaching its end, a further ten Starfish were closed: these were sites on the 'B' list – the second stage of the block closure programme – drawn up in January, though since modified in detail. Like the 'A' list sites closed in February, these were sites in peripheral positions with poor records of attack, and most served northern targets. Edinburgh lost two sites, while one each was removed from the layouts at Glasgow, Lancaster, Leeds, Warrington, Wolverhampton, Leicester, Stoke on Trent and Middlesbrough, the last being the Strategic Starfish at Osmotherly, SF10(c).[19] No Starfish operations were recorded by 80 Wing in June 1943 and only one in July, when SF38(a) was fired at Ipswich, while by now attacks on other decoy types had again slumped to monthly figures in the ones and twos. The last heavy raid of this minor campaign came on the night of 25/26 July, when a force of 50 aircraft operating against Hull managed to miss their target entirely.[20]

The ineffectiveness of this new round of German raiding was explained in part by the RAF's established air superiority over Britain by the summer of 1943. Three years on from *Adlertag*, when the battle for dominance in the skies might have gone either way, Britain's air defences could call upon a mature layout of radar stations, effective night fighters – themselves using increasingly sophisticated GCI and airborne radars – and anti-aircraft gunnery which was both well drilled and itself largely radar controlled. Faced with these defences the Luftwaffe by summer 1943 found any kind of daylight operation over Britain particularly hazardous: and this during the very period when reconnaissance of ports and assembly areas for whatever landing operation the Allies were planning was becoming critical. Ironically, the strength of the air defences acted in one way to the Allies' disadvantage, since it was at this time that the first strategic feints connected with the invasion of Europe were played out. These displays, plainly, could not mislead unless the Luftwaffe had an opportunity to see them.

As we have seen, the deceptive preparations for the continental landing which would be mounted in June 1944 eventually fell into two parts: first, a series of displays designed to convince the Germans that landings were actually to be made in 1943; and second, further operations in the run-up to the real landing in 1944. The 1943 *Cockade* plan was divided into three sections: a spoof cross-Channel landing (code-named *Starkey*), a series of displays intended to suggest preparations for a landing in Norway (*Tindall*), and a similar operation to imply an imminent American landing in Brittany (*Wadham*). As originally conceived these three elements were to interlock in a complex feint to keep the Germans guessing over the site of a landing in 1943, which would itself be mounted as a spoof on 8 September (as part of *Starkey*) when a substantial force of ships and aircraft would advance on the French coast, lure the Germans into battle, and then withdraw.

Almost from the start, however, scepticism from commanders invited to play the *Cockade* game forced reductions in this plan. The Admiralty refused to commit its precious battleships to the mock invasion fleet, while Harris at Bomber Command resisted any diversion from the campaign against Germany. Portal, as CAS, was dubious about the whole enterprise, while the Special Operations Executive and Political Warfare Executive faced questions of immense delicacy in deciding what to tell agents, resistance movements in occupied Europe, and the world's public about the spoof invasion, and by what means. Nor was anyone sure, for a time, how much to tell the troops who would actually sail toward France. All strategic deceptions, it is true, brought such problems; but they proved especially troublesome in *Cockade*, and launched the operation amid doubt and uncertainty.

The script for the play called for the action to begin in July, when dummy aircraft and gliders would be exposed at airfields in Scotland – this was the opening gambit of *Tindall* – while the south coast would see troops concentrate under an exercise called *Harlequin*, the display of real and dummy landing craft at ports, and further dummy aircraft displayed at airfields; these southern measures were the first stages of *Starkey*. Turner's department, in theory, was to co-ordinate the dummy aircraft for both operations, as well as providing deceptive night lighting displays simulating concentrations of troops near south coast ports. But it was soon obvious that a shortage of real and dummy landing craft ruled out night lighting to mimic high troop concentrations, since suggesting an invasion force too large for the number of vessels visible would probably be counter-productive. Already by mid July, therefore, Turner's lighting plans had been cut merely to protective displays – decoys proper – to cover embarkation points and the real camps occupied by troops assembling under *Harlequin*. Plans for *Tindall*, too, were soon reworked, when Turner realised that he was expected in a matter of a few weeks to conjure up protective hides for 210 gliders to be displayed at Scottish airfields. Protesting on 14 July that the material for these hides equated to a rectangle one mile long by half a mile wide, Turner declared that *Tindall* as planned to start on the following day was 'frankly impossible.' So it was, for this and other reasons. There was, for example, no means of ferrying the gliders to Scotland without borrowing aircraft from Bomber Command to serve as tugs; and Harris had already made it clear what he thought of *Cockade* and its ruses.

Three months earlier, it will be recalled, Turner had foreseen most of these problems. 'I submit', he wrote on 14 July, 'that it is useless for Chair-borne Contrivers to prepare schemes on subjects of which they have no personal knowledge (eg, gliders, deception), without consulting those who know something about them.' He made other submissions, too: that 'no operational scheme can be successful unless the equipment and time is available to carry it out'; that long-term, co-ordinated planning was essential; and that 'deception is best obtained by the slow and natural building up of a scheme'. Turner's chief anxiety was that self-erected obstacles of the kind already jeopardising *Cockade* would reappear when the deception plan for the real invasion was put in train. He was right,

Plate 17 Dummy Boston aircraft of the type used in Operations *Tindall* and *Fortitude North*, 1943–44.

and it was partly on the failings of *Cockade* that the success of *Fortitude* would be built.

In the event the display and decoy layout for *Tindall* and *Starkey* went ahead during August in a reduced form, whilst *Wadham* was begun and then prematurely curtailed. In the last week of July officers from Turner's department arrived in Scotland to oversee the erection of dummy Boston aircraft at Fordoun, Peterhead and Fraserburgh. These were formally 'exposed' to enemy view from 7 August, while dummy gun emplacements and tented camps were set out at the three airfields to give the impression of heightened occupation: so began *Tindall*. Meanwhile, down in the south, *Starkey* got underway with the exposure of dummy aircraft at ten airfields – these were handled by six-man detachments from nearby Starfish – and the laying out of lighting decoys at 33 sites on the south coast in four clusters spread along the coast from Portsmouth to Dover. Each of these contained an inland group of sites equipped with what Turner dubbed 'Assault QLs' (ASQLs), giving protective cover to areas used by the *Harlequin* troops with lights replicating dumps, vehicle convoys, and camps, and a coastal group of MQLs, mostly occupying positions for hard decoys (the 'NC' Series) built in skeleton form earlier in the year and now activated for the first time.[21]

The distribution of Turner's decoys (Fig 41) gives a good impression of the geography of *Starkey*. Of the five positions making up the Southampton MQL coastal group, sites 606 and 607 (the hard lighting at Sowley Pond and Chilling) and NC609 (the port lighting at Pennington Marshes, decoying Lymington) originated earlier in the year, while Newtown Bay East and West, which now accommodated hard lighting, were newly-found and became sites 611 and 612. The inland ASQL sites around Southampton consisted of six positions; one of these made use of the existing permanent QL at Durley – C93(d) – and another was originally overlain on SF17(c) at Lee, though this was later switched to a new site at nearby Brook.[22] A little further to the east, the seven sites of the Portsmouth group were the three hard decoys at Cobnor Point, East Head and Itchenor (600–602), and four inland positions at Meonstoke, Ramsdean and Stoughton (where there were two sites). The established QL at Cuckmere Haven was the only coastal site in the Newhaven group, which otherwise consisted of four inland sites around Brighton, one at Seaford and the established QL at Alciston, earmarked earlier in the year for use in coastal lighting operations. All three coastal sites in the easternmost, Dover, group decoyed hards: these were 650 and 652, at Worth and Sandwich Flats, together with a new site at West Hythe. Five inland sites completed this group, spread between Burmarsh, Wigmore and West Langdon, variously imitating camps, convoys and dumps.

These sites completed the rather modest decoy component of *Starkey*, which was otherwise confined largely to displays of landing craft and a certain amount of deceptive signals traffic; a series of minor amphibious raids on the northern French coast and cross-channel bombing operations were also mounted as preliminaries to the spoof invasion itself. The dummy landing craft, which were supplied by the army, were of two types. Measuring 160 feet long by 30 feet wide, the larger 'Bigbobs' used a canvas covering on a tubular steel frame fitted with floats to replicate landing craft designed for tanks (LCTs). Personnel-carrying assault landing craft (LCAs) were dummied by the smaller 'Wetbobs', which were made from inflatable rubber. In all 75 of the larger and 100 of the smaller

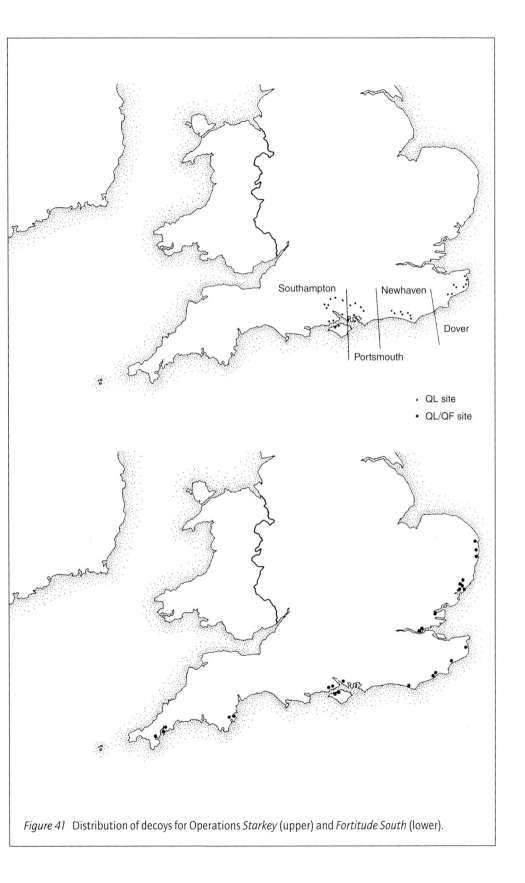

Figure 41 Distribution of decoys for Operations *Starkey* (upper) and *Fortitude South* (lower).

types were intermixed with a force of 360 real landing craft to suggest a sizeable invasion fleet moored between Falmouth and Rye.
Carefully timed assembly and launching of the dummies at different ports was intended to suggest movement within the fleet,
while radio signals (which would be monitored by the Germans)
were broadcast from different stations to achieve the same end.

The dummy landing craft, of course, could play no part in the
sailing of the invasion fleet, which ventured forth from the Dunge-
ness area on 9 September (like D-Day the following summer, it was
delayed for 24 hours by weather), under cover from a moderate
force of 72 fighter aircraft, and supported by some bombing of
coastal targets. Coming to a halt ten miles off Boulogne, this bogus
armada met silence from the defences: no gun was fired, no aircraft seen, and no ship sighted. At that they went home, to begin a
post-mortem which concluded that the Germans had simply not
been fooled. Turner's lighting decoys were dismantled on the following day, and *Starkey* came to an end.

On the same day that *Starkey* tried and failed to convince the
Germans that an invasion was underway, the third element of
Cockade, Operation *Wadham*, was called off. Like *Starkey*, *Wadham*
had used dummy landing craft and aircraft to suggest a forthcoming operation against the French coast (in this case Brittany)
which the Germans were supposed to believe would be mounted
later in the autumn, if the supposed invasion play-acted by *Starkey*
proved unsuccessful. One genuine commando raid was mounted
in support of the ruse, when Operation *Pound* made a brief landing on the Isle of Ushant, supposedly to reconnoitre the defences,
while air reconnaissance was stepped up and the submarine pens
in western France were bombed.[23] But none of this was enough,
and *Wadham* perished prematurely when it was realised that the
Germans had not been deceived.

Up in the north, the dummy aircraft assembled under *Tindall*
had been dismantled and hidden at dates between 25 August and
the end of the month, to give the impression of forces moving
southward to join the invasion which was supposed to be threatened by *Starkey*. A week or so after the Channel sailing, they were
re-erected according to a prearranged plan to switch attention back
towards an apparent threat to Stavanger. From 19 September the
aircraft were again on view, accompanied by simulated camp

activity of the kind developed for K sites three years earlier. But
once again the Germans refused to take the bait. There was no
detectable increase in reconnaissance activity over Scotland, and
no apparent effect on the disposition of forces across the water.
Tindall was nonetheless allowed to run its course, and lingered on
until November, when the dummy aircraft began to be dismantled.
But long before the last were packed up at the end of the month it
was accepted that *Cockade* as a whole had failed.

The much lengthier timetable for preparing deception operations
supporting *Overlord* itself suggests that Turner's plea for more gradual evolution of schemes had been accepted even as *Cockade* was
launched on its uncertain path in the summer of 1943. Planning
for the domestic operation eventually known as *Fortitude*, and the
range of ancillary strategic deception schemes surrounding it,
began in July 1943, almost a year ahead of the Normandy landings
themselves. The staff at Shepperton had little to do with these
early preparations, and became fully involved in the operation
only towards the end of the year; but in the year before D-Day decisions on domestic decoy policy were increasingly influenced by
the approaching landing.

The most important of these affected the Air Ministry Starfish
layout, which lost a further 38 sites between September 1943 and
January 1944 and still more in the month before the landing itself.
The fourteen Starfish to go in September reached down into the 'C'
list prepared in January, and comprised nine permanent sites
ranging from Reading to Glasgow, TSFs at Andover, Oxford, Cambridge and Glastonbury/Wells and the Strategic site at Huttoft.
One new site was opened in September, when SF81(a) at Hart,
serving Hartlepool, became the last Starfish of the war, but otherwise the trend was now firmly downward.[24] One further closure
followed in November, when the previously very active site
SF43(a) – Little Plumstead for Norwich – was shut, before a further
23 sites were abandoned over the winter. In result, by the end of
January 1944 only nineteen of the original Baedecker targets had
Starfish still in place, and major layouts covering the more
northerly cities were in general pruned to between a half and two-

thirds of their original densities. Nationally, some 144 Starfish in the Air Ministry layout remained active, together with most of the naval examples, of which 39 were operable in the autumn of 1943.

One of Turner's purposes in imposing these cuts was to release personnel for C&D units newly forming to serve the mobile air-field detachments destined to operate on the continent after the invasion.[25] As always, pressure on manpower tended to rob Starfish first, since, despite the reductions in their establishments arranged by Dowding and subsequently, these of all the decoys operated directly by Turner's department still claimed the greatest number of men. In other respects the decoy layout was not greatly depleted in the last months of 1943, despite the level of attacks remaining low. By autumn 1943 all the Q sites in Northern Ireland had been abandoned, but elsewhere they were retained in num-bers and some were actually developed further. In July the T-type displays which had not been converted to Drems began to be replaced by new single-line hooded flarepaths (see Fig 5, p.44), which lacked the approach funnel of the Drem and used lights screened from directly overhead.[26] Once again, this brought Q dis-plays into line with real airfields, though even the old T-types con-tinued to do their job despite no longer resembling any variant of genuine lighting still in use. Q sites of all types claimed half the attacks directed at RAF stations or Qs between March and August 1943 inclusive. This total, it is true, amounted to only 24 raids, but of the twelve directed at real stations, eleven were on airfields which either had no Q site, or had not lit their decoy on the night of the attack. Only one station was attacked when its Q was show-ing, and this was Donna Nook (itself a converted decoy) which was in an exposed position on the east coast and had been bombed on a moonlit night.[27] These continuing returns persuaded the Air Staff that Q site closures should initially be confined to the less exposed areas of the north and west. The RAF Q site layout accord-ingly contracted from 165 sites in August 1943 to 146 in December, where it remained virtually unchanged until D-Day had passed; additionally, around eight Q sites for Fleet Air Arm airfields remained in these months. More than three years after the first were opened, Qs remained the most profitable decoys of the war.

In mid October 1943 a meeting was held at Sound City to exam-ine the potential for cuts among the 'C' Series and army sites,[28] with the result that the number of civil QLs was reduced from September's total of 181 to 169 at the end of October, and the civil QFs from 73 to 61.[29] Further reductions in the following months were not great, however, partly because many of the 'C' Series decoys were manned by civilians, and partly too because QFs provided some second-degree protection for urban targets which had lost Starfish. At this time the navy operated 44 QLs and 28 QFs and the army respectively five and twelve decoys in these categories; there were, in addition, sixteen QFs still in place to protect RAF stations, and seven oil QFs.[30] Though cuts were imposed in the army layout – which was never extensive and now practically vanished – the naval decoys were in general left in place until well after *Overlord*, chiefly because many covered harbours with an important role in the invasion. Beyond the Starfish cuts, in fact, the only sharp reductions at this time were in the QFs for RAF stations, whose numbers fell from 20 in September 1943 to thirteen in December.[31] For the most part, therefore, Britain entered 1944 with a solid layout of decoys still in place.

Much as the Baedecker raids followed the economies in Starfish in 1942, so this new phase of cuts came immediately before the start of a renewed night bombing campaign against the cities. Bringing its first heavy raid on the night of 21/22 January, the 'Little Blitz', as it came to be called, would develop over the following three months into a sequence of raids chiefly aimed at London, but occasionally reaching further afield. Fortunately for the defenders London was one of the few major cities where Starfish cover had largely survived the economies of the preceding months: SF8(e) at Lullingstone had gone in September 1943, but six sites remained in place, most of which had originated early in the programme. One of these was lit on no fewer than four occasions between 6th and 22nd February, when seven major raids were launched against London. This site was SF8(c) at Rainham Marshes, which collected just one unexploded bomb on the night of 13/14 February (its second firing), and one HE and a scatter of incendiaries on the 22nd. This same night saw sixteen HEs fall on SF25(b) at Stanwell Moor, where Dowding had made his ignition experiments a year earlier, and an unproductive lighting at SF44(a) in the Luton layout. A London Starfish was in action again on the 24/25th January, this time SF8(b) at Farleigh; there was no result, but as in 1943 the Luftwaffe's bombing in this and other raids was poor.

The reappearance of the Luftwaffe over Britain's cities was not altogether unexpected as invasion preparations were under way early in 1944, though by this time greater anxieties surrounded the looming threat from pilotless weapons – V1s and V2s – than bombing by orthodox means. As things turned out the first V1 flying bomb would not arrive on British soil until June, in the weeks following D-Day, but this new round of conventional attacks did bring one new tactic, if not one that was wholly unexpected. By January 1944 the Luftwaffe had been known for some time to have been studying methods of marking with target indicator (TI) flares similar to those used by the RAF, and these tactics were brought into play for the first time during the Little Blitz. The Luftwaffe's TIs were yellowish-white flares which, dropped in groups of five or six from pathfinder aircraft, slowly cascaded from about 5000 feet to mark the target for subsequent crews. They were altogether more reliable than the fire-raising incendiaries dropped by KGr 100 during the main Blitz of 1940–41, though incendiaries, high explosives, and some ground-marking flares were often dropped by the lead crews in addition to the new TIs themselves.

Plainly, these tactics could potentially be decoyed, if not without difficulty. The Germans, indeed, were already doing so. Bomber Command's own Pathfinder Force squadrons had been using similar 'skymarking' tactics for some time, and by spring 1944 evidence suggested that the Germans were responding by exploding rocket-launched dummy TIs over their own decoys.[32] No dummy skymarkers had been prepared in Britain, but the habit of the German pathfinder crews to drop a small number of conventional incendiaries along with the cascading flares was soon identified as the weak point in the technique. The skymarkers burned only briefly, but not so the incendiaries; and these could be decoyed in the conventional way. The result was another variation on Starfish lighting, involving the ignition of just eight to sixteen baskets to represent minor fires started by odd incendiaries from the lead aircraft. Introduced at the end of February 1944, this 'Minor Starfish' procedure was confined to sites south of a line between King's Lynn, Bletchley and St David's Head, and added to the existing repertoire of Full, Short, and Medium Starfish – the latter previously introduced as an intermediate level between Full and Short firings – brought the number of possible ignition patterns to four. The decision to light was at first given to the site NCO, who would set off the baskets when TIs, incendiaries or HEs fell nearby and then ask 80 Wing at Radlett to judge whether further elements were needed.[33] Within a few weeks, however, a more subtle system had been developed in which site NCOs had authority to light at eleven Starfish serving London and selected sites at Slough, Luton and Southampton – the last because of the *Overlord* preparations – while the remaining 47 decoys remained under the control of 80 Wing, who also decided when to enlarge locally-initiated Minor Starfish firings at the other eleven sites.[34]

The eight weeks remaining until the Little Blitz concluded at the end of April brought something of a swan-song for the Starfish layout.[35] Fires were lit on twelve occasions, and with no fewer than eight firings the thirteen nights between 14 and 27 March were their busiest period since the winter of 1940–41. It is not clear how many of these incidents used the new Minor Starfish procedure, but all took place on sites south of the King's Lynn–Bletchey–St David's line, where the system was in force. Five of the eight firings in March were on London sites, and three of those were at SF8(b) at Farleigh, which had already been lit on one occasion in January and, with a further lighting in April, became the busiest Starfish of the Little Blitz. Incendiaries and phosphorus bombs were drawn to Farleigh on the night of 24/25 March, while SF8(d) at Lambourne End collected three HEs on the 14th/15th. Starfish outside London lit in March included Colchester's TSF58(a) at Great Bromley – which drew a couple of HEs – SF38(a) for Ipswich and, on the night of 27/28 March, SF1(d), one of the oldest Starfish, at Kenn Moor in the Bristol layout. No bombs landed here, but this same night the nearby QL at Bleadon, C86(a) for Weston-super-Mare, collected twelve HEs and a scatter of incendiaries, the largest haul of the campaign. London sites were again in action during April, when in addition to Farleigh, Lambourne End was ablaze, drawing two 500kg HEs on 18th/19th. This was London's last raid of the Little Blitz, which by now was reaching its end. The closing raids fell on Hull and Bristol during the nights of the 20th and 23rd April, on the latter occasion prompting the ignition of SF1(e), the Strategic Starfish at Cheddar, though without result.

Two nights later TSF76(a) for Chichester became the final Tempo-rary Starfish to be lit during World War Two.

As the Little Blitz rumbled on during the early months of 1944 the deception plan for the forthcoming continental landing gradually took shape. The final decision to mount *Overlord* in 1944 was taken at the Cairo and Tehran conferences in November and December 1943, when Churchill, in course of discussions with Stalin, made his famous remark that truth was 'so precious' in wartime that 'she should always be attended by a bodyguard of lies'.[36] *Bodyguard* duly became the codeword for the overall deception operations sur-rounding the landings, of which the domestic component – *Forti-tude* – was but one part. The overall pattern for this complex web of lies was drafted by the London Controlling Section under Colonel Bevan, who began work as soon as the Cairo conference broke up and presented his scheme to the Chiefs of Staff on 24 December. The principal objectives were twofold: first to persuade the Germans that, while a cross-Channel landing was indeed loom-ing in 1944, it would be only one element of a much larger series of operations extending into several other theatres; and secondly that the landing itself would come much later than the date actu-ally planned, which at this stage was 1 June.

As the official historian records, the first part of this scheme was never likely to succeed: despite a series of complex diversions mounted through diplomatic and other means, Hitler's attention remained firmly anchored to the cross-Channel axis as the most likely venue for the decisive operation in 1944. But the second ele-ment was altogether more promising, and here the crucial trick was to persuade the Germans that the genuine landing would be delivered elsewhere on the Channel front, and later, than was in fact the case. Practical measures to put over this ruse lay in the hands of the operational formations responsible for the landing itself. The original 'Ops B' section of COSSAC, which had handled *Cockade* in 1943, was expanded and became part of Eisenhower's Supreme Headquarters Allied Expeditionary Force (SHAEF) which formed in January 1944. Beneath the level of Supreme Headquarters, the operational commanders for *Overlord* assembled deception staffs of their own: Montgomery's 21 Army Group formed a team known as 'R' Force – modelled on the 'A' Force which had planned deception operations for the Battle of Alamein – under Lieutenant Colonel David Strangeways, while the Americans had an equivalent body known as 'Special Plans' under Colonel William A Harris.[37] It was these staffs who planned and controlled Operation *Fortitude*.

As approved towards the end of February 1944, *Fortitude* was divided into two elements, closely connected in operational intent but widely separated in space, and both to some extent indebted to ancestors in *Cockade*. Chronologically the first operation was *Fortitude North*, a spoof threat to Norway which would come into force during April and May to persuade the Germans that the cross-Channel force in the south would not be launched until these operations had reached a conclusion, and certainly not before mid July (six weeks after D-Day). The second element was *Fortitude South*, another notional operation designed to convince Germany that the decisive cross-Channel landing, when it came, would take place in the Pas de Calais rather than on the beaches of Normandy, and that the Normandy landing – Operation *Neptune* – was itself a diversionary spoof. This part of the operation would peak only after the real landings had taken place. Both elements of *Fortitude* depended upon convincing the Germans that sizeable forces existed in the areas concerned. In Scotland this was a notional Fourth Army, whose presence would be simulated chiefly by spoof radio traffic and confirmed by the activities of double agents. In the south-east the ruse would depend upon faking the existence of a fictitious First United States Army Group (FUSAG), using deceptive displays as well as radio, agents' reports and so on. Together, and in summary, these two operations would act to convince the Germans that the important landing was destined for the Pas de Calais on D + 45, with the overall aim of weakening their dispositions at the site of the true assault, and pinning down reserves elsewhere.

The role of Turner's staff in these operations was important but subsidiary, and took some time to define in detail. An early plan anticipated that Turner's job would begin as early as February 1944, when for two months QLs would be activated around hards on the south coast to accustom German reconnaissance to seeing lights in these areas: against this background lights showing from real activities in the run-up to the genuine operation would appear as nothing new.[38] A good deal of planning went into this scheme, which was intended to make use of real hards, decoys in the 'NC' Series built a year earlier, and new positions, and many sites were actually occupied and equipment issued in the first week of February.[39] But the plan was cancelled at the insistence of 21 Army Group, who argued that unless concentrations of landing craft appeared around the ports in daytime the night lighting ruse would be spotted.[40] No real landing craft were available for this work and Bigbobs could not be produced in time, so the idea was dropped, though many of the sites remained in occupation.

In the preparatory stages of this first plan Turner continually pressed the Admiralty to confirm exactly what type of lighting would be used on true hards, but since this information was long delayed Turner was obliged to develop the systems speculatively. When the true hard lighting was finally decided in mid February it was at once apparent that the decoy lights developed for the original scheme – by now cancelled – were in any case far too bright. Fixed lights would be screened to the point of invisibility and the only illumination likely to show was the sidelights of vehicles and the flashes of torches held by the men guiding them as they boarded the landing craft. In these circumstances it was decided to use the MQLs to simulate those lights which would be seen if the hard came under attack – sidelights left on, torch flashes – and to bolster the illusion by adding QFs (using small clusters of baskets) to selected sites.[41] In this way, by mid February, what had originally been conceived as first degree decoys – to divert attack – became second degree sites, designed to draw subsequent bombs once a raid had begun.

These decisions affected the QLs to be used for 'protective' purposes, that is to cover the hards *actually* used to embark troops for the operation. But in addition the *Fortitude South* cover plan required a degree of purely 'deceptive' lighting – as it now rather opaquely came to be called – intended to simulate concentrations assembling for the bogus mission against the Pas de Calais (but without necessarily drawing attack) in areas also to be occupied by dummy landing craft. The distribution of lighting in these two forms – protective and deceptive – was settled at the end of February, and in broad terms called for three more or less distinct types of displays on the coast from Cornwall to Norfolk.[42] Sites between the Helford River and Newhaven would be purely protective, using lights and fires to cover the genuine hards used in *Overlord*. Out to the east, another frontage would run from the River Colne to Yarmouth, where purely deceptive lighting would be displayed, along with dummy landing craft, to give the impression of a force assembling to sail toward Calais. Between these two sections – from Newhaven to the Colne – there would be an intermediate section of mixed function, where most of the sites would be protective (in the manner of those to the west), but where decoys would not generally be used until the feint attack represented by the deceptive displays in the easterly section came into use.[43] This was the plan to which Turner's staff worked in the two months or so before the real operation on 6 June.

To implement this scheme the layout of sites which had earlier been readied for the south coast deceptive lighting display was remoulded, several new positions were found, and QFs were added. A closer look at the layouts in the three sections (Fig 4, page 189) shows how this was done.[44] In the western (purely protective) section, existing hard decoy sites at Helford, St Mawes, Ruan Lanihorne, East Cornworthy and Churston in Plymouth Command had all been occupied during the first week of February, along with Newtown Bay East and West, Pennington Marshes and Gravelly Marsh in Portsmouth Command. Under orders of mid February QFs were added at all of these sites except those in Newtown Bay,[45] while by early April two additional positions had been activated, at Sowley Pond and Menabilly (606 and 555 in the existing stock of hard decoy positions). Fires were then added at these sites, and at the Newtown Bay positions where they had been omitted under the original orders. Thus by the last week in April, the western section consisted of eleven sites, all equipped with protective lighting decoys and fires.[46]

The middle section from Newhaven to the Colne – again, largely protective – began at the established QL at Cuckmere Haven and by the end of April included six further sites extending round the coast as far as a new position at East Tilbury. Like those to the west, some of these sites had been occupied earlier in the year. Cuckmere Haven QL had been manned with special lighting in early February, along with Lower Hope Point (703) in the

Thames, while the site at Camber Castle was in any case overlain on the Temporary Starfish for Rye. Of the remaining sites in this group all but the newcomer at East Tilbury (713) had been earmarked for the earlier deceptive display, though none seems to have reached occupation before it was cancelled: these sites were at Pett Level (654), West Hythe (653) and Worth (650). All the sites in this group were specially provided with basket fire QFs (except Camber, already a Temporary Starfish), and those positions not occupied earlier were manned from early May.

Most of the sites in the easternmost, purely deceptive group were begun only in the last week of April. This group included three positions inherited from the skeleton hard decoy layout of early 1943, at Kirton, Long Reach and Steeple (700–702), to which were added six new sites at Breydon Water (Yarmouth), Oulton Broad and Benacre Ness (Lowestoft), Whitehall Farm and Falkenham Marshes (on the River Deben) and Trimley Marshes (on the River Orwell); additionally the new site at East Tilbury in the central group was reconnoitred along with these positions, and its building was contemporary with theirs.[47] All of these positions were scheduled to be occupied and ready for operation on 1 May – not much more than a week after the new sites were found – when all would be equipped with basket fires.[48] This, then, was the Turner contribution to *Fortitude* in the south of England: a mixture of conventional decoys, ready to protect hards used in the real embarkation, and deceptive displays to serve the higher-level strategic plan which would come fully into force after *Neptune* had been launched.

By the time the last of these sites was ready to play its part in *Fortitude South*, the deceptive operation in the north was under way. Though the simulation of an impending operation against Scandinavia was, as we have seen, achieved largely through radio traffic and other non-physical means, like *Tindall* before it the operation did involve an element of deceptive display. This was Turner's main contribution to *Fortitude North*, for which dummy aircraft – Bostons and Spitfires – were erected at Peterhead and Fraserburgh from the second week in April, and others at Fordoun from early May.[49] And by the time these were dismantled in early June, the first displays of *Fortitude South* were beginning. The dummy landing craft came first. Lieutenant-Colonel Strangeways launched the first few Bigbobs at Yarmouth on 20 May, followed on the next day by more on the Deben, near Harwich.[50] Thereafter this spectral force gradually accumulated, and by 12 June a total of 255 dummy landing craft were displayed at Yarmouth, Lowestoft, on the Orwell and Deben, and at Dover and Folkestone.[51] Carefully timed to support these displays, Turner's deceptive lighting was switched on a few days after the first assault force for the Normandy landings had sailed.

CHAPTER 7

The final year

JUNE 1944 – MAY 1945

At five minutes to midnight on Monday, 5 June 1944 gliders carrying the men of the British 6th Airborne Division landed a few miles to the north of Caen, at the village of Bénouville. By dawn they were joined by eighteen thousand parachute troops, British and American, whose task it was to attack targets supporting communications in the Normandy battlefield. *Neptune* made landfall on the northern French coast at 06.30. First in were the American amphibious tanks, at the westernmost invasion beach codenamed *Utah*; more Americans landed at *Omaha*, while British and Canadian troops followed at *Gold*, *Sword* and *Juno*. By midnight some 155,000 Allied troops were ashore, around ten thousand of whom were casualties.

The first equipment for tactical deception supporting *Neptune* was already in action by nightfall on D-Day. The orders for the operation called for a 100-yard stretch of beach in the British XXX Corps landing area around *Gold* to be protected by ASQL lighting on D-Night and a further 300-yard beach exit to the west of Arromanches to be covered 24 hours later. Further to the west, in the area to be captured by the British I Corps, more lights were to be set out by D-Night to cover beaches at Luc sur Mer, Langrune, and between the Rivers Orne and Dives, while bridges were to be decoyed on the Caen Canal and Orne. All but one of these layouts were installed according to plan, the exception being the Orne–Dives beaches, which remained in German hands throughout June. Laid out by 556 Field Company RE with a small component from 1 and 2 C&D Units RAF – formed from redundant

Starfish – most of these decoys were handed over to full RAF manning within ten days, thereafter coming under control of the C&D Officer of 83 Group. All four sites were attacked, and by the time *Neptune* had officially run its course on 30 June, officers on the ground estimated that at least half the bombs intended for the beaches had been diverted by decoys. It was noted, however, that 'contrary to expectations', enemy bombing was light.[1]

One reason for this was that, just as intended, the Germans refused to believe that *Overlord* was genuinely the opening of the second front: and that belief was fostered largely by *Fortitude*, which continued to play its tricks until mid September. The purely tactical decoys protecting the south-coast hards remained poised for action throughout June, though Luftwaffe activity over the embarkation areas was practically nil and only one attack was drawn in this period, on the established QL at Cuckmere Haven, covering Newhaven.[2] Up in East Anglia, the deceptive displays intended to keep alive the bogus threat against the Pas de Calais came into operation on D + 2 (8 June), when the QLs were lit to suggest troops in the area. Lighting intensity was increased between 25 June and 5 July to imply that troops were embarking, toned down again between 6 July and 30 July, and then cut altogether to suggest that the areas had been vacated. During this period the displays in the Yarmouth and Lowestoft areas were genuinely abandoned and the dummy landing craft removed, before the focus of the building invasion force was shifted southward into Essex. In this phase of the operation, which began on 15 August, lights only were displayed and Turner's layout gained three new sites, two fringing the River Crouch at Canewdon and Burnham and the third at East Mersea. This display continued until 12 September.[3]

Closure of these sites finally on 15 September marked the end of *Fortitude South*. It was certainly a huge success, though initial analysis suggested that there had been plenty of mistakes. For one thing, the Air Ministry believed that the lighting displays had been operated for far too long; and for another, Turner suspected that the whole deceptive display in East Anglia had been fatally compromised from the start, through Lieutenant Colonel Strangeways of 21 Army Group having assembled the Yarmouth Bigbobs in public and unscreened. The first judgement was probably right, though it is not clear how an over-lengthy display of lights might have damaged the operation, while Turner's (particularly acidic) comments on the Yarmouth incident do appear to have been justified. Despite these weaknesses, however, *Fortitude South* did succeed in holding down German troops to cover the Pas de Calais area, just as intended, though in all probability its victory owed more to the false information fed to German intelligence through double agents than it did to dummy landing craft and lights.[4] Air reconnaissance over East Anglia during the life of *Fortitude South* was very sparse, but no one could have predicted this when the operation was planned.

The three additional *Fortitude* sites in Essex were the last new positions established by Colonel Turner's Department during the Second World War, and already by the high summer of 1944 Turner was looking ahead to his department's impending dissolution. Events of these months, indeed, illustrated the limitations of the sites built and operated in the previous four and a half years, for the flying bombs which were by now striking London daily were blind to decoys. Strategic deception did have a role in this battle, and misinformation on the sites of V1 landings continued to be supplied to German intelligence throughout the campaign; but this was not Turner's field, and from August 1944 his staff's work at home was directed toward dismantling what they had laboriously built up.

And so the axe was swung. Towards the end of July Turner asked for permission to close down all the decoys operated by his department in Scotland, and in the No 3 Priority Area north of a line running from Falkirk to Goole, through Bletchley to St David's Head.[5] Taken together with a contraction of the naval decoy layout on similar lines decided earlier in July,[6] this policy shaved the total number of decoy functions operating in Britain from 445 in mid August 1944 to 252 at the end of September, and the number of sites from 328 to 193.[7] Urban layouts went completely at Glasgow and Edinburgh, around the cities of the industrial north – Manchester, Leeds, Huddersfield, Sheffield and their neighbours – and at Birmingham, Nottingham, Coventry, Rugby, Leicester and

Derby.[8] Q sites were abolished everywhere north and west of the new line, while Starfish functions nationally were reduced from 109 to 66, QLs were more than halved from 122 to 57, QFs cut from 69 to just 27, and the 'A' Series decoys abolished altogether. Progressive dismantling of the Naval Coast sites reduced their numbers to seven from sixteen in the same period. Indeed, the only category of decoy to be untouched by these changes was the dummy building; for the two W/T stations at Leighton Buzzard and Dagnall built by Sound City in the summer of 1940 stayed put, the only day decoys remaining on Turner's books.

This round of cuts also reduced the number of Q sites from 127 in mid August to 93 at the end of September, but these last positions were not allowed to remain for long. On 2 October the Air Staff approved Turner's proposal to abolish all the remaining Qs, which now became the second category of decoy to be lost *in toto*, following the decommissioning of the last Ks in June 1942.[9] Two days later the Admiralty approved further contractions in its own layout, scrapping all decoys at Plymouth and Portland, together with others south of the line defined in July, notably at Pembroke, Milford Haven and Falmouth.[10] By the end of the year, in consequence, decoy cover had contracted very largely to a coastal front from Tyneside to Brighton, with concentrations remaining at Newcastle, Middlesbrough, the Humber, Yarmouth and Lowestoft, the Thames Estuary and London; additionally, a few QFs and QLs remained for important inland targets.

The procedure for decommissioning decoys in this and earlier cuts was thorough, partly in order to preserve secrecy, though – as we shall see – it was not so comprehensive as to eliminate all traces.[11] Equipment which could be economically salvaged was stripped and carted away to regional stores maintained by the Air Ministry's Directorate of Works, so all sites lost their generators and switchgear, while Qs and QLs were robbed of their lights, light fixtures, shelter fittings, and above-ground wiring (though buried cables were left). The fire equipment on Starfish and QFs was dismantled and much was salvaged (especially the fuel) though some of the baskets were simply fired *in situ* and the incinerated debris scattered. Hard standings and all newly-built roads were left in place, while the decommissioning teams – from Turner's department and the Directorate of Works, never civilian contractors –

Plate 18 SF35(e), Hameldon Hill (for Accrington), 9 May 1946.

were authorised to undertake limited reinstatement of field boundaries, though in general the Air Ministry preferred to pay compen-
sation rather than become too involved with hedge and fence
work. Payment in the opposite direction, however, was expected
for the empty carcass of the shelter. In a remarkably audacious
piece of officialdom, landowners whose property had been com-

mandeered for decoys were invited to render the Air Ministry a sum of money for the brick and concrete shelter, in the expectation that it could serve a secondary agricultural purpose. Those who declined, however – and these were surely the majority – were generously allowed to keep the shelter free of charge. Either way, the one thing the Air Ministry would not do was demolish the building themselves; so many remained.

For a brief period in January 1945 it appeared that the wholesale closure of Q sites may have been premature. News that the Germans might be about to launch a campaign of intruder operations against Bomber Command airfields forced Turner to examine whether Qs in Lincolnshire and Yorkshire could be reinstated with mobile lighting of overseas type.[12] Nothing came of this, however, and January instead saw the national layout shrink further. By the end of the month 362 Air Ministry sites had been completely vacated or were being actively dismantled, leaving 55 positions still in place: eleven to protect London, a further 22 covering Newcastle, Middlesbrough and Hull – mostly Starfish and associated QLs – and 22 more at isolated targets elsewhere. In addition, just ten sites were still occupied by the navy and two oil QFs remained in place, making 67 occupied decoy sites accommodating 105 functions.[13]

Reviewing his commitments at the end of January Turner suggested that it would not be long before the department at Shepperton could itself be disbanded.[14] Turner's idea was that a small residuary staff should be moved across to the Directorate of Works to handle any outstanding demands for mobile equipment from overseas, and that the remaining decoys at home should be retained for just one month further unless events took an unexpected turn for the worse. In fact by now some of the sites established across the Channel had become permanent, and by January 1945 at least six fully-built Q sites were operating to cover airfields in northern France (Fig 42, page 208).[15] Turner, in the meantime, was at work on three projects to document his department's achievements and ensure that its accumulated expertise was not lost. One was a history of activity over the past five years; another – very appropriately – was a film of the department's work (this was possibly the only footage shot at Shepperton during the war); and the third was a technical and policy paper intended to set a course for the future. In fact more than a year would pass before

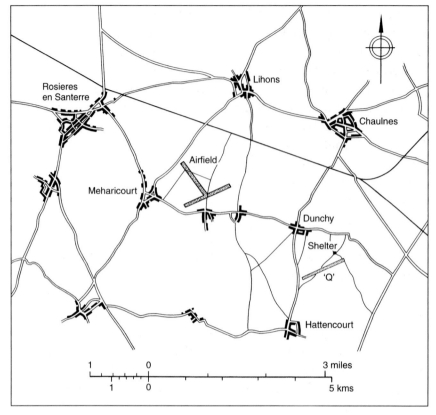

Figure 42 On the offensive. Allied airfield B87, south-west of Amiens, and its Q site, early 1945.

the department could be finally closed, but Turner's proposals for releasing the remaining decoys were largely accepted. In mid February the 22 Air Ministry sites protecting Newcastle, Middlesbrough and Hull were listed for closure, along with the 22 still covering isolated vital points.[16] Three weeks later the Admiralty issued orders to close its remaining decoys on the Humber, at Yarmouth and Lowestoft, and on the Medway.[17] By the final month of the war in Europe, the only decoys left in Britain were eight serving London; and in May 1945 these, too, were closed.[18]

The decommissioning of the last sites is a suitable point at which to ask what bombing decoys did contribute to Britain's defences during the Second World War. In principle the answer should be straightforward: attacks on decoys and genuine targets were recorded, usually in some detail, so theoretically we could simply compare one with the other to yield an index of success. As we saw in Chapter 4, however, expectations of this kind are simplistic. Some decoy attacks were dramatically self-evident, but the majority were comparatively minor affairs, whose admission to the tally is partly a matter of definition. Throughout the war Colonel Turner's Department worked with admirably rigorous criteria for measuring attacks though, as we have seen, other collectors of raid data applying more liberal rules and wider margins produced higher figures than Turner himself allowed. The decoy men's caution was explained as a mechanism to resist self-deception, and this was probably so. But we should also remember that the catchment area for scoring attacks was obliquely related to the safety distances observed when decoys were sited. If Turner's department had claimed bombs landing two miles away as having been aimed at a decoy, then they would have been obliged to increase safety clearances accordingly. Juggling a decoy into position within the existing limits often proved troublesome enough, so Turner's staff had an interest in keeping the attack/safety radius fairly tight, even if they were probably quite happy for others to embellish their results.

Counting attacks brought a number of common difficulties regardless of the catchment area used. The failure of crews to notice that some minor attacks had taken place at all has already been noted. To this must be added a degree of uncertainty in the reporting system, which resulted in some attacks escaping record at Shepperton; this problem apparently worsened in the later war years when some stations parenting Q sites were taken over by USAAF staff unfamiliar with the system, and indeed with the decoys themselves. Then there was the ability of decoys to displace attacks by many miles – way outside any agreed catchment radius – by muddling navigation. The classic instance of this phenomenon was the attack on 8/9 May 1941 discussed in Chapter 4, when the burning Cropwell Butler Starfish serving Nottingham was probably mistaken for a fire at Derby, and bombing was displaced by twelve miles. It is impossible to tell how frequently raids were foiled by similar errors, but we should note that in this case the phenomenon was discovered only through unusually close analysis of events, to counter an accusation that the Starfish organisation had failed. Nor can we tell how often QL sites displaced raids in this way, as they were suitably poised to do; diligent as they may have been, analysts of raids could not reconstruct the train of thought which led every Luftwaffe crew to release its bombs precisely where it did.

Most of these technicalities were carefully considered by the Air Historical Branch, whose analysis at the end of the war concluded that correction factors should be applied to amplify the attack totals compiled at Shepperton. These are considered in a moment, but taking the 'raw' figures first we find that 728 attacks were registered on the sites run or co-ordinated by Colonel Turner's Department between the first in 1940 and the last in 1944. Q sites were by far the most successful, their 443 attacks contributing 61 per cent of the total – approaching two-thirds. Starfish came in a distant second, with 101 attacks (79 on Air Ministry sites in 176 lightings and the remainder on naval), followed by Air Ministry QLs, which drew 72. Air Ministry QFs were the least successful of the night sites, drawing only nine raids in just 25 lightings (though this figure appears to have excluded night operations against the QFs at day dummy factories), while the naval QFs and QLs combined managed 33 (separate totals are not available). Two attacks were additionally drawn by the Naval Coast QLs operating in 1943–44. Among the day decoys – all of which but the dummy W/T stations had been closed by April 1943 – the K sites were the most productive group, drawing 36 attacks in the period from July 1940 to June 1941. Their average of only one attack per site was eclipsed, however, by operations against the four dummy factories, which drew nine day raids, plus fourteen at night (aimed at their QFs or QLs). Lastly, eleven attacks early in 1941 were attracted by dummy aircraft displayed at real airfields.

Since it was Turner's audit of attacks which shaped the Department's evolving decoy policy during the war, it is these 'certainty' figures which have been quoted consistently throughout this book. But the probability that some at least were underestimates was recognised almost as soon as bodies other than Turner's department began to collect figures. Comparing Turner's 'certainties' with the records of the Key Points Intelligence Directorate and the

Air Warfare Analysis Section, post-war analysts reckoned that the score for Q sites and Starfish logged at Shepperton probably captured only 85 per cent of the real total, while for QL and QF sites the proportion dropped to only 75 per cent. (Attacks on day decoys of all kinds were, however, taken as fully logged.) Applying these correction factors to the Department's data, it was suggested that the total score was more in the order of 869 attacks, within which Q sites had drawn 521 raids, Starfish 119 and QLs and QFs (combined) some 173. As the results of statistical manipulation, these figures now of course become artificially precise; but the general point is that night attacks probably *were* higher than Turner's methods allowed, perhaps by as much as a fifth.

What did this contribute to the defeat of the Luftwaffe? Again, the AHB analysis provides a basis for assessment. Taking average figures derived from real attacks on decoys, it was judged that – for the purposes of calculation – some 2221.13 tonnes of bombs had been diverted during the war, of which 2091.9 tonnes (94 per cent) had been drawn by night decoys and the remaining 129.2 tonnes by day (the calculations supporting these figures are shown in Appendix III). As a proportion of the total bomb tonnage delivered by the Luftwaffe, these figures were fairly modest – 3.73 per cent of the 56,000 tonnes estimated to have been dropped by night and just 1.03 per cent of 12,500 tonnes delivered during the day. Taken together with the small number of individual attacks, the figures emphasise the relative weakness of the day decoys. For the night sites, on the other hand, the AHB study was inclined to see the figure of 3.73 per cent as an underestimate because poor navigation and inaccurate aiming sent many bombs astray into open country and the weight actually striking towns and other targets was a good deal less than 56,000 tonnes. Despite the obvious danger of circularity in this argument – some bombs, after all, fell in open country *because* of decoys – the suggestion that roughly 5 per cent of bombs dropped at night was deflected does not seem wildly unreasonable. And this figure was an average for five and a half years of war: short-term figures for some phases were of course lower and others higher. Close analysis showed that proportions greater than 5 per cent could readily be calculated over discrete periods. For 1942, for example, it was calculated that Turner's 'certainties' might have drawn 7.84 per cent of the 2,761 tonnes of bombs dropped by night; applying the correction factors for unobserved and unreported attacks would push this proportion as high as 9.95 per cent. In the light of these figures the AHB was inclined to regard the 'war-average' figure of 5 per cent as 'very conservative' and the overall contribution of the layout as 'very considerable'.

The figures for attacks and bomb tonnages drawn have much to say about the relative performance of decoys of different types, and can be set against the resources invested in their construction and manning to reach a judgement on the value of each technique. The most obvious distinction here is between day and night decoys, and in particular between K and Q sites which, without straining the contrast, emerge respectively as a costly failure and a brilliantly economical success. Britain's 36 K sites absorbed a substantial tract of land, much of which could have been used for agriculture, required hundreds of men to operate them, and depended upon costly and elaborate equipment – the dummy aircraft – which in turn spawned a training organisation in support. For this they drew just 36 attacks which may have averaged 2.5 tonnes of bombs apiece – 90 tonnes in all, or just 4 per cent of the total calculated draw by decoys. Q sites, by contrast, offered no disruption to agriculture, required only two men drawn from the parent station, and drew 61 per cent of decoy attacks with elementary equipment. Judged in those terms K sites failed to yield a sufficient return on resources which could have been expended elsewhere. All the same, we should always be wary of judgements based on mere statistics. The K sites' *indirect* contribution could be seen more charitably – not least because it was the requirement for dummy aircraft which first led Sound City Films to apply their genius for artifice to decoy work. Overall, however, the type of day deception represented by K sites reflected misplaced pre-war expectations, both over the practicalities of building dummy satellite airfields, and the tactics which would be used by the Luftwaffe.

Starfish, as we have seen, were chiefly of value when the draw of bombs was large. Although each attack, in the AWAS's estimate, averaged some 5.61 tonnes of bombs, this figure tends to obscure the fact that many Starfish attacks were light. Every bomb drawn by a Starfish, of course, was a bomb wasted, but given that many were diverted from substantial raids no very great saving of life and property resulted from many of the 101 recorded attacks. The Starfish performance was also geographically inconsistent. Many were never lit, and even some of the larger systems saw almost no action. Liverpool's layout, for example, contributed little to the city's defence, probably because the decoys were rather too far out; similar problems affected Birmingham. Some cities with many Starfish, such as Leeds, were seldom bombed. As the AHB survey found, the most successful Starfish systems were at Portsmouth, Plymouth, Bristol, the Humber and Middlesbrough (to which we might be justified in adding Cardiff, given the star success at Lavernock in March 1941). These targets, oddly enough, were all in coastal positions where under normal conditions the manifest contrast between sea and land should have given attacking crews clear orientation on their objectives, and thus exposed the decoys for what they were. Quite why this was not so is difficult to say, though the presence of cloud or ground haze during some of the most successful operations is the most likely explanation.

There can be no doubt that the performance of Q sites and Starfish relative to QLs and QFs owed much to their simply being in place in the peak periods of German bombing. Coming later on the scene – generally from August 1941 onwards – QFs and QLs hardly stood a chance of matching their predecessors in the action. QLs, as we have seen, did not do too badly, though the rather indifferent performance of the QFs might imply that they were generally rather too small to serve. Indeed, if there was an overall weakness in Britain's decoy strategy, it lay in timing. The Air Ministry's hesitancy to seize the initiative in decoy building during the summer of 1938 is perhaps understandable, given that other aspects of the air defence system, either proven or promising, claimed attention in these months. But the policy on airfield decoys decided in the year after Munich should certainly have been given material effect before the war began, and without the happy reprieve of the 'phoney war' no sites would have been in place when raiding began to bite. That the neglect of decoy precautions before the war was so rapidly reversed is, of course, to the credit of Turner, Loudon and their colleagues. With more time they could perhaps have done more, but in the simple arithmetic of total war, the 5 per cent of the German bombing effort wasted on decoys may have spared 3160 injured and 2596 dead.

CHAPTER 8

Traces

THE DECEPTIVE LEGACY

With the run-down in decoy work in the year after *Overlord*, Loudon was able to reopen part of Sound City before the war ended. Limited space was available from the spring of 1945, and by September three stages were ready for filming. New work came quickly, and within months the Rank Organisation, squeezed out of Pinewood, had hired Sound City for its first post-war film. By the time Colonel Turner's Department was finally closed, on 28 February 1946,[1] the pearly kings and queens who would dance their way through Wesley Ruggles's musical *London Town* were already practising their steps. An upbeat pseudo-Hollywood burlesque of Cockney life, *London Town* starred Sid Field and a host of wartime favourites, including Kay Kendall, Sonnie Hale and Claude Hulbert. The film opened in September 1946, unfortunately to withering reviews.

The surprising point about *London Town* is less that the film failed, than that it was made at all. Five years of decoy work, damage from at least two air raids, and a number of additional war functions – sugar storage and aircraft servicing among them – had left Sound City a battered shell by the end of the war (*London Town* was reportedly made amid the wreckage of aircraft awaiting repair). It was Loudon's last project, for already by the spring of 1946 Sound City had begun to pass from his control. The rebirth of the studio in the two years after the war instead lay in the hands of Alexander Korda, whose approach to the Air Ministry in 1937 had first hinted at the film industry's potential in decoy work. As head of British Lion Films, Korda had representatives on the

Sound City board from April 1946, and in November struck a deal with Loudon to buy the studio outright. Shepperton thus became the British Lion Studio Company, part of the British Lion Group which under Korda's management soon came to dominate post-war British films. By the summer of 1946 a huge rebuilding programme was under way, buttressed by a government policy which ranked cinema investment high in the economic priorities of reconstruction.[2]

Never one to accept second best, Loudon seized upon the commercial potential of the post-war building boom as readily as he had the demand for quota quickies fifteen years earlier.[3] Along with his works manager, Percy Bell, Loudon formed an attachment to a firm known as Bellrock Construction and, after buying up an engineering works in Chertsey, hired craftsmen from Shepperton to make moulds for plaster panels. Before long Loudon had prospered sufficiently to invest in a factory at Harefield, where he made panels for sale, while the Chertsey works concentrated on prefabricating panel construction plants for export. Next came a venture in Jamaican gypsum and then a firm making plasterboard, before Loudon's business activities began to decline, along with his health, in the mid 1960s. He certainly did well in the post-war years, continuing to indulge a passion for shooting and making enough money to lease country property in Scotland and maintain a permanent suite at the Carlton Tower Hotel. And this is where he died, on 13 March 1967.

Shepperton of course lives on. In the half-century or so since the end of the war, under several changes of management, the studio which Loudon founded has become one of the beacons of the British film industry, in most years producing up to twenty major features for cinema and, latterly, for television. The '50s and '60s saw directors crafting the images of war in several films. Dirk Bogarde was at Shepperton in the early '50s to star in Philip Leacock's *Appointment in London* (1953), a film whose quietly understated portrayal of Bomber Command's war included, *inter alia*, some convincing scenes of a burning city seen from the air. David Lean's *The Sound Barrier* (1952) was made at Shepperton, so too was *The Colditz Story*, directed by Guy Hamilton and released in 1954. The next decade saw Shepperton enter the Cold War with Kubrick's *Dr Strangelove* (1963) and Martin Ritt's *The Spy Who*

Came in from the Cold (1965). More peaceably, by the 1990s Turner's old headquarters was making *Inspector Morse*.

At the end of the war Turner was keen that the expertise built up over the previous five years should not be allowed to atrophy, and his last duty before retiring for the third time was evangelical. In a paper written a fortnight after VE day, Turner drafted a prospectus for a new joint-service visual deception research centre and school.[4] The nucleus of the RAF Component of VISTRE – the Visual Inter-Service Training and Research Establishment – was duly formed at Erlestoke Camp in December 1945, in time to allow a formal handover from the residuary staff of Colonel Turner's Department, before moving to its first permanent home at RAF Netheravon in November 1947.[5] The RAF Component's initial jobs were to study deception in numerous applications, only some of which had their roots in the war: concealment methods for radar stations, urban decoy lighting, countermeasures to reconnaissance, and means of deceiving the enemy over the strength and deployment of Fighter Command.[6] This last was to include pneumatic dummy aircraft of rubber – a similar technology to that used for the 'Wetbobs' of 1943–44 – and by 1952 prototype Vampire jet fighters were ready (Plate 19). A new generation had begun.

Plate 19 The next generation. Pneumatic Vampire fighter under test, 1952.

VISTRE was reformed as the Joint Concealment Centre in January 1952, and it was under this title that the unit inspected the last Starfish – or something like it – to be built in Britain. In the autumn of 1951 the Air Ministry decided that the time was ripe to bring up to date the techniques for building decoy fires developed by Turner in the last war, largely in order to hold the technology ready for quick deployment if the need arose.[7] Where the first Starfish of 1940 had been commissioned in a matter of hours, however, arrangements to build this final site took two and a half years, during which time departments found themselves unable to agree whether the work should properly fall to the Air Ministry, the Ministry of Supply or – for no better reason than that oil was involved – to the Ministry of Fuel and Power.[8] Eventually the Air Ministry arranged the trials, the first of which took place at Netheravon in February 1954. The original drawings for baskets, boiling oil fires and other types were dusted off, the newly manufactured equipment was wired up to electrical igniters, and the switch was thrown. Everything sprang to life as expected, and the inspecting officers – none of whom appears to have seen a wartime Starfish – declared themselves impressed. Further experiments were held in May and a large-scale trial was scheduled for November 1954, though it is uncertain whether it went ahead; for by June it was realised that advances in Soviet blind bombing techniques – the successors to *X-Gerät* – were rapidly making visual decoy fires obsolete.[9]

Turner, no doubt, would have been gratified to learn how well his equipment performed in these tests, though there is no reason to suppose that he knew anything about them. In the twelve years remaining to him after the department's closure in 1946, Sir John Turner lived in London, remained unmarried, and devoted much of his still considerable energy to charitable works. The Church of England Children's Society claimed much of his attention, and this former Air Ministry Director of Works appropriately enough served as chairman of the Homes Committee, touring the country to meet staff and children at the society's various homes. He did not change. 'Headquarters staff were devoted to him', recalled Lady Ismay, 'and all his fellow committee members loved him. There will be a lump in all our throats when we look back on some of his caustic, and sometimes almost unprintable, entries in the minute books. He joked about his work, but I think it became his greatest interest. Certainly the society owe him more gratitude than they can ever express, and he will never be forgotten.'[10] Lady Ismay was one of two friends who were moved to write to *The Times* in the days after Turner's sudden death on 21 May 1958, adding personal tributes to the paper's brief obituary notice.[11] The other was Air Chief Marshal Sir Guy Garrod, who recalled Turner's work on RAF buildings in India and at home.[12] But neither correspondent could say anything of Turner's war work – or indeed that he had any war work – and even the *Royal Engineers Journal* confined itself to the circumspect note that Sir John had been 'specially employed' by the Air Ministry from 1939–45.[13] In 1958 the deception war in all its aspects remained secret, thanks to a Chiefs of Staff ruling that this must be so.[14] In these circumstances the official history of Britain's home defences, which appeared in 1957 – in time for Turner to read it, had he been so minded – could do little more than note the existence of decoys, with no elaboration.[15] So Turner's death brought no public recognition of the last and most singular phase of his remarkable career.

Today, sixty years on from the building of the first airfield decoys, several memorials to Turner's and Loudon's war work do survive. One, of course, is the substantial body of documents preserved in the Public Record Office and elsewhere; but the decoy programme has also left us a less obvious legacy in those sites which, in varying degrees, have survived the vicissitudes of development, agriculture, coastal erosion, forestry, and the allied agencies which continuously remake the face of Britain's landscape. Interest in these sites did not wholly vanish after the war, not least because decoys, in common with all wartime sites, often held poignant associations for those whose lives were bound up in them. But it was only in the 1990s that the remains of Britain's wartime defences began to win acceptance as places of national significance, worthy of study and selective preservation – in short, as historic monuments in their own right. The drive to discover what remains of this huge volume of building, to understand its character and the motivations which brought it into being, underpins the series to which this book belongs.

As we might expect, the first studies of Britain's surviving decoys were locally conceived. Sites such as the Temporary Starfish for York, and its permanent counterparts in the Leeds system were rediscovered by fieldwork and aerial photography during the 1980s,[16] while more recently decoys have been included in regional surveys of wartime remains, for example in the Plymouth area and in Essex.[17] At the same time, a few decoy sites have made their way onto the Sites and Monuments Records maintained by local authorities as databases for historical research and development control. Among other things, these investigations have shown how difficult it can be to recognise the remains of decoys without secure corroborative evidence, ideally from contemporary documents. The surviving firebreak trenches of the York Temporary Starfish, for example, puzzled local archaeologists for many years (at one point they were written down as the remains of a medieval rabbit warren) before more expert eyes saw them for what they were.[18] Elsewhere, the fields occupied by Turner's decoys have proved fertile soil for legend and myth. One rumour, for example, holds that a local decoy consisted of a fully-built dummy town, erected by a film company, whose alleged scale would rival the set of *Ben Hur* (disappointingly, the site was actually a standard QL). Decoys, it seems, continue to deceive, and assessing the full range of surviving examples demands an informed, nationally-based approach.

Responsibility for the study and preservation of historic monuments respects the national divisions within the United Kingdom, and while heritage agencies in England, Wales, Scotland and Northern Ireland share a common sense of purpose in evaluating the built legacy of the Second World War, their methods have differed. English Heritage's approach was initially to commission, in 1994, a survey of the documentary records on defence works in several categories – decoys among them – to discover as far as possible the full 'population' of sites occupied, the principles of their design, and their histories.[19] In an allied project, similar work to establish site locations in the remainder of the UK was subsequently sponsored by the Royal Commission on the Historical Monuments of Scotland, the Department of the Environment (Northern Ireland) and Cadw (Welsh Historic Monuments).[20] With a few additions arising from subsequent research the resulting consolidated gazetteer (Appendix I) shows that within the UK as a whole 797 individual locations were occupied by the decoys studied in this book, between which there were distributed around 1100 decoy functions. For the English sites the next step was a systematic study of aerial photographs to discover what had become of each site since the war. Using the air photo collection of the National Monuments Record in Swindon, wartime images were examined (where available) to delineate the features of each decoy on the ground, and were then compared with the most recent cover to see what, if anything, remained of the site.[21] There were gaps in the post-war cover, of course, while in some areas the absence of recent photographs meant that the fortunes of their sites could be followed only as far as the 1970s or '80s. But in all, the 558 English sites which could be examined proved an intriguing exercise in rediscovery.

In seeking remains of Britain's wartime decoys it is necessary to hold two considerations in mind: first that the potential for survival varies with the type of site; and secondly that many caveats will always surround the very definition of 'survival'. One abiding lesson which archaeology teaches is that few of the works of man ever *wholly* disappear: apart from rare cases in which sites are removed wholesale by quarrying or open-cast mining, something usually lingers, even if – for modern sites at any rate – that something may not at the moment be of much historical interest. As we have seen, lights and fire equipment were cleared as the sites were closed, and there is no possibility that any would be discovered in place today. But several decoy types were characterised by built structures and, particularly, by excavated features with some inherent potential to survive. All decoys except K sites had a solidly-built control and generator building of one kind or another, while Starfish and many standard QFs had shallow firebreak trenches and oil QFs used substantially-built concrete features to contain their liquid fuel. Fire decoys generally were linked to roads with metalled tracks, to admit supply lorries, and some Starfish at least had small clutches of hutting. K sites had dugout shelters, ground defences – real and dummy – and a host of locally-improvised works introduced to add realism. In contrast, the surface features of Q and QL sites were by far the most ephemeral. In all, then, diversity is the rule: all decoy sites were fragile, and some are inherently more likely to leave traces than others. Nor is the evidence always straightforward of interpretation.

We are not yet in a position to quantify the exact survival rate of these features, but we do know that a great many decoy sites have been so reduced by post-war land uses as to be unrecognisable as decoys today. The latest available aerial photographic cover shows that at least 384 of the 558 English sites examined (68.8 per cent) have been destroyed to the point where characteristic traces have vanished. As we might expect, the vast majority of these sites – 341 in total – had been lost to agriculture, while a further 43 were claimed by other agencies, chiefly coastal erosion, development, extractive industries, forestry, wetlands, continuing military activity, and land uses connected with recreation (notably golf courses, some of which were active before the war and temporarily supplanted by decoys). These, it must be stressed, are minimum figures for destruction: a good proportion of the aerial photographic cover used in their compilation belongs to the 1970s and '80s, and the attrition must be assumed to have continued, if perhaps more gently than in the immediately post-war years. There is nothing to regret in this: sites have been lost, as they always are, through the natural evolution of the landscape. But these figures do mean that the equally natural impetus to preserve a selection for the future already works with a much depleted population – and one which is diminishing still.

How have the surviving decoys fared since the war? Starfish still recognisable in the form in which Turner and Loudon conceived them are most readily found in the uplands, where erosion by ploughing is limited. One of the most extensive system of firebreak trenches surviving in England is that belonging to SF10(e) at Sneaton Moor, one of the Strategic Starfish attached to the Middlesbrough system. Seen from the air in July 1992 (Plate 20, page 222), Sneaton Moor's strange, quasi-lunar firebreak rings survive practically complete, if much cut about by tracks. Similarly, Hameldon Hill – SF35(e) in the Accrington layout – was still recognisable as a Starfish when photographed under melting snow in February 1979 (Plate 21, page 223). In both cases, however, it is the airborne view which reveals survival; little or nothing of these fragile and eroded features can be seen on the ground.

Plate 20 SF10(e), Sneaton Moor (for Middlesbrough), 28 July 1992. Though much disturbed by track activity, the firebreaks of this Strategic Starfish remain intact.

Although plentiful remains are hardly to be expected from QL sites, exceptions can occur when the lighting devices were unusually substantial. The most striking example is the survival of the reflective basins for the QL representing the Humber docks – the naval site HU3 at Paull – where these features still stand, remote and mysterious, in the plain bordering the Humber Estuary, in some cases complete with poles for their lights (Plate 22, page 224). The shelter abides here, too, and in general it is these little brick and concrete structures which remain most plentifully from decoys of all types. In large part this must be due to Turner's disposal policy – sell them if possible, but in any case avoid the trouble of demolition – and the uses to which farmers and others have put them since. Upstanding shelters are usually the only physical clue that a decoy was present nearby, and fairly obtuse clues they are, when seen by themselves. As the photographs here show (Plates 23–25, pages 224–5), overgrown decoy shelters are hardly eloquent of their original function: many remain, dotted around field boundaries and hedgerows, with little but local tradition to suggest what they are, and why they are there. Britain's landscape, in fact, is full of remains from the Second World War whose original purpose is not at all easy to read from the structural evidence

Plate 21 SF35(e), Hameldon Hill (for Accrington), 6 February 1979. The same site 33 years earlier appears as Plate 18 (page 206).

Plate 22 QL light post and basin on the Humber, surviving in the 1990s.

Plate 23 A Starfish control shelter surviving today. Figure 19 (page 104) shows the design of this building type.

Plate 24 A Drem Q control shelter surviving today. Figure 36 (page 152) shows the design of this building type.

Plate 25 A decoy control shelter surviving in the 1990s.

alone. An integrated approach, using documents to illuminate the surviving fragments is the only secure means to understand this weighty historic legacy.

That is very much the approach which English Heritage has taken to Second World War remains generally, and early in the new century a selection of surviving sites, decoys among them, will be recommended for statutory protection as historical monuments. It is right that this should be so. On the face of things the drive to preserve wartime remains may seem to sit oddly with the more familiar objects of heritage management. These sites, after all, are recent in date, generally unprepossessing, and often so clearly illuminated by surviving documents that study of the built structures themselves is not essential to understand the strategy and technology which underlay them – something which would certainly be untrue of Roman forts or medieval castles, which are precious historical sources in their own right. But selective preservation can be justified on other grounds, among them the very special and particular character of the 1939–45 war itself. So large does this episode loom in the history of the twentieth century that its sites, today, stand as monuments to a massive, collective experience which future generations should be given the opportunity to understand by witness to its everyday places. No one can say what value may be placed on these remains in fifty, a hundred or a thousand years' time; but unless steps are taken now to safeguard a selection for the future, no one will have the opportunity to judge.

Notes

List of Abbreviations used in Notes

AA	Anti-Aircraft
ACAS(G)	Assistant Chief of the Air Staff (General)
ACAS(Ops)	Assistant Chief of the Air Staff (Operations)
ACAS(P)	Assistant Chief of the Air Staff (Policy)
ACAS(R)	Assistant Chief of the Air Staff (Research)
AEAF	Allied Expeditionary Air Force
AM	Air Ministry
AMSO	Air Member for Supply and Organisation
CA	Coast Artillery
CAS	Chief of the Air Staff
C&D	Concealment and Decoy
CDC	Civil Defence Committee
C-in-C	Commander-in-Chief
CIU	Central Interpretation Unit
Cmd	Command
COHQ	Combined Operations Headquarters
COS	Chiefs of Staff
CTD	Colonel Turner's Department
DF Ops	Director(ate) of Fighter Operations
DDF Ops	Deputy Director of Fighter Operations
DFW	Director(ate) of Fortifications and Works
DGW	Director(ate) General of Works
D of I	Director(ate) of Intelligence
D Org	Director(ate) of Organisation
D Plans	Director(ate) of Plans
D Works	Director(ate) of Works
D Ops	Director(ate) of Operations

DCOS	Deputy Chiefs of Staff
DD Ops(H)	Deputy Director of Operations (Home)
DDWO	Deputy Director of War Organisation
DE	Director(ate) of Engineering
DOR	Director(ate) of Operational Requirements
E1(a)	Engineering 1(a) (designation of an official post)
EPM	Expansion Progress Meeting
FO3(b)	Fighter Operations 3(b) (designation of an official post)
GHQ	General Headquarters
Gp	Group
GPO	General Post Office
IO	Intelligence Officer
OR	Other ranks
ORB	Operations Record Book
PS to CAS	Private Secretary to CAS (*qv*)
PS to S of S	Private Secretary to S of S (*qv*)
RA	Royal Artillery
SHAEF	Supreme Headquarters Allied Expeditionary Force
S of S	Secretary of State
TI	Target indicator
VCAS	Vice Chief of the Air Staff
VISTRE	Visual Inter-Services Training and Research Establishment
Wg	Wing
WO2	War Organisation 2 (designation of an official post)
WOC	War Organisation Committee

Preface

1. This simple distinction between tactical and strategic deception is, at any rate, that widely recognised during WWII itself, though today's military theorists tend to work with more subtle gradations: see particularly Handel 1982; Whaley 1982.
2. Notably Howard 1990.
3. Cruickshank 1979.
4. For example by Hartcup 1979; Dewar 1989; Smith 1989; Brettingham 1997 and Lloyd 1997.
5. An introduction to the scope and objectives of the Monuments Protection Programme (MPP) can be found in Darvill *et al* 1987, with a recent summary of progress in Nieke 1997. MPP's approach to the modern military heritage is further described in Schofield & Lake 1995; Dobinson 1998; Dobinson *et al* 1997 and English Heritage 1998.

Acknowledgements

1. The original research for the English sites and those in Wales, Scotland and Northern Ireland was commissioned by the bodies concerned through the Council for British Archaeology.

Chapter 1

1. O'Brien 1955, 11. The exact figures were 4820 casualties, of which 1413 were killed.
2. O'Brien 1955, 96.
3. AIR 2/34/X8621/1916, Rear Admiral Commanding East Coast of England to Admiralty, 3 Mar 1916.
4. AIR 2/34/X8621/1916, Naval Base Lowestoft to Admiralty, 10 Mar 1916.
5. AIR 2/34/X8621/1916, Naval Base Lowestoft to Admiralty, 6 Aug 1916.
6. AIR 2/2878, f 14b, Appendix III to 1932 decoy report, accompanying D Org letter to RAF commands, 18 Mar 1939, p 2.
7. AIR 2/2878, f 14b, Appendix III to 1932 decoy report, accompanying D Org letter to RAF commands, 18 Mar 1939.
8. AIR 2/2878, Denham Studios – recruiting and use of buildings etc in war, 13 Jan 1937.
9. AIR 2/2878, Minute 1, DDWO to DD Ops (H), 11 May 1938.
10. Quoted in Hyde 1976, 284.
11. See particularly Smith 1984.
12. Thetford 1995, 219, 304.
13. AIR 5/1377, War Organisation Committee, Note on the organisation of heavy and medium bomber stations in the UK in war, WOC No 6, 17 Jan 1936, revised 18 Jun 1936.

14. Myerscough 1985.
15. AIR 2/2878, Minute 1, DDWO to DD Ops (H), 11 May 1938.
16. AIR 2/2878, Minute 3, DDWO to DD Ops (H), 1 Nov 1938.
17. AIR 2/2878, f 4b, Bomber Cmd letter, 9 Nov 1938.
18. AIR 2/2878, f 5a, Coastal Cmd letter, 5 Nov 1938.
19. AIR 2/2878, f 8.
20. AIR 2/3447, f 6a, Specification 23/38 for the manufacture of dummy aircraft, 17 Dec 1938.
21. For the date of issue see Meekcoms & Morgan 1994, 264–5.
22. AIR 2/2878, Minute from WO2 to DDWO, 23 Feb 1938.
23. AIR 2/2878, f 9a, AM letter S44682/WO2, 8 Mar 1939.
24. AIR 2/2878, f 15a, Fighter Cmd to Air Ministry, 18 Mar 1939.
25. AIR 2/2878, f 15c, Coastal Cmd to Air Ministry, S7000/9/8A/Air, 30 Mar 1939.
26. AIR 2/2878, f 15b, Bomber Cmd to Air Ministry, BC/S21817/Org/AOA, 29 Mar 1939.
27. AIR 2/2878, Minute 10, DDWO to DOR and DE, 15 Mar 1939.
28. AIR 2/2878, Minute 12, DOR to DE, 27 Mar 1939; f 11, Copy of Specification 23/38, 14 Sep 1938.
29. AIR 2/2878, DD Ops (H) to D Ops, 25 May 1939.
30. AIR 2/2878, f 18a, Note on Air Staff policy, dummy aerodromes, 8 Jun 1939.
31. AIR 2/3180, CAM (P&O) Paper 3 (Final), 5 Apr 1940.
32. HO 186/208, Report on the Humber black out, 14 Jun 1939.
33. AIR 2/3447, f 8a, Specifications for Decoy Aircraft, 28 Jun 1939.
34. AIR 2/2878, Minute 26, DD Ops (H) to D of O, 25 Aug 1939.
35. AIR 14/254, f 1a, copy of cypher message from AM to all RAF Cmds originated 03.30, 7 Sep 1939.
36. AIR 2/2878, f 30a, Bomber Cmd letter, 9 Sep 1939.
37. AIR 2/2878, f 49a, Fighter Cmd letter, 18 Sep 1939.
38. AIR 6/40, Air Council EPM 184, 13 Sep 1939, item 3(b).

Chapter 2

1. Faithfull 1958; *Who Was Who* V, 1106; *Army List* and *Air Force List*, 1900–1931, *passim*.
2. AIR 6/40, Air Council EPM 184, 13 Sep 1939, item 3(b); Air Council EPM 185, 26 Sep 1939, 3(b).
3. Faithfull 1958, 301.
4. Wheatley 1980, 141.
5. AIR 2/3180, R S Crawford to J F Turner, 15 Sep 1939.
6. AIR 2/2878, Minute 32, E1(a) to RDQ4, 19 Sep 1939.
7. AIR 2/2878, Minute 34, AD RDT to RDQ4, 28 Sep 1939.
8. AIR 2/2878, Description of dummy landing grounds (night), 11 Oct 1939; Description of dummy landing grounds (day), 12 Oct 1939.

9. AVIA 15/281, f 47a, Turner to D of O, 1 Nov 1939.

10. This account of Sound City in the 1930s is based largely upon Threadgall 1994, 4–23. For Loudon see *ibid*, 33; Brunel 1949, 173; Low 1985, 170–80.

11. Brunel 1949, 173.

12. Robinson 1937.

13. See, for example, Carrick 1941.

14. AVIA 15/281, f 47a, Turner to D of O, 1 Nov 1939.

15. AVIA 15/281, f 70b, Loudon to Turner, 14 Nov 1939.

16. AIR 2/3705, f 10b, RAF Dishforth to Bomber Cmd, DS/S82/1/Air, 14 Nov 1939.

17. AVIA 15/281, f 79a, RDQ4(a) to ADOP, 18 Nov 1939.

18. AIR 2/3212, f 14a, Turner to Dowding, 1 Nov 1939.

19. AIR 2/3212, f 32a, Turner to Linnell, 17 Nov 1939.

20. AVIA 15/281, RDQ4(a) to Turner, 10 Dec 1939.

21. AIR 6/40, Air Council EPM 190, item 2(e), 12 Dec 1939.

22. AIR 2/3212, f 41a, Turner to Dowding, S58776, 1 Dec 1939.

23. AIR 2/3180, f 16a, Turner to CAS, 29 Dec 1939.

24. AIR 2/3180, f 16a, Turner to CAS, 29 Dec 1939.

25. Richards 1953, 63.

26. AIR 6/41, Air Council EPM 191, item 2(e), 2 Jan 1940.

27. AIR 2/3705, f 51a, Report on visit to Sound City Film Studio, 3 Jan 1940; AIR 29/62 ORB No 2 Balloon Depot, 3 Jan 1940.

28. AIR 29/62 ORB No 2 Balloon Depot, 21 Jan 1940.

29. AIR 2/3212, Lecture on dummy aerodromes [by Turner], nd [but *c* Jan 1940].

30. AIR 2/3212, f 95a, Turner to commands, S58776, 22 Jan 1940.

31. AIR 6/41, Air Council EPM 194, item 1(a), 13 Feb 1940.

32. AIR 2/3212, f 116b, Schedule of day dummies, 13 Mar 1940.

33. AIR 6/41, Air Council EPM 199, Appendix A, Progress of dummies: report by Colonel Turner, 23 Apr 1940.

34. AIR 2/2878, DOR to Turner, 14 Feb 1940.

35. AIR 28/171, ORB Coningsby.

36. AIR 2/3212, f 135a, Board to K Area officers, S58776, 30 Apr 1940.

37. AIR 2/3212, f 110a, Turner to PS to S of S, 9 Mar 1940.

38. AIR 6/41, Air Council EPM 199, Appendix A, Progress of dummies: report by Colonel Turner, 23 Apr 1940.

39. AIR 2/3212, f 173a, K and Q sites, 19 Jun 1940.

40. AIR 2/8021, f 12a, D Works to Supt Engineers, S 58447/W7a/QJ, 9 Feb 1940.

41. AIR 2/8021, f 9b, RAF Abingdon to 6 Gp, AB/S/36, 4 Mar 1940.

42. AIR 2/8021, f 13b, Explanatory note on Q lighting, 15 Mar 1940.

43. AIR 6/41, Air Council EPM 194, item 1(g), 13 Feb 1940.

44. AIR 2/3180, Note on the question of dummy factories, J F Turner, nd [but *c* Jan 1940].
45. AIR 6/41, Air Council EPM 197, item 2(c), 26 Mar 1940.
46. AIR 2/3180, CAM (P&O) Paper 3 (Final), 5 Apr 1940.
47. AIR 6/41, Air Council EPM 199, Appendix A, Progress of dummies: report by Colonel Turner, 23 Apr 1940.
48. AIR 2/3212, f 146a, Instructions on defence of K sites, 18 May 1940.
49. AIR 2/3705, f 89a, Don to Turner, 9380/4/E/DO, 23 Apr 1940.

Chapter 3

1. Richards 1953, 158.
2. AIR 14/647, Turner to multiple recipients, 10 Jun 1940.
3. Eg AIR 14/647, f 4a, Bomber Cmd to groups, BC/S 23485/Ops 1(c), 14 Jun 1940.
4. AIR 14/647, f 26b, Brief notes on the tactical use of K and Q sites, 15–[30] Jun 1940; AIR 14/647, f 18a, 3 Gp to Bomber Cmd, Q and K sites – reports on tactical use, 3G/S2032/1/Ops, 29 Jun 1940; AIR 14/647, f 31b, Fortnightly summary of attacks on Q and K sites in Bomber Cmd for fortnight ending 1 Jul 1940, BC/S 22567/1/Ops 1(c), 12 Jul 1940.
5. Attack figures quoted throughout this book are tabulated in Appendix II.
6. AIR 14/647, f 26b, Brief notes on the tactical use of K and Q sites, 15–[30] Jun 1940.
7. Collier 1957, 156.
8. AIR 2/8022, f 20a, Note on RAF deception policy, J F Turner, 23 Jun 1940.
9. Cooper 1981, 127.
10. AIR 2/8022, f 20a, Note on RAF deception policy, J F Turner, 23 Jun 1940.
11. AIR 2/8022, f 20a, Note on RAF deception policy, J F Turner, 23 Jun 1940.
12. AIR 2/8022, f 3a, Turner to commands, 24 Jun 1940.
13. AIR 20/2806, Turner to PS to S of S *et al*, 2 Jul 1940.
14. AIR 2/5179, FO3(b) to ACAS(G), 2 Jul 1940.
15. HO 186/391, Decoy lighting. Note of a discussion with representatives of the Air Staff, 3 Jun 1940.
16. AIR 2/5179, FO3(b) to ACAS(G), 2 Jul 1940.
17. AIR 2/4597, f 23b, Pickard to Lucas, 28 Jun 1940.
18. AIR 2/4597, f 26a, Turner to Lucas, 2 Jul 1940.
19. HO 186/173, Sinclair to Anderson, 4 Jul 1940.
20. AIR 2/5179, f 16a, Interdepartmental Meeting. Minutes of meeting held at the Home Office, 10 Jul 1940.

21. AIR 2/3180, f 35a, DCOS (40) 94, War Cabinet Deputy DCOS Sub-Committee. Co-ordinated planning, construction and operation of decoy schemes, dummy fires and smoke, 15 Jul 1940; AIR 2/3180, f 36a, DCOS (40) 95, 21 Jul 1940.
22. AIR 2/3180, f 37a, Air Staff note on decoy lighting policy, 30 Jul 1940.
23. HO 186/391, CDC draft minutes, item 7(iii), 31 Jul 1940.
24. AIR 2/3180, f 39b, Decoys 1.8.40, J F Turner, 1 Aug 1940.
25. AIR 2/3180, f 39b, Decoys 1.8.40, J F Turner, 1 Aug 1940.
26. AIR 2/5179, f 33a, ACAS(G) to multiple recipients, S 62596, 13 Aug 1940.
27. AA gunsite decoys are discussed in WO 166/2075, Notes on camouflage, accompanying AA Cmd letter AAC/Z/1267/SD, 7 Aug 1940, and those for coast artillery batteries in WO 166/11, GHQ Home Forces (CA) letter CRHF 1/3098 (RA), 7 Jul 1940.
28. AIR 14/271, f 13b, Notes on Q sites, J F Turner, 4 Nov 1940.
29. AIR 2/3212, f 16b, Turner to K detachments, S 58776/11, 12 Jul 1940.
30. AIR 2/3213, f 27a, Turner to DCAS, 26 Jul 1940.
31. AIR 2/3213, f 26a, Turner to ACAS(G), 26 Jul 1940; AIR 2/3213, f 27a, Turner to DCAS, 26 Jul 1940.
32. AIR 2/3213, f 26a, Turner to ACAS(G), 26 Jul 1940.
33. AIR 20/2806, Decoys: report by Colonel Turner, 17 Aug 1940, para 5.
34. ADM 199/69, p 38, DCOS Cttee: memorandum on decoys, 19 Sep 1940.
35. ADM 199/69, p 38, DCOS Cttee: memorandum on decoys, 19 Sep 1940.
36. AIR 2/3706, Turner to ACAS(G), 6 Sep 1940; AIR 2/3706, Turner to commands, 26 Sep 1940.
37. AIR 2/3213, f 77a, AMSO to CAS (with addendum by J F Turner), 24 Sep 1940.
38. AIR 14/271, f 13b, Notes on Q sites, J F Turner, 4 Nov 1940.
39. AIR 19/499, f 10c, Report on decoys, J F Turner, 23 Jan 1941, Appendix 1.
40. AIR 14/271, f 13b, Notes on Q sites, J F Turner, 4 Nov 1940.
41. HO 186/391, CDC (40) 40, War Cabinet Civil Defence Committee: Decoy lighting, 5 Aug 1940; HO 186/391, Stradling to Johnson, 17 Aug 1940.
42. AIR 2/5129, f 60c, Baillie to Curtis, 29 Sep 1940.
43. HO 186/391, Turner to Rucker, S 64171, 5 Nov 1940.
44. AIR 2/5179, f 34a, letter from Ministry of Home Security Civil Defence Establishment, Leamington, to Air Ministry FO3(b), 22 Aug 1940.
45. AIR 20/4355 contains extensive photographic coverage of these and other decoy experiments, including those on QF variants held at the Middle East Camouflage Centre in May 1942.

46. AIR 2/5129, f 48a, Memorandum on decoys submitted by the Air Ministry in pursuance of conclusions of a Meeting of the Deputy Chiefs of Staff Committee held on July 21st, 1940, 19 Sep 1940.

Chapter 4

1. Wakefield 1981, 115–7; 212.
2. Quoted in Motion 1993, 49.
3. Longmate 1979, 32.
4. The US Strategic Bombing Survey put the death toll for this raid at 87,793: quoted in Schaffer 1985, 132.
5. Summarised in Hinsley 1979, 552–64. A more detailed technical appraisal is given in Wakefield's important but often overlooked (1981) history of KGr 100.
6. AIR 26/580, ORB 80 Wg, Jun 1940.
7. AIR 8/317, Copy of minute from Lindemann to Churchill, 24 Oct 1940.
8. AIR 8/317, ACAS(R) to PS to CAS, 4 Nov 1940.
9. AIR 8/317, Whitworth Jones to Turner, 30 Oct 1940.
10. AIR 8/317, Turner to Whitworth Jones, 1 Nov 1940.
11. Cooper 1981, 169–70.
12. Harris's own account of these events is at AIR 2/5181, f 24a, Harris to DF Ops, 19 Nov 1941. Harris places this event on 'about' the 24th November, though contemporary sources show the date to have been the 23rd.
13. AIR 20/2806, FO3(b) to VCAS *et al*, 23 Nov 1940.
14. AIR 20/5213, f 2a, Ward to Harris, 7 Dec 1940.
15. Wakefield 1981, 213.
16. AIR 20/2806, Harris to VCAS *et al*, 23 Nov 1940.
17. AIR 2/3180, f 59a, CTD letter, 30 Nov 1940.
18. AIR 26/580, ORB 80 Wg, 26 Nov 1940.
19. AIR 20/4354, Notes on Starfish, nd.
20. AIR 20/5213, f 2a, Ward to Harris, 7 Dec 1940.
21. AIR 2/3182, Turner to Harris, 6 Dec 1940.
22. Jones 1998, 153.
23. Saward 1985, 112.
24. AIR 8/317, Harris to Portal, 4 Dec 1940; italics indicate a ms addendum by Harris.
25. AIR 8/317, Harris to Portal, 4 Dec 1940.
26. ADM 199/733, p 88, Decoy fires: Plymouth area, 1 Jan 1941.
27. AIR 19/499, f 10c, Report on decoys, J F Turner, 23 Jan 1941.
28. AIR 2/5179, f 86a, CTD to FO3(B), 19 Jan 1941.
29. AIR 26/580, ORB 80 Wg, Apr 1941.

30. AIR 20/4354, Part D.
31. AIR 20/4352, f 5a, Schedule of decoys, 1 Aug 1941.
32. AIR 2/4598, Memo to PAS (G), 5 Jan 1941.
33. AIR 19/499, Harris to S of S, 1 Feb 1940.
34. AIR 19/499, Harris to S of S, 1 Feb 1940, original emphasis.
35. AIR 2/4761, F5b, Night Decoys Part IVA, 24 May 1941.
36. AIR 19/499, f10c, Report on decoys, J F Turner. 23 Jan 1941.
37. Wakefield 1981, 128.
38. Summarised in AIR 41/3, pp 238–46.
39. AIR 41/3, p 238.
40. AIR 41/3, p 244.
41. AIR 40/1556, ACAS(G) to DCAS, 19 Mar 1941.
42. Summarised in AIR 14/1242, f 102c, Decoys, 8 Jan 1942.
43. AIR 2/8022, Starfish, J F Turner, nd [but evidently Jan 1941].
44. Summarised in AIR 14/1242, f 102c, Decoys, 8 Jan 1942. It might be noted that this figure, which was derived from the definitive post-raid survey, markedly exceeds that given in the ORB of 80 Wing, which was presumably compiled before the full facts had been collected.
45. AIR 26/580, ORB 80 Wg, Mar 1941; AIR 40/1556, ACAS(G) to DCAS, 19 Mar 1941.
46. AIR 41/3, 86.
47. AIR 2/4708, f 8a, Turner to Addison, S 70123, 6 May 1941.
48. AIR 2/4708, f 10a, Addison to Turner, 80W/S3035/Sigs, 9 May 1941.
49. AIR 2/4708, f 10a, Addison to Turner, 80W/S3035/Sigs, 9 May 1941.
50. AIR 2/4708, f 10a, Addison to Turner, 80W/S3035/Sigs, 9 May 1941.
51. AIR 2/4766, f 1a, Memo to Turner, 10 Jun 1941.
52. AIR 2/4708, f 14a, Addison to Turner, 80W/S3035/Sigs, 26 May 1941.
53. HO 186/391, Bomber Cmd to AM, BC/S24093/Org, 19 Jun 1940.
54. AIR 14/242, f 5a, Bomber Cmd to Gp IOs, BC/S20574/Int, 17 Dec 1940.
55. AIR 14/1242, f 19a, CIU Special Report Z3: Bomb Decoys, 12 Aug 1941.
56. AIR 14/1889, f 44a, Bomber Cmd Operational Research Section Report S244, 5 Jul 1945.
57. Wakefield 1981, 239–40.
58. This at any rate is the date implied by the department's correspondence, which in late November 1940 began to appear with 'c/o GPO Shepperton' overtyped on standard Air Ministry stationery.
59. AIR 19/499, f 10c, Report on decoys, J F Turner, 23 Jan 1941; AIR 14/254, f 65a Schedule of decoys, 15 Jul 1941.
60. Howard 1990, 10.
61. AIR 2/3706, f 19a, Turner to commands, 27 Apr 1941.
62. AIR 15/320, Turner to D of I, 19 Dec 1940.

63. AIR 19/499, f 10c, Report on decoys, J F Turner, 23 Jan 1941.
64. AIR 2/3706, f 19a, Turner to commands, 27 Apr 1941.
65. AIR 2/4770, Schedule of War Office night decoy sites, nd.
66. AIR 14/254, f 65a, Schedule of decoys, Col Turner's Dept, 15 Jul 1941.
67. These reports are scattered through ADM 199/733 and ADM 199/734.
68. All figures from AIR 41/3, Chap X, App II.
69. AIR 2/8022, f 65a, AM letter S.58447/W7a/HO, 24 Jul 1940. This problem was overcome in older Q site shelters by fitting a baffle silencer to the generator exhaust outlet.

Chapter 5

1. Bekker 1966, 217–222; Cooper 1981, 218–22.
2. Wakefield 1981, 227.
3. AIR 26/580, ORB 80 Wg, Jul 1941
4. AIR 26/580, ORB 80 Wg, Aug–Dec 1941.
5. AIR 2/4767, f 16a, Turner to local controls, S72946, 5 Aug 1941.
6. AIR 2/4767, f 27a, Ridley to Dick, S72946, 23 Aug 1941.
7. AIR 2/4767, f 49a, Conference with AA Cmd, 19 Sep 1941.
8. AIR 26/580, ORB 80 Wg, Sep 1941 – Mar 1942; AIR 20/4352, Schedule of decoys, 9 Mar 1942.
9. AIR 26/580, ORB 80 Wg, Jun 1942.
10. AIR 20/2806, FO3(b) to PS to CAS, 21 Nov 1940.
11. AIR 20/4354, part L.
12. AIR 20/4354, part L.
13. The shelter was covered by Air Ministry Drawing CTD 151/41.
14. AIR 2/4761, f 130b, AM letter S 72931, 13 Feb 1943.
15. AIR 2/4761, f 20a, Instructions to QL operators at the site: furnace and loco glows, 25 Aug 1941.
16. AIR 20/7628, illustration at p 20.
17. AIR 2/5179, f 56a, report to War Cabinet COS Committee, 11 Oct 1940.
18. AIR 2/5180, f 20a, letter from ACAS to Col Turner, 16 May 1941.
19. AIR 2/5180, f 69d.
20. AIR 2/5180, f 69b, Turner to DCAS, 22 Aug 1941.
21. AIR 20/4354, part B.
22. AIR 14/3340, f 38b, 'Q' Lighting of Drem Type Flarepaths, description, policy and operation, CTD, 22 Aug 1941, p 3.
23. AIR 2/8023, f 105a, Slessor to Turner, 5G/111/1/Air/DO, 16 Sep 1941.
24. AIR 2/5180, f 102a, minutes of meeting at Bomber Cmd Headquarters, High Wycombe, 3 Oct 1941.
25. AIR 2/5181, f 1a, Turner to DF Ops, 10 Oct 1941.
26. AIR 2/5182, f 13b, Minute from DDF Ops, 27 Oct 1941.

27. AIR 41/3, Chapter X, App I.
28. AIR 2/5181, f 16a, DDF Ops to D Plans, 3 Nov 1941.
29. AIR 20/4354, Chronological sequence, Section I, 11 Jun 1942.
30. AIR 41/3, Chapter X, Appendix II.
31. AIR 2/4785, f 25a, Note on organization and duties of Colonel Turner's Department and the C & D Service, Nov 1941.
32. Sturtivant *et al* 1997, 86.
33. CAB 121/226, f 3a, COS(41)617, Material for the construction and maintenance of decoys, 10 Oct 1941.
34. AIR 2/5181, f 27a, Turner to PAS, 19 Nov 1941.
35. Wright 1970, 269.
36. CAB 120/319, Dowding to S of S *et al*, S 76111, 12 Dec 1941.
37. CAB 120/319, Memo from Dowding, S 7611, 21 Jan 1942.
38. AIR 2/5181, f 47b, Dowding to S of S *et al*, S 76111, 4 Feb 1942.
39. CAB 120/319, Turner to Ismay, 10 Feb 1942.
40. AIR 2/5181, Turner to DCAS, 10 Feb 1942.
41. CAB 120/319, VCAS to DCAS, 25 Feb 1942.
42. AIR 2/5181, f 53a, Turner to DF Ops *et al*, 27 Feb 1942.
43. AIR 26/580, ORB 80 Wg, Jan–Mar 1942.
44. AIR 2/5181, f 53a, Turner to DF Ops *et al*, 27 Feb 1942.
45. AIR 41/3, pp 245–6.
46. Harris 1947, 105–6.
47. Harris 1947, 105.
48. Quoted in Cooper 1981, 190.
49. Collier 1957, 305.
50. AIR 2/8024, f 48a, Turner to commands, 1 May 1942.
51. AIR 2/5182, f 15b, Turner to Whitworth Jones, 1 May 1942.
52. AIR 2/5182, f 15b, Turner to Whitworth Jones, 1 May 1942.
53. AIR 2/5182, f 18a, Jacobs-Larkcom to Whitworth Jones, 9 May 1942.
54. Collier 1957, 307.
55. ADM 1/17816, DLD minute, 14 Jul 1942.
56. Collier 1957, 307–8.
57. AIR 20/5227, f 11a, Final Report on Op No 106, SF61(a) Bridge for Canterbury, 1/2 Jun 1942.
58. AIR 20/5227, f 10a, Attack on Canterbury on night of 6/7 Jun 1942.
59. AIR 2/5182, f 48b, Whitworth Jones to ACAS(Ops), 9 Jun 1942. Summary of operations from AIR 26/580, ORB 80 Wg, Jun–Oct 1942.
60. AIR 26/580, ORB 80 Wg, Nov 1942.
61. The figures in this paragraph are derived from a summary compiled by Colonel Turner's Department late in 1944: AIR 20/4354, Part L.
62. AIR 41/3, p 15.
63. AIR 20/4352, f 67a, Schedule of decoys, 12 Aug 1942.
64. AIR 2/5182, f 55b–c, Turner to Whitworth Jones, 23 Sep 1942.

65. AIR 2/5182, f 63a, DF Ops II to Turner, 19 Oct 1942.

66. Attack figures are from AIR 41/3, Chap X, App II.

67. ADM 1/17816, DLD minute, 14 Jul 1942.

Chapter 6

1. The official account is in Howard 1990, 103–33, 185–200; and see Cruickshank 1979, 61–113, 170–89; Cubbage 1987; Müller 1987; Reymond 1994.

2. WO 199/2264, f 3a, DFW letter 118/General/4439 (FW4d), 6 May 1942.

3. WO 199/2264, f 40a, DFW letter 118/Southern/6050 (FW4 R&A), 20 Sep 1942.

4. WO 199/339, f 4b, COHQ to Turner, M0024, 24 Sep 1942.

5. AIR 2/6016, f 4a, Ridley (Section III) to Board (Section I), NS439, 11 Feb 1943.

6. AIR 2/4771, f 77a, CTD to DLD Admiralty, S72956, 22 Feb 1943.

7. AIR 20/964, Turner to DF Ops, 6 Apr 1943.

8. AIR 20/964, ACAS (Ops) to ACAS (P), 13 Apr 1943, refers.

9. Wheatley 1981, 141.

10. AIR 2/6016, f 64b, Memo by Ridley (Section III), 7 Apr 1943.

11. AIR 20/964, Turner to ACAS (Ops), 27 Apr 1943.

12. AIR 2/7183, f 7b, Notes of proposed cuts of OR RAF personnel on decoys, J F Turner, 6 Jan 1943.

13. AIR 26/581, ORB 80 Wg, Feb 1943.

14. AIR 2/7183, f 7c, Notes of proposed cuts of OR RAF personnel on decoys, J F Turner, 6 Jan 1943, Appendix.

15. Collier 1957, 313.

16. AIR 26/581, ORB 80 Wg, Jan 1943.

17. Collier 1957, 314.

18. AIR 2/6016, f 72a, CTD to K Areas, 13 May 1943.

19. AIR 26/581, ORB 80 Wg, Jun 1943.

20. Collier 1957, 317.

21. ADM 179/272, Scheme for decoy lighting for 'Starkey', 25 Jul 1943.

22. ADM 179/272, CTD to C-in-C Portsmouth, 15 Aug 1943.

23. Cruickshank 1979, 84.

24. AIR 26/581, ORB 80 Wg, Sep 1943–Jan 1944.

25. AIR 2/5183, f 51a, Turner to DF Ops, 10 Sep 1943.

26. AIR 2/4688, f 211b, Instructions for operating single line hooded flarepath Q site, 15 Oct 1943.

27. AIR 2/8024, f 93a, Turner to Harris, S59939/IV, 17 Sep 1943.

28. AIR 2/4766, f 47a, Notes on meeting at Sound City, 18 Oct 1943.

29. AIR 20/4354, Part L.

30. AIR 2/5183, f 71a, Summary of decoy sites, 1 Nov 1943.

31. AIR 20/4354, Part L.

32. AIR 14/1890, Observations on enemy decoy TI markers, Bomber Cmd Operational Research Section Report, 14 Apr 1944.

33. AIR 2/5184, f 14a, Minute from Turner, 28 Feb 1944; AIR 2/4760, f 2a, Starfish and new enemy tactics, S67000, 1 Mar 1944.

34. AIR 26/581, ORB 80 Wg, Mar 1944; AIR 2/4760, f 4d, 'Minor' Starfish, CTD, 21 Mar 1944, Apps A–B.

35. AIR 26/581, ORB 80 Wg, Mar–Apr 1944.

36. Howard 1990, 106–7.

37. Howard 1990, 110.

38. AIR 2/6021, f 18, Turner to B H Churchill, 17 Dec 1943.

39. AIR 2/6021, f 29, SHAEF to Admiralty and GHQ Home Forces, 27 Jan 1944; AIR 2/6021, f 30, Turner to AEAF *et al*, 1 Feb 1944; AIR 2/6017, f 11a, CTD to Freeth, 2 Feb 1944.

40. AIR 41/3, p 148.

41. AIR 41/3, p 149; AIR 2/6017, f 46a, Turner to area officers, 12 Feb 1944.

42. AIR 41/3, p 151–2.

43. AIR 2/6022, Instructions for display lights and fires for Overlord, J F Turner, 20 Apr 1944.

44. A summary of the layout at the end of April is in AIR 2/6018, f 8a, CTD coastal sites, 27 Apr 1944.

45. AIR 2/6017, f 47a, CTD letter, 10 Feb 1944.

46. AIR 2/6017, Coast sites, progress report, 18 Apr 1944.

47. AIR 2/6017, f 90a, Bengough (CTD Section I) to Cranmer, 20 Apr 1944.

48. AIR 2/6017, f 94a, CTD (Section I) to C&D Area 7, 21 Apr 1944.

49. AIR 20/4354, Part K.

50. Cruickshank 1979, 183.

51. Howard 1990, 127.

Chapter 7

1. AIR 20/4259, Report on the activities of the C&D Units on the Western Continental Front up to and including June 29th, 1944, HQ 83 Group, 30 Jun 1944.

2. AIR 2/6022, Turner to ACAS(G), 26 Jun 1944.

3. AIR 41/3, pp 155–6.

4. See particularly Cubbage 1987.

5. AIR 2/5184, f 38a, Ops(AD)4 to D Ops, 23 Jul 1944.

6. ADM 1/18005, Admiralty to multiple recipients, 4 Jul 1944.

7. Figures in this summary from AIR 2/5184, f 43a, Analysis of decoy sites, 15 Aug 1944; AIR 2/5184, f 55a, Analysis of decoy sites, 30 Sep 1944.

8. ADM 1/18005, Turner to Durst, 5 Aug 1944.

9. AIR 2/8024, f 110a, Turner to DGW, 2 Oct 1944.
10. ADM 1/18005, Admiralty to multiple recipients, 4 Oct 1944.
11. Instructions for decommissioning during this period can be found in ADM 1/18005, Turner to Durst, 5 Aug 1944; AIR 2/8024, Turner to DGW, 22 Sep 1944; AIR 2/8024, f 116a, DGW to Superintending Engineers, S 58700/W2A, 16 Oct 1944.
12. AIR 2/8024, f 121a, Turner to D Ops(AD), 11 Jan 1945.
13. AIR 2/5184, f 71a, Analysis of decoy sites, 31 Jan 1945.
14. AIR 2/6022, f 71, Turner to DCAS *et al*, 29 Jan 1945.
15. AIR 20/965, Summary of Q sites in northern France, 2 Mar 1945.
16. ADM 1/18005, AM to Admiralty, CS5640/VI/S6, 15 Feb 1945.
17. ADM 1/18005, Admiralty to C-in-C Nore Cmd, 8 Mar 1945.
18. AIR 26/581, ORB 80 Wg, May 1945.

Chapter 8

1. AIR 20/965, f 20a, ACAS(Ops) to S1, 1 Mar 1946.
2. The papers on this project are in BT 177/34.
3. See Threadgall 1994, 34–5.
4. AIR 20/4259, f 11a, The future of RAF visual deception, J F Turner, 23 May 1945.
5. Sturtivant *et al* 1997, 308.
6. AIR 20/965, D Ops to VISTRE (RAF), C 32224/46/DD Ops, 4 Nov 1946.
7. AIR 20/7628, f 4, D Ops 1 to DOR(B), 5 Sep 1951.
8. AIR 20/7628, f 41, Ops(AD)5 to DD Ops (AD), 9 Dec 1953.
9. AIR 20/7628, D Ops(1) to DO *et al*, 21 Jun 1954.
10. *The Times*, 26 May 1958, 8.
11. *The Times*, 24 May 1958, 8.
12. *The Times*, 28 May 1958, 13.
13. Faithfull 1958.
14. Cruickshank 1979, ii.
15. Collier 1957.
16. See Crawshaw 1992 for the York site and Haigh 1993 for two of those serving Leeds.
17. Pye & Woodward 1996 survey the Plymouth decoys, and Nash 1999 those in Essex.
18. Crawshaw 1992.
19. Dobinson 1996 was the report on this stage of the process.
20. In the hands of Neil Redfern: Redfern 1998.
21. This work was in the hands of Michael Anderton: Anderton 1999.

Gazetteer of sites

The following tables provide listings of the locations of decoy sites throughout the United Kingdom, with each identified by its code number, name, type, and location. Altogether, 797 separate sites appear, among which National Grid References are available for 769 – some 96.5 per cent. The information has been collated from many sources, but principally the comprehensive national 'schedules' of decoys regularly issued by Colonel Turner's Department during the war.* There can be little doubt that the listing is complete, or very nearly so, in the sense of including practically every decoy site built by Turner's department or co-ordinated by it under the national decoy scheme.

For the most part these tables are self-explanatory, but the complexity of the decoy system itself is necessarily reflected by some complications in the tabulation of its component parts. Sites are broken down between nine separate tables, respecting the divisions usually made in their listing during the war. These are:

Table I.1   RAF airfield decoys
Table I.2   Dummy buildings (M Series)
Table I.3   Oil QFs (P Series)
Table I.4   Civil Starfish (SF Series)
Table I.5   Naval decoys (N Series)

* The main schedules on which this listing is based are in AIR 20/4352 and AIR 14/254, while the QLs for *Starkey* can be found in ADM 179/272, Scheme for decoy lighting for 'Starkey', 25 Jul 1943.

Each table shows the 'parent' target or grouping for the decoys – the airfield, city, or other locale to be protected – followed by the decoy serials and names, the type present on the site (where the series includes more than one type), and the grid reference. In addition, each table includes a final column headed *Co-located* showing cross-references for the code letters of decoys from *other* tables which share the site. Individual grid references are thus duplicated *between* tables where the position is occupied by a decoy in more than one series; while only 797 *different* grid references occur in the tables, these duplicates mean that the number of references printed is substantially larger.

A complexity is introduced by periodic shifts of decoys between parent targets within a single series: thus a Q site might have begun its life attached to a particular airfield, later to be assigned to another, further down the sequence. In these cases the grid reference for the site is shown on the *first* occasion when it appears in the table, while subsequent entries for the same site under a new parent are shown as ' = [the former site number]' *in the NGR column.*

The shifting of sites introduces a further complexity when this occurs *between* series – some Starfish were shifted between civil and naval lists, for example, while around half of the decoys originally in the army series were transferred to the civil series early in their lives. In these cases the dual identity is shown as ' = [the alternative site number]' *in the Co-located column.* Put simply, any decoy whose number is prefixed by ' = ' in this column has been moved to or from another series at some point in its existence. Numbers in the Co-located column without the ' = ' sign indicate decoys in another series which simply occupy the same site; typically these are urban Starfish and QL sites, though in some cases more exotic admixtures occur. The cardinal rule is that grid references are never repeated *within* tables, but they can be *between* tables, both through the co-location of sites in different series, and the shifting of sites between them.

A few less common complications should be noted. One is the occasional shifting of a decoy on the ground, without change of name, series or site number – typically the moving of a Q site to a better position a few fields distant from its original position. In these cases the site is simply listed with the code and name shown twice, and two separate grid references. Another point to note is the handling of omissions from the list. These occur in two forms. In the first, the original schedules of sites show a parent and a code number allocated to it, but no details of a decoy code or name – a typical example is RAF Netheravon in the airfield decoys list, which was coded 63 early in the programme but in no source has a decoy site or grid reference attached. In these cases it appears that intentions to establish a decoy for the site were simply cancelled, so this is what the listing says. The second form of omission is those cases where a decoy clearly *was* established, but the grid reference for one reason or another cannot be traced. Again, this is reflected in the entry made against site in the listing. These cases are few and – as we have seen – all but 29 of the 797 decoy sites known to have been occupied yield a grid reference for their positions.

It is worth noting finally that these grid references are given here in different form from that used during the war, and in which they occur in the sources. Wartime references were quoted on a system known as the 'Cassini grid', a map projection differing markedly in geometry and orientation to the National Grid in use by the Ordnance Survey in Britain today (though the older system survives practically unchanged in Northern Ireland). In order to derive National Grid References from their Cassini equivalents the original references have been converted by using two sets of maps and relating the point on the Cassini grid to the modern system by visual or photographic means. The 797 grid references shown here are only a small proportion of the total which we have converted in this way: equivalent information for sites in other categories – anti-aircraft batteries, radar stations, coast batteries and so on – will appear in later volumes of the present series.

Table I.1 RAF airfield decoys

No.	Parent	Decoy(s)	Type(s)	NGR	Co-located
1	Wick	(a) Sarclet	Q/K	ND 155438	—
2	Lossiemouth	(a) Milltown	Q	NJ 264661	—
		(b) Kingston	Q	NJ 309665	—
3	Dyce	(a) Harestone Moss	Q	NJ 928195	—
4	Leuchars	(a) Craigie	Q/K	NO 437235	—
		(b) Eden Mouth	Q	NO 488213	—
5	Turnhouse	(a) Ratho	Q	NT 110700	—
6	Drem	(a) Black Loch	Q	NT 670734	—
		(b) Spittal	Q	NT 482768	—
7	Acklington	(a) Long Houghton	Q/K	NU 259132	—
		(b) Widdrington	Q	NZ 268942	—
8	Thornaby	(a) Grangetown	Q/K	NZ 572218	C2(a)
		(b) Middleton	Q/QF	NZ 481114	C2(j)
9	Catterick	(a) Low Moor	Q	SE 393984	—
		(b) Birkby	Q	NZ 318003	—
10	Dishforth	(a) Cold Kirby	Q/K	SE 510836	—
		(b) Boltby	Q	SE 512852	—
		(c) Raskelf	Q	SE 488723	—
11	Linton	(a) Bossall	Q/K	SE 727613	—
		(b) Wigginton	Q	SE 552615	—
12	Driffield	(a) Skipsea	K	TA 183537	—

No.	Name		Place	Grid reference		
		(b)	Skerne	TA 034552	Q	—
		(c)	Kilham	TA 083634	Q	—
13	Leconfield	(a)	Routh	TA 077427	Q	—
14	Church Fenton	(a)	Kelfield	SE 592396	Q	—
		(b)	Hambleton	SE 569321	Q	—
		(c)	Menthorpe	SE 694353	Q/K	—
15	Finningley	(a)	Owston Ferry	SE 792012	Q/K	—
		(b)	Armthorpe	SE 645040	Q	—
16	Hemswell	(a)	Caenby	*Not traced*	Q	—
		(b)	Toft Grange	TF 033869	Q/K	—
		(c)	Glentham	TF 011893	Q	—
17	North Coates	(a)	Donna Nook	TA 403002	Q/K	—
18	Coningsby/Manby	(a)	Hagnaby	TF 352618	Q/K	—
		(b)	Frithville	TF 298496	Q	—
		(c)	Sibsey	TF 367528	Q	—
19	Scampton	(a)	Rand	TF 133796	Q	—
20	Waddington	(a)	Potter Hanworth	TF 079667	Q	—
		(b)	Branston Fen	TF 078693	Q/QF	C72(a)
		(c)	Gautby	TF 170714	Q/K	—
21	Digby	(a)	Ruskington	TF 111514	Q	—
		(b)	Dorrington	TF 095543	Q	—
22	Grantham	(a)	Folkingham	TF 064325	Q/K	—
23	Sutton Bridge	(a)	Terrington Marsh	TF 555226	Q	—
24	Bircham Newton	(a)	Coxford Heath	TF 828307	Q/K	—
		(b)	Sedgeford	TF 737363	Q	—

No.	Parent	Decoy(s)	Type(s)	NGR	Co-located
25	West Raynham	(c) Salthouse	Q	TG 080425	—
		(d) Burnham Sutton	Q	TF 840391	—
		(a) Fulmodestone	Q/K	TG 009306	—
		(b) Gately	Q	TF 952245	—
26	Swanton Morley	(a) North Tuddenham	Q/K	TG 034134	—
27	Marham	(a) Swaffham	Q/K	TF 832038	—
		(b) South Acre	Q	TF 796122	—
		(c) Wormegay	Q	TF 649125	—
28	Honington	(a) Thetford	Q/K	TL 896810	—
		(b) Ixworth	Q	TL 948714	—
29	Feltwell	(a) Lakenheath	Q/K	TL 735814	—
		(b) Stanford	Q	TL 849938	—
		(c) Southery	Q	TL 672948	—
30	Mildenhall	(a) Cavenham	Q/K	TL 750692	—
		(b) Littleport	Q	TL 584852	—
31	Stradishall	(a) Ashfield Green	Q	TL 772561	—
		(b) Poslingford	Q	TL 787496	—
		(c) Lidgate	Q	TL 712584	—
32	Wattisham	(a) Boxford	Q/K	TL 955385	—
		(b) Gislingham	Q	TM 064731	—
		(c) Nedging	Q	TM 007476	—
33	Cottesmore	(a) Swayfield	Q/K	SK 979218	—
34	Wittering	(a) Maxey	Q	TF 143077	—

No.	Station	Site	Type	Grid ref.	
35	Upwood	(b) Alwalton	Q/K	TL 152949	—
36	Wyton	(a) Benwick	Q	TL 345918	—
		(a) Haddenham	Q/K	TL 467775	—
		(b) Somersham	Q	TL 345760	—
		(c) Colne	Q	TL 389776	—
37	Bassingbourn	(a) Barley	Q	TL 396399	—
38	Upper Heyford	(a) Otmoor	Q	SP 581139	—
39	Duxford	(a) Horseheath	Q/K	TL 587482	—
		(b) Great Eversden	Q	TL 337536	—
40	Debden	(a) Stambourne	Q	TL 727394	—
41	Northolt	(a) Barnet	Q/K/QF	TQ 234980	—
42	North Weald	(a) Nazeing	Q/K/QF	TL 421055	—
		(b) Blackmore	Q	TL 619043	—
43	Hornchurch	(a) Bulphan	Q/K	TQ 656857	—
44	Martlesham	(a) Hollesley	Q/K	TM 335462	—
45	Bicester	(a) Grendon Underwood	Q/K	SP 678198	—
46	Benson	(a) Pyrton	Q/K	SU 662982	—
47	Harwell	(a) Beedon	Q	SU 472779	—
48	Biggin Hill	(a) Lullingstone	Q/K/QF	TQ 526648	—
49	Detling	(a) Lenham	Q/K/QF	TQ 920534	—
50	Manston	(a) Monkton	Q	*Not traced*	—
		(b) Ash Level	Q	TR 299621	—
51	Tangmere	(a) Gumber	Q/K	SU 958120	—
		(b) Colworth	Q	SU 926027	—
52	Thorney Island	(a) West Wittering	Q/K	SZ 770983	—

No.	Parent	Decoy(s)	Type(s)	NGR	Co-located
53	Coltishall	(a) Beeston St Lawrence	Q	TG 318227	—
		(b) Suffield	Q	TG 242320	—
54	Horsham St Faith	(a) Crostwick	Q	TG 264148	—
55	Llandow	(a) Marcross	Q	*Not traced*	—
56	South Cerney	(a) Ashton Keynes	Q	SU 028927	—
57	Aston Down	(a) Horsley	Q	ST 865963	—
58	Pembrey	(a) Kidwelly	Q	SN 431069	—
59	Old Sarum	(a) Pitton	Q	SU 199319	—
60	Hullavington	(a) Allington	Q	ST 885768	—
61	St Eval	(a) Trelow Down	Q	SW 924683	—
		(b) Tregonetha Down	Q	SW 958631	—
		(c) Colan	Q	SW 872585	—
62	Warmwell	(a) Knighton	Q	SY 812866	—
63	Netheravon	*Cancelled?*	—	—	—
64	Exeter	(a) Woodbury	QF	SY 048882	—
		(b) Clyst Hydon	Q	SY 037869	—
		(c) Aylesbeare Common	Q	ST 056012	—
		(d) Clyst St Mary	Q/QF	SY 056902 SX 993917	—
65	Boscombe Down	(a) South Newton	Q	SU 096356	—
66	Brize Norton	(a) Chimney	Q	SP 345006	—
67	Upavon	(a) All Cannings	Q	SU 080608	—
68	Middle Wallop	(a) Houghton	Q	SU 331343	—

No.	Name	Sub-site	Type	Grid reference	Notes
69	Odiham	(a) Froyle	Q	SU 726435	—
70	Andover	(a) Thruxton	Q	*Not traced*	—
		(b) Hurstbourne Tarrant	Q	SU 401536	—
71	Ternhill	(a) Chipnall	Q	SJ 721326	—
72	Shawbury	(a) Withington	Q/QF	SJ 548142	= A43
73	Little Rissington	(a) Farmington	Q	SP 146171	—
74	Kidlington	(a) Enstone	Q	SP 399247	—
		(b) Fawler	Q	SP 378183	—
		(c) Glympton	Q	*Not traced*	—
75	Reading	(a) Warfield	Q	SU 863744	—
76	Silloth	(a) Pelutho	Q	NY 109496	—
		(b) West Newton	Q	NY 105449	—
77	Montrose	(a) Warburton	Q	NO 739627	—
78	Carew Cheriton	(a) Begelly	Q	SN 106075	—
79	Castletown	(a) Barrock	Q	ND 244696	—
80	Cranfield	(a) Hardmead	Q	SP 923483	—
81	Oakington	(a) Rampton	Q	TL 466697	—
		(b) Boxworth	Q	TL 330663	—
82	Kenley	(a) Woldingham	Q/QF	TQ 388560	—
		(b) South Godstone	Q	TQ 336476	—
		(b) South Godstone	QF	TQ 335479	—
		(c) Walton Heath	QF	*Not traced*	—
		(d) Farleigh	Q	TQ 375610	SF8(b)
83	Abbotsinch	(a) Glennifer Braes	Q	NS 446600	C15(k)
84	Bramcote	(a) Wibtoft	Q	SP 472864	—

No.	Parent	Decoy(s)	Type(s)	NGR	Co-located
85	Binbrook	(a) Wyham	Q	TF 258939	—
		(b) Kelstern	Q	*Not traced*	—
		(c) Ludborough	Q	TF 284960	—
86	Colerne	(a) West Littleton	Q	ST 767764	—
		(b) Monkton Farleigh	Q/QF	ST 820661	—
87	Lindholme	(a) Belton	Q	SE 759100	—
		(b) Eastoft	Q	SE 789167	—
88	Topcliffe	(a) Raskelf	Q	= Q10(c)	—
		(b) Cold Kirby	Q/K	= Q10(a)	—
		(c) Boltby	Q	= Q10(b)	—
89	Leeming	(a) Burneston	Q	SE 326859	—
90	Kirton in Lindsey	(a) Cadney	Q	TA 015050	—
		(b) Thornton le Moor	Q	TF 029956	—
91	Newton	(a) Cotgrave	Q	SK 659358	—
		(b) Tithby	Q	SK 709347	—
92	Swinderby	(a) Bassingham	Q	SK 943612	—
		(b) Brant Broughton	Q	SK 905552	—
93	Catfoss	(a) Skipsea	Q/K	= Q/K11(a)	—
		(b) Dunnington	Q	TA 144528	—
		(c) Beeford	Q	TA 124524	—
94	Kinloss	(a) Burghead	Q	NJ 103645	—
95	Ouston	(a) Berwick Hill	Q	NZ 181767	—
96	Gravesend	(a) Cliffe Marshes	Q	TQ 727778	—
		(b) Luddesdown	Q	TQ 688662	—

No.	Site				
97	Kingscliffe	(a) Warmington	Q	*Not traced*	—
		(b) Alwalton	Q	TL 152949	—
98	Honiley	(a) Wolverton	Q	SP 218616	—
		(b) Wootten Wawen	Q	SP 129611	—
99	West Malling	(a) Collier Street	Q	TQ 700464	—
		(b) Hammer Dyke	Q	TQ 642463	—
100	Fairwood	(a) Reynoldstone	Q	SS 500900	—
		(b) Kidwelly	Q	= Q58(a)	—
101	Chivenor	(a) Braunton Burrows	Q	SS 454338	—
102	Cranage	(a) Betchton	Q	SJ 787602	—
103	Elsham Wolds	(a) Great Limber	Q	TA 140074	—
		(b) South Ferriby	Q	TA 000203	—
104	Goxhill	(a) Burnham	Q	TA 044177	—
105	Hibaldstow	(a) Thornton le Moor	Q	= Q90(b)	—
106	Syerston	(a) Kneeton	Q	SK 717457	—
107	Wellesbourne M'fd	(a) Pillerton Priors	Q	SP 309480	—
108	Pershore	(a) Netherton	Q	SP 001421	—
109	Aldergrove	(a) Corbally	Q	J 137837	—
110	Limvady	(a) Crindle	Q	C 654280	—
111	Portreath	(a) Tehidy	Q	SW 622428	—
112	Hunsdon	(a) Braughing	Q	TL 411261	—
113	Charmy Down	*Cancelled?*	—	–	—
114	Foulsham	(a) Fulmodestone	Q	= Q25(a)	—
115	Predannack	(a) Kynance	Q	SW 676140	—
		(b) Goonhilly Downs	Q	SW 732185	—

No.	Parent	Decoy(s)	Type(s)	NGR	Co-located
116	Perranporth	(a) Penhale Sands	Q	SW 770567	—
117	Bodney	Cancelled?	—	—	—
118	Waterbeach	(a) Haddenham	Q	= Q36(a)	—
		(b) Soham	Q	TL 566730	—
119	Langham	(a) Salthouse	Q	= Q24(c)	—
		(b) Warham St Mary	Q	TF 938433	—
120	Pocklington	(a) Burnby	Q	SE 834476	—
121	Donna Nook	(a) Marsh Chapel	Q	= Q17(a)	—
122	Ayr	(a) Newark Hill	Q	NS 298162	—
123	East Fortune	(a) Black Loch	Q	NT 670734	—
124	High Ercall	(a) Kinnersley	Q	SJ 673182	—
125	Snaith	(a) Drax	Q	SE 664238	—
126	Scorton	(a) Birkby	Q	= Q9(b)	—
127	Barkston Heath	(a) Willoughby Walks	Q	TF 035409	—
128	Middleton St George	(a) Crathorne	Q	NZ 443064	—
129	East Kirkby	(a) Sibsey	Q	TF 367528	—
130	Polebrook	(a) Little Gidding	Q	TL 116817	—
131	Doncaster	(a) Armthorpe	Q	= Q15(b)	—
132	Sumburgh	(a) Quendale	Q	HU 383130	—
		(b) Scatness	Q	HU 390098	—
133	Woolfox Lodge	(a) Pickworth	Q	TF 002122	—
		(b) Swinstead	Q	TF 019236	—
134	Penrhos	(a) Porth Caered	Q	SH 319250	—

135	Valley	(a) Newborough	Q	SH 411637	—
136	Wrexham	(a) Minera	Q	SJ 255486	—
137	Holme	(a) South Newbald	Q	SE 956373	—
138	Wombleton	*Cancelled?*	—	—	—
139	Bottesford	(a) Tithby	Q	= Q91(b)	—
		(b) Belvoir	Q	SK 805342	—
		(c) Foston	Q	SK 872408	—
140	York	(a) Bugthorpe	Q	SE 781593	—
141	Nutts Corner	(a) Groganstown	Q	J 245704	—
142	Eglington	(a) Faughanvale	Q	J 634524	—
143	Ballyhalbert	(a) Kearney	Q	C 577219	—
144	Chelveston	(a) Swineshead	Q	TL 062635	—
145	Molesworth	(a) Grafham	Q	TL 177688	—
146	Tempsford	(a) Boxworth	Q	= Q81(b)	—
147	Hawkinge	(a) Wootton	Q	TR 238481	—
148	Abingdon	(a) Pyrton	Q	= Q46(a)	—
149	Docking	(a) North Creake	Q	TF 896392	—
		(b) Burnham Sutton	Q	= Q24(d)	—
150	Yatesbury	(a) Easton Down	Q/QF	SU 056663	—
151	St Athan	(a) Penmark	Q/QF	*Not traced*	—
		(b) Marcross	Q/QF	= Q55(a)	—
		(c) Flemingston	Q/QF	ST 032704	—
152	Halton	(a) Puttenham	Q/QF	SP 883135	—
153	Sealand	(a) Puddington	Q/QF	SJ 313734	—
154	Peterhead	(a) St Fergus	Q	NK 055536	—

No.	Parent	Decoy(s)	Type(s)	NGR	Co-located
155	Atcham	(a) Cressage	Q	SJ 587019	—
156	Crosby	(a) Scaleby	Q	NY 438614	—
157	Hawarden	(a) Bretton	Q	SJ 366629	—
158	Weston-super-Mare	(a) Bleadon	Q	ST 310567	C86(a)
159	Ossington	(a) Upton	Q	SK 738564	—
160	Hurn	(a) Ridley Plain	Q	SU 210072	—
		(b) Verwood	Q	SU 100066	—
161	Ibsley	(a) Woodgreen	Q	SU 185162	—
		(b) Verwood	Q	= Q160(b)	—
162	Manby	(a) Mablethorpe	Q	TF 477845	—
163	Gatwick	(a) Lower Beeding	Q	TQ 236299	—
164	Woodvale	(a) Great Altcar	Q	SD 329076	—
165	Lakenheath	(a) Brandon	Q	Not traced	—
166	Great Ashfield	(a) Gislingham	Q	= Q32(b)	—
		(b) Ixworth	Q	= Q28(b) & Q182(a)	—
167	Watchfield	(a) Kingston Warren	Q	SU 314842	—
168	Redhill	(a) South Godstone	Q	= Q82(b)	—
		(b) Lower Beeding	Q	= Q163(a)	—
169	Watton	(a) West Bradenham	Q	TF 912070	—
		(b) Breckles	Q	TL 952950	—
170	Snetterton	Cancelled?	—	—	—
171	Cranwell	(a) Willoughby Walks	Q	= Q127(a)	—
172	Hardwick	(a) Hempnall	Q	TM 256952	—

173	Talbenny	(a) Marloes	Q	SM 769082	—
174	Ridgewell	(a) *Cancelled?*	—	—	—
		(b) Stambourne	Q	= Q40(a)	—
175	Defford	(a) Longdon	Q	SO 816365	—
176	Bungay	(a) Rumburgh	Q	TM 356825	—
177	Wickenby	(a) Rand	Q	= Q19(a)	—
178	Wing	(a) Wingrave	Q	SP 869173	—
179	Charter Hall	(a) Swinton	Q	*Not traced*	—
180	Milfield	(a) Lowick	Q	*Not traced*	—
181	Brunton	(a) Elford	Q	*Not traced*	—
182	Bury St Edmunds	(a) Ixworth	Q	= Q28(b) & Q166(b)	—
183	Holmesley South	(a) Ridley Plain	Q	= Q160(a)	—
184	Ballykelly	(a) Faughanvale	Q	= Q142(a)	—
185	Warboys	(a) Benwick	Q	= Q35(a)	—
186	Sculthorpe	(a) Coxford Heath	Q	= Q24(a)	—
187	Lydd	(a) Midley	Q	TQ 982208	—
188	New Romney	(a) Romney Salts	Q	TR 064223	—
189	Newchurch	(a) Burmarsh	Q	TR 086326	—
190	Chipping Ongar	(a) Blackmore	Q	TL 619043	—
191	Downham Market	(a) South Acre	Q	TF 796122	—
		(b) Wormegay	Q	= Q27(c)	—
192	Ludford Magna	(a) Rand	Q	= Q19(a)	—
201	Filton	(a) Patchway	Q/QF	ST 630819	= C1(g)
202	Brooklands	(a) Wisley	QF	TQ 057589	= C41(a)
203	Brockworth	(a) Shurdington	QF	*Not traced*	—

No.	Parent	Decoy(s)	Type(s)	NGR	Co-located
204	Quedgeley	(a) Haresfield	QF	*Not traced*	—
		(b) Longney	QF	SO 774120	SF14(d); C20(a)
205	Sealand	(a) Puddington	Q/QF	= Q/QF153(a)	—
206	Weston-super-Mare	(a) Bleadon	Q/QF	= Q158(a)	= C86(a)
207	Hawarden	(a) Bretton	Q/QF	SJ 366629	= C42(a)
208	Yeovil	(a) Chinnock	Q/QF	ST 496146	= SF42(a); C30(a)
209	Gloucester	(a) Twigworth	QF	SO 841243	—
210	Cosford	(a) Boningale	QF	SJ 814019	—
211	Langley	(a) Longford	QF	TQ 047778	= C43(a)
212	Woodford	(a) Mottram	QF	SJ 866796	= C44(a) & A44
213	Burtonwood	(a) Bold Heath	QF	SJ 546897	—
214	Kirkham	(a) Westby	QF	*Not traced*	—
215	Carlisle	(a) Rockcliffe	QF	NY 335618	= A23
216	Yatesbury	(a) Easton Down	Q/QF	= Q/QF150(a)	—
217	Hartlebury	(a) Elmbridge	QF	SO 891666	SF26(c)
218	Hereford	(a) Bishopstone	QF	SO 428446	—
219	Milton	(a) Steventon	QF	SU 445935	—
220	Cardington	(a) Cople	QF	TL 125480	C28(a)
221	Henlow	(a) Astwick	QF	TL 202396	—
222	St Athan	(a) Flemingston	Q/QF	= Q151(c)	—
223	Rochester	(a) Chatham	QF	TQ 779638	= C102(a); M1
224	Wolverhampton	(a) Coven	QF	SJ 894058	= C98(a); M2
225	Hatfield	(a) Holywellhyde	QF	TL 269132	C99(a); M3

226	Baginton	(a) Leamington Hastings	QF	SP 452680	SF7(a); M4; = C7(g)
227	Halton	(a) Puttenham	Q/QF	= Q/QF152(a)	—
228	Dumfries	(a) Cathart Moor	QF	NX 810779	—
229	Redhill	(a) South Godstone	QF	= QF82(b)	—
230	West Malling	(a) Hammer Dyke	QF	= Q99(b)	—
231	Kenley	(a) Woldingham	Q/QF	= Q82(a)	—

Table I.2 Dummy buildings (M series)

No.	Parent	Decoy	NGR	Co-located
1	Rochester	Chatham	TQ 779638	QF223(a); C102(a)
2	Wolverhampton	Coven	SJ 894058	QF224(a); C98(a)
3	Hatfield	Holwellhyde	TL 269132	QF225(a); C99(a)
4	Baginton	Leamington Hastings	SP 452680	QF226(a); C7(g); SF7(a)
5	Leighton Buzzard	—	SP 938242	—
6	Dagnall	—	SP 978158	—

Table I.3 Oil QFs (P Series)

No.	Parent	Decoy(s)	NGR	Co-located
1	Isle of Grain	All Hallows	TQ 855774	—
2	Shell Haven	Fobbing	TQ 731838	—
3	Thames Haven	Stanford-le-Hope	TQ 700811	—
4	Grangemouth	Polmont	NS 968805	—
5	Stanlow	Ince	SJ 471766	—
6	Preston	Clifton Marsh	SD 470288	SF33(b); C21(a)
7	Killingholme	East Halton	TA 137229	—
8	Salt End	Paull	TA 198246	—
9	Avonmouth	(a) Sheepway	ST 497779	= C1(a)
		(b) Severn Beach	ST 542836	= C1(e)
10	Fawley	Lynes Common	SU 445058	—
11	Hamble	Tichfield	SU 520049	—

Table I.4 Civil Starfish (SF Series)

No.	Parent	Decoy(s)	NGR	Co-located
1	Bristol	(a) Stockwood	ST 629679	C1(d)
		(b) Chew Magna	ST 573649	–
		(c) Downside	ST 478659	C1(i)
		(d) Kenn Moor	ST 434686	–
		(e) Cheddar	ST 466557	–
		(f) Yeomouth	ST 368670	C1(h)
2	Birmingham	(a) Ballsall	SP 213768	–
		(b) Holt End	SP 080777	–
		(c) Maxstoke	SP 224868	C4(f)
		(d) Fairfield	SO 938754	–
		(e) Bickenhill	SP 180816	C4(g)
		(f) Peopleton	SO 947522	–
		(g) Halford	SP 283453	–
		(h) Silvington	SO 613803	–
3	Sheffield	(a) Curbar	SK 270743	–
		(b) Thorpe Salvin	SK 521799	–
		(c) Ringinglow	SK 278816	–
		(d) Norton	SK 369804	C10(c)
		(e) Bramley	SK 504933	C10(f)
		(f) Ulley	SK 472886	C10(e)

No.	Parent	Decoy(s)	NGR	Co-located
4	Derby	(a) Ticknall	SK 336240	—
		(b) Diseworth	SK 465247	—
		(c) Swarkestone	SK 363299	C17(a)
5	Crewe	(a) Chorlton	SJ 736504	—
		(b) Hack Green	SJ 663473	—
6	Wolverhampton	(a) Shipley	SO 818955	—
		(b) Blakes Hall	SO 840819	—
7	Coventry	(a) Leamington	SP 452680	QF226(a); C7(g); M4
		(b) Hunningham	SP 364676	C7(b)
		(c) Bretford	SP 418777	C7(f)
8	London	(a) Richmond Park	TQ 204730	—
		(b) Farleigh	TQ 375610	Q82(b)
		(c) Rainham Marshes	TQ 529800	—
		(d) Lambourne End	TQ 493938	—
		(e) Lullingstone	TQ 519642	—
		(f) Hampstead Heath	Not traced	—
		(g) Kenn Wood	Not traced	—
9	Manchester	(a) Chat Moss	SJ 695957	C25(a)
		(b) Tatton Park	SJ 765823	—
		(c) Park Moor	SJ 969805	—
		(d) Chunal Moor	SK 036908	—
		(e) Mossley	SD 996017	—
		(f) Carrington Moss	SJ 753919	C25(b)
		(g) Ludworth Moor	SK 002908	—

		(h)	Reddish	SJ 912939	—
		(i)	Elkstone	SK 045610	—
10	Middlesbrough	(a)	Middleton	NZ 480113	C2(h)
		(b)	Kirkleatham	NZ 616193	—
		(c)	Osmotherley	SE 476987	—
		(d)	Guisborough	NZ 608118	C96(b)
		(e)	Sneaton Moor	NZ 903029	C2(f)
		(f)	Newton Bewley	NZ 475260	C6(f)
11	Liverpool	(a)	Hale	SJ 454833	C6(g)
		(b)	Ince	SJ 472767	C6(h)
		(c)	Brimstage	SJ 297833	—
		(d)	Wallasey	SJ 283914	C6(a)
		(e)	Formby	SD 284048	C6(b)
		(f)	Little Crosby	SD 307017	C6(m)
		(g)	Heswall	SJ 245826	C6(k)
		(h)	Moreton	SJ 247909	—
		(i)	Llandegla	SJ 222535	—
		(j)	Llanasa	SJ 096821	—
		(k)	Fenn's Moss	SJ 491365	C6(n)
		(l)	Little Hilber	SJ 189872	C6(o)
		(m)	Burton Marsh	SJ 286749	C6(p)
		(n)	Gayton	SJ 269796	C85(a)
12	Warrington	(a)	Hatton	SJ 594821	—
		(b)	Appleton	SJ 643821	—
		(c)	Arley	SJ 669793	

No.	Parent	Decoy(s)	NGR	Co-located
13	Glasgow	(a) Renton	NS 367778	C15(a)
		(b) Douglas Muir	NS 516751	C15(d)
		(c) Craigmaddie	NS 594759	C15(g)
		(d) Glennifer Braes	NS 449602	C15(k)
		(e) Eaglesham	NS 541523	—
		(f) Parknewk	NS 664533	—
		(g) Condorrat	NS 722734	—
		(h) Townhead	NS 701661	—
		(j) Auchenreoch	NS 423781	C15(b)
14	Gloucester	(a) Coberley	SO 972168	C20(d)
		(b) Standish	SO 832085	C20(b)
		(c) Brimpsfield	SO 927125	C20(c)
		(d) Longney	SO 774120	C20(a); Q204(b)
15	Newcastle	(a) New York	NZ 308691	—
		(b) Beamish	NZ 228554	C12(c)
		(c) Boldon Colliery	NZ 332618	C12(i)
		(d) Ryhope	NZ 419519	C12(f)
		(e) Whitburn	NZ 395631	C12(a)
16	Portsmouth	(a) Farlington	SU 687041	= N14 PO1
		(b) Sinah Common	SZ 695992	= N14 PO4
17	Southampton	(a) Longdown	SU 356084	—
		(b) Beaulieu	SU 409038	C93(b)
		(c) Lee	SU 354172	—

	(d)	Nutburn	SU 392213	C93(a)
	(e)	Chilworth	SU 395177	—
	(f)	Durley	SU 534162	C93(d)
	(g)	Botley	SU 515116	C93(c)
18 Swansea	(a)	Bishopston	SS 599902	—
	(b)	Felindre	SN 630011	—
	(c)	Baglan Higher	SS 775939	C9(c)
	(d)	Llantwit Lower	SS 788980	C9(b)
	(e)	Morfa	SS 776858	C9(a)
19 Boscombe Down	(a)	Winterslow	SU 225310	—
20 Cardiff	(a)	Leckwith	ST 140739	C11(a)
	(b)	Lavernock	ST 173689	C11(b)
21 Newport	(a)	Llanwern	ST 365866	C8(d)
	(b)	Duffryn	ST 276854	—
	(c)	St Brides Wentloog	ST 310829	C8(c)
22 Rugby	(a)	Barby	SP 536712	C84(a)
	(b)	Claycoton	SP 600783	—
23 Leeds	(a)	Wintersett	SE 371162	C16(d)
	(b)	Emley	SE 259138	C16(f)
	(c)	Pudsey	SE 207316	—
	(d)	Barwick in Elmet	SE 399360	C16(b)
	(e)	Clifton	SE 167236	—
	(f)	Cragg Vale	SE 004205	C16(i)
	(g)	Meltham Moor	SE 095083	C16(h)
	(h)	Swillington	SE 402309	C16(c)

No.	Parent	Decoy(s)	NGR	Co-located
23	Leeds (continued)	(j) Thorner	SE 386397	C16(a)
		(k) Chidswell	SE 279234	C16(e)
		(l) Slaithwaite	SE 042135	—
		(m) Ingbirchworth	SE 197052	C16(g)
24	Scunthorpe	(a) Risby	SE 929158	C23(a)
		(b) Twigmoor	SE 921058	C23(b)
		(c) Brumby	SE 849096	—
25	Slough	(a) Dorney	SU 928782	—
		(b) Stanwell Moor	TQ 037738	—
26	Stourport	(a) Ribbesford	SO 789721	C4(n)
		(b) Shrawley	SO 787659	C4(m)
		(c) Elmbridge	SO 891666	QF217(a)
27	Redditch	(a) Morton Bagot	SP 103646	C4(p)
		(b) Feckenham	SP 010606	—
28	Leicester	(a) Galby	SK 694020	C31(a)
		(b) Beeby	SK 656076	C31(b)
		(c) Newton Harcourt	SP 635982	C31(c)
		(d) Willoughby Waterless	SP 577939	C31(d)
29	Reading	(a) Binfield	SU 831732	—
		(b) Arborfield	SU 755687	—
		(c) Sulham	SU 637736	—
30	Nottingham	(a) Clipston	SK 643337	C18(c)
		(b) Barton in Fabis	SK 535314	= A41; C18(d)
		(c) Cropwell Butler	SK 653364	C18(b)

		(d) Lowdham	SK 650455	C18(a)
31	Hull	(a) Ganstead	TA 139340	= N8 HU1
		(b) Bilton	TA 161317	= N8 HU2
		(c) Paull	TA 188240	= N8 HU3
		(d) Aldbrough	TA 258373	C96(a)
32	Stoke on Trent	(a) Caverswall	SJ 931452	C35(a)
		(b) Swynnerton	SJ 853361	C35(b)
		(c) Keele	SJ 813430	C35(c)
		(d) Beech	SJ 855371	—
33	Preston	(a) Farington	SD 523240	C21(b)
		(b) Clifton Marsh	SD 470288	C21(a); P6
		(c) Hoghton	SD 622278	—
		(d) Brinscall	SD 639202	C21(c)
34	Edinburgh	(a) Cramond	NT 199769	—
		(b) Liberton	NT 256697	—
		(c) Millerhill	NT 333689	—
		(d) Craigmillar	NT 295706	—
		(e) Kinleith	NT 199673	—
35	Accrington	(a) Haslingden	SD 763238	C22(a)
		(b) Accrington	SD 796279	C22(b)
		(c) Burnley	SD 845288	C22(c)
		(d) Worsthorne	SD 891325	C22(d)
		(e) Hameldon Hill	SD 809287	C22(e)
36	Cowley	(a) Denton	SP 605021	C36(a)
		(b) Sandford	SP 548010	C36(b)

No.	Parent	Decoy(s)	NGR	Co-located
37	Northwich	(a) Bostock	SJ 686693	—
		(b) Little Budworth	SJ 610650	C39(a)
38	Ipswich	(a) Shottisham	TM 313427	C32(a)
		(b) Bucklesham	TM 238410	C32(b)
39	Doncaster	(a) Tickhill	SK 603951	—
		(b) Armthorpe	SE 643044	—
40	Darlington	(a) Great Burdon	NZ 326155	—
		(b) Eryholme	NZ 338077	—
41	Swindon	(a) Liddington	SU 213790	C71(a)
		(b) Barbury	SU 149747	C71(b)
42	Yeovil	(a) Chinnock	ST 496146	C30(a); Q/QF208(a)
43	Norwich	(a) Little Plumstead	TG 299121	C33(a)
		(b) Bramerton	TG 305052	C33(b)
44	Luton	(a) Bendish	TL 163205	C29(a)
		(b) Flamstead	TL 085127	C29(b)
45	Northampton	(a) Kislingbury	SP 708586	—
		(b) Hardingstone	SP 802581	—
46	Peterborough	(a) Eye	TF 264009	C24(a)
		(b) Stanground South	TL 233958	C24(b)
47	Worcester	Not traced	—	—
48	Lancaster	(a) Lainsley Hill	SD 528560	—
		(b) Overton	SD 445581	= C13(a)
49	Belfast	(a) Clady Corner	J 275793	—

No.	Location		Site	Grid Ref	Code
50	Londonderry	(b)	Hightown	J 300799	—
		(c)	Carnmoney Hill	J 334831	—
		(d)	Millbank	J 440754	—
		(e)	Holywood	J 426787	—
		(f)	Knock Breckan	J 385682	—
		(a)	Glebetown	C 435131	C87(a)
		(b)	Lisglass	C 453116	—
51	East Coast	(a)	Huttoft	TF 534773	C97(a)
52	Lincoln	(a)	Branston Fen	TF 077689	—
		(b)	Canwick	TF 011694	—
53	Salisbury	(a)	Odstock	Not traced	—
		(b)	Clearbury Down	SU 148240	—
54	Cambridge	(a)	Fulbourn	TL 527545	—
		(b)	Comberton	TL 398569	—
		(b)	Comberton	TL 399573	—
		(c)	Babraham	TL 518522	—
55	Bath	(a)	Monkton Farleigh	ST 818661	—
		(b)	Wellow	ST 758587	—
56	Winchester	(a)	Hursley	SU 452254	—
57	Basingstoke	(a)	North Waltham	SU 576473	C19(a)
58	Colchester	(a)	Great Bromley	TM 076257	C75(a)
59	Redhill & Reigate	(a)	South Godstone	TQ 335479	—
60	Andover	(a)	Houghton	SU 333340	—
61	Canterbury	(a)	Bridge	TR 166544	—
		(b)	Hacklington	TR 146625	—

No.	Parent	Decoy(s)	NGR	Co-located
62	Guildford	(a) Wanborough	SU 926491	—
63	Taunton	(a) Nynehead	ST 145230	A3(a)
		(b) Dipford	ST 193223	A3(b)
64	Chelmsford	(a) Little Baddow	TQ 758064	C74(a)
65	Ashford	(a) Brabourne	TR 109428	C14(a)
66	Maidstone	(a) Lenham	TQ 920534	QF49(a)
		(b) Broomfield	TQ 826524	—
67	Tonbridge	(a) Hammer Dyke	TQ 643469	—
68	Hayle	(a) Upton Towans	SW 569396	—
69	Penzance	(a) Mousehole	SW 454257	—
70	Truro	(a) Merther	SW 883441	—
71	York	(a) Fulford	SE 636474	—
72	Durham	(a) Sherburn	NZ 325397	—
73	Glastonbury	(a) Southway	ST 535419	—
74	Oxford	(a) Cumnor	SP 448064	—
75	Exeter	(a) Ide	SX 902893	—
76	Chichester	(a) Colworth	SU 927034	—
77	Tunbridge Wells	(a) Frant	TQ 573346	—
78	Rye	(a) Camber Castle	TQ 917183	NC651
79	Sussex Coast	(a) Alciston	TQ 504043	C91(a)
80	Grantham	(a) Boothby Pagnall	SK 953305	C63(a)
81	Hartlepool	(a) Hart	NZ 494364	C101(a)

Table I.5 Naval decoys (N Series)

No.	Area	Code	Decoy(s)	Type(s)	NGR	Co-located
1	Orkneys	OR1	Plain of Fidge	Q/QF	HY 710411	—
		OR2	Shapinsay	Q/QF	HY 518170	—
		OR2	Cot on Hill	Q/QF	HY 516168	—
		OR3	Isbister	QF/QL	HY 395168	—
		OR4	Burn of Grid	Q/QF	HY 326210	—
		OR5	Deasbreck	Q/QF	HY 307255	—
		OR6	Grit Ness	QL	HY 367267	—
		OR7	Rousay Searchlight	QL	HY 381292	—
		OR8	Skatequoy	Q/QF	HY 386347	—
2	Invergordon	IN1	Dalmore Distillery	QF	NH 658685	—
		IN1	Balinstraid	QF/QL	NH 737711	—
3	Arbroath	AR1	Kellie Moor	Q/QF	NO 579410	—
4	Crail	CR1	Boghall	Q/QF	NO 587139	—
5	Dundee	DU1	West Dundee	QF	NO 379343	—
6	Rosyth	RO2	Donibristle Moss	QF	NT 160863	—
		RO4	Midhope	SF/QL	NT 066789	—
		RO5	Preston Island	SF/QL	NT 007852	—
		RO6	Bannockburn	QF	NS 840931	—
		RO7	Leith Harbour	QF	NT 261777	—
		RO9	Letham Moss	SF/QL	*Not traced*	—
7	Leadburn	LD1	Auchencorth Moss	QF	NT 201565	—

No.	Area	Code	Decoy(s)	Type(s)	NGR	Co-located
8	Humber	HU1	Ganstead	SF	TA 139340	= SF31(a)
		HU2	Bilton	SF	TA 161317	= SF31(b)
		HU3	Paull	SF/QL	TA 188240	= SF31(c)
		HU4	Little Humber	SF/QL	TA 197237	—
		HU5	Thorney Crofts	SF/QL	TA 210227	—
		IM1	Immingham Range	SF/QL	TA 235136	—
		KI1	East Halton	QF	TA 138231	—
		GR1	Humberston	SF/QL	TA 333057	—
		GR1	Grimsby	SF/QL	TA 331061 to TA 340048	—
9	Great Yarmouth	YA1	Winterton Ness	SF/QL	TG 478219	—
		YA2	Lound	SF/QL	TM 525991	—
10	Lowestoft	LO1	Burgh Marsh	SF/QL	TM 489948	—
11	Harwich	WR1	Spinnels Farm	QF	TM 162298	—
		HA1	Walton on Naze	SF/QL	TM 262247	—
		HA2	Kirby le Soken	SF/QL	TM 222239	—
		BR1	Brightlingsea	QF/QL	TM 091144	—
		BR2	East Mersea	QF/QL	TM 052157	—
12	Chatham	VI1	Binney Farm	QF	TQ 851772	—
		VI2	Harty Ferry	QF	TR 013657	—
		LO1	Stoke	QF	TQ 816761	—
		LH1	Stoke	QF	TQ 822760	—
		CH1	Nore Marsh	SF/QL	TQ 812702	—

13	Newhaven	SH1	Cleve Marshes	SF/QL	TR 047645	—
		NH1	Cuckmere Haven	QL	TQ 530036 to TV 514975	NC604–5
14	Portsmouth	PO1	Farlington Marshes	SF	SU 687041	= SF16(a)
		PO2	North Binness Island	QL	SU 695046	—
		PO2	40 Acre Farm	SF/QL	SU 696035	—
		PO3	Hayling Island (W)	SF/QL	SU 715012	—
		PO3	Long Island	QL	SU 702042	—
		PO4	Sinah Common	SF	SZ 695992	= SF16(b)
		PO4	Bakers Islands	QF	SU 696035	—
		PO5	South Binness Island	QF	SU 698033	—
		PO6	Round Nap	QF	SU 705034	—
		PO7	Old Oyster Bed	QL	SU 705033	—
		PO8	Hayling Island West	QF	SU 717023	—
		PO9	Sinah Sands	QL	SU 693009	—
		PO10	Sinah Common	SF	= N14 PO4	—
15	Portland	PT1	Fleet	SF/QL	SY 637791	—
		PT1	Speed Beacon	QF	SY 637791	—
		PT2	Littlemore	SF	SY 682823	—
		PT2	Wyke Oliver	QF	SY 682823	—
16	Poole	PE1	Brownsea Island	SF	SZ 011878	—
	Holton Heath	HH1	Arne	QF	SY 963868	—
		HH2	Gore Heath	QF	SY 922914	—
17	Yeovilton	YE1	Kings Moor	Q/QF	ST 503245	—
18	Worthy Down	WO1	Micheldever	Q/QF	SX 497499	—

No.	Area	Code	Decoy(s)	Type(s)	NGR	Co-located
19	Plymouth	PL1	Down Thomas	SF/QL	= N18 WO1	–
		PL2	Roborough Down	Q/QF	SX 513644	–
		PL3	Boringdon	QF/QL	SX 532583	–
		PL4	Cofflete	QF/QL	SX 548510	–
		PL5	Wembury	SF/QL	SX 530488	–
		PL6	Worswell	QF/QL	SX 525473	–
		PL7	Earth	QF/QL	SX 382558	–
		PL8	Southdown	SF/QL	SX 438533	–
		PL9	Shapley Tor	QL	SX 700818	–
		PL10	Hillsons House	QL	SX 635623	–
20	Falmouth	FA1	Nare Point	SF/QL	SW 800251	–
		FA2	Cancelled?	–	–	–
		FA3	Halvos	QF	SW 748332	–
		FA4	Nare Head	SF/QL	SW 916370	–
21	Caerwent	CA1	Rhyd-y-Fedw	QF/QL	ST 472955	–
22	Milford Haven	MH1	Sandy Haven Farm	SF/QF	SM 853083	–
		MH2	Herbrandston Hall	FmSF/QF/QL	SM 859073	–
		MH3	South Hook Farm	QF/QL	SM 870059	–
		PD1	Cosheston Hall	QF	SM 999045	–
		PD2	East Popton Farm	SF/QF/QL	SM 909033	–
		PD3	Sawdern Farm	SF/QF	SM 891033	–
23	Trecwm	TR1	Esgyrn	QF/QL	SM 966345	–
24	Ditton Priors	DP1	Neenton	QF	SO 651889	–

25	Barrow	MI1	Whicham Valley	SF/QL	SD 148836	—
		BA1	Lowsy Point	SF/QL	SD 181749	—
		BA2	Westfield Point	SF/QL	SD 235670	—
		BA3	Snab Point/ Wylock Marsh	SF/QL	SD 201640	—
26	Broughton Moor	BR1	Broughton	QF	NY 077328	—
		BR1	Broughton	QF	NY 078331	—
27	Cambeltown	SC1	Westport	Q/QF	NR 659265	—
28	Greenock & Gourock	BU1	Isle of Bute	SF/QL	NS 011748 to	—
		BU2	Isle of Bute		NS 034730	—
		GG1	Auchmead	SF	NS 234760	—
		GG2	Whitelees	SF	NS 276732	—
		GG3	Whitelees	SF	NS 267733	—
29	Stretton	ST1	Budworth	Q	SJ 705806	—

Table I.6 Army decoys (A Series)

No.	Parent	Decoy	Type	NGR	Co-located
1	Box Bridge	Monkton Farleigh	QF/QL	ST 819659	= C83(a)
2	Ash Church	Fiddington	QF	SO 943306	—
3	Norton Fitzwarren	(a) Nynehead	QL	ST 145230	SF63(a)
		(b) Dipford	QF	ST 193223	SF63(b)
4	Thingley	Lacock	QF/QL	ST 923673	—
5	Bridgend	Colwinston	QF/QL	SS 932763	= C45(a)
6	Glascoed	Coel-y-Paen	QF/QL	ST 346971	= C46(a)
7	Hereford	Holme Lacy	QF/QL	SO 549339	= C47(a)
8	Pembrey	Whiteford Burrows	Q/QF/QL	SS 448956	= C48(a)
9	Swynnerton	Whitgreave	QF/QL	SJ 885293	= C49(a)
10	Donington	(a) Kinnersley	QF/QL	SJ 677183	—
		(b) Sheriff Hales	QF/QL	SJ 741120	—
11	Ebbw Vale	Trefil	QF	SO 129137	= C50(a)
12	Severn Tunnel	Redwick	QF/QL	ST 434846	= C3(a)
13	Branston	Yoxhall	QF/QL	SK 147174	—
14	Banbury	Tadmarton	QF/QL	SP 401358	= C52(a)
15	Carlisle	Aglionby	QF/QL	NY 432571	= C53(a)
16	Crewe	Chorlton	QL	SJ 736504	= C54(a)
17	Toton	Diseworth	QF/QL	SK 463247	= C55(a)
18	Chorley	Belmont	QF/QL	SD 658162	= C51(a)
19	Blackburn	Oswaldtwistle Moor	QF/QL	SD 736238	= C56(a)

20	March	Coldham	TF 452011	QF/QL	= C57(a)
21	Peterborough	Eye	TF 264009	QL	SF46(a); = C24(a)
22	Doncaster	Tickhill	SK 600947	QL	= C34(a)
23	Longtown	Rockcliffe	NY 335618	QF/QL	QF215(a)
24	Didcot	Moulsford	SU 539831	QF/QL	–
25	Thatcham	Kingsclere	Not traced	–	–
26	Weedon	Preston Capes	SP 585559	QF	–
27	Poole	Cranford Magna	SZ 027963	QF	= C58(a)
28	Ardeer	West Kilbride	NS 200497	QF	= C59(a)
29	Aldershot	Wanborough	SU 927488	QF	–
30	York	Upper Poppleton	SE 545548	QL	= C60(a)
31	Tidworth	Shipton Bellinger	SU 217445	QF	–
32	Bramley	Monk Sherborne	SU 598554	QF	–
33	Bridgewater	Bawdrip	ST 351386	QF/QL	= C61(a)
34	Mold	Cilcain	SJ 172635	QF	= C62(a)
35	Grantham	Boothby Pagnall	SK 953305	QF/QL	SF80(a); = C63(a)
36	Marchviel	Worthenbury	SJ 444471	QF	= C64(a)
37	Spennymoor	Cornforth	NZ 317326	QF	= C65(a)
38	Aycliffe	Elstob	NZ 323233	QF	= C66(a)
39	Thorp Arch	Wighill	SE 481479	QF	= C67(a)
40	Ironbridge	Leighton	SJ 624057	QF	= C68(a)
41	Chilwell	Barton in Fabis	SK 535314	SF	= SF30(b); C18(d)
42	Catterick	Hunton	SE 184914	QF	–
43	Harlescott	Withington	SJ 548142	QF	= QF72(a)
44	Handforth	Mottram	SJ 866796	QF	= C44(a) & QF212(a)

Table I.7 Civil QLs and QFs (C Series)

No.	Parent	Decoy(s)	Type	NGR	Co-located
1	Bristol	(a) Sheepway	QF	ST 497779	= P9(a)
		(b) Long Ashton	QF/QL	ST 543717	—
		(c) Chew Magna	QL	ST 575648	—
		(d) Stockwood	QF/QL	ST 629679	SF1(a)
		(e) Severn Beach	QF	ST 542836	= P9(b)
		(f) Lawrence Weston	QF	ST 538787	—
		(g) Patchway	QF/QL	ST 630819	= QF201(a)
		(h) Yeomouth	QF/QL	ST 368670	SF1(f)
		(i) Downside	QL	ST 478659	SF1(c)
		(j) Kenn Moor	QL	ST 436685	—
2	Middlesbrough	(a) Grangetown	QF/QL	NZ 572218	Q8(a)
		(b) Bran Sands	QF/QL	NZ 559236	—
		(c) Seal Sands	QF/QL	NZ 513246	—
		(d) Greenabella	QF	NZ 514261	—
		(e) Cowpen Bewley	QF/QL	NZ 494241	—
		(f) Newton Bewley	QL	NZ 475260	SF10(f)
		(g) Wolviston	QF/QL	NZ 437263	—
		(h) Elton	QF	NZ 394180	—
		(j) Middleton	QF	NZ 481114	= QF8(b)
		(k) Kirkleatham	QF	NZ 616193	= SF10(b)
3	Severn Tunnel	(a) Redwick	QF/QL	ST 434846	= A12

4	Birmingham	(a) Newtown	QL	SK 002052	—
		(b) Little Aston	QF/QL	SK 100017	—
		(c) Great Barr	QF/QL	SP 051971	—
		(d) Overgreen	QF/QL	SP 162936	—
		(e) Kingsbury	QF/QL	SP 228966	SF2(c)
		(f) Maxstoke	Q	SP 224868	SF2(e)
		(g) Bickenhill	QL	SP 180816	—
		(h) Alvechurch	QF/QL	SP 041740	—
		(j) Illey	QF/QL	SO 975814	—
		(k) Stourbridge	QF/QL	SO 864832	—
		(l) Uphampton	QL	SO 828652	SF26(b)
		(m) Shrawley	QF/QL	SO 787659	SF26(a)
		(n) Ribbesford	QL	SO 789721	—
		(o) Mappleborough	QF/QL	SP 107674	SF27(a)
		(p) Morton Bagot	QL	SP 103646	—
		(q) Meriden	QF/QL	SP 272829	—
		(r) Tile Cross	—	*Not traced*	—
5	Slough	(a) Wexham	*Cancelled*	—	—
		(b) Hedsor	*Cancelled*	—	—
6	Liverpool	(a) Formby	QL	SD 284048	SF11(e)
		(b) Little Crosby	QL	SD 307017	SF11(f)
		(c) Lydiate	QF/QL	SD 347038	—
		(d) Knowsley	QF/QL	SJ 421955	—
		(e) Halewood	QF/QL	SJ 461866	—
		(f) Hale	QF/QL	SJ 454833	SF11(a)

No.	Parent	Decoy(s)	Type	NGR	Co-located
6	Liverpool (continued)	(g) Ince	QF	SJ 472767	SF11(b)
		(h) Brimstage	QL	SJ 297833	SF11(c)
		(k) Moreton	QL	SJ 247909	SF11(h)
		(l) Hoylake	QF	SJ 229882	—
		(m) Heswall	QL	SJ 245820	SF11(g)
		(n) Little Hilber	QL	SJ 189872	SF11(l)
		(o) Burton Marsh	QL	SJ 286749	SF11(m)
		(p) Gayton	QL	SJ 269796	SF11(n)
7	Coventry	(a) Eathorpe	QL	SP 395680	—
		(b) Hunningham	QF/QL	SP 364676	SF7(b)
		(c) Bubbenhall	QF/QL	SP 358706	—
		(d) Meriden	QF/QL	= C4(q)	—
		(e) Astley	–	Not traced	—
		(f) Bretford	QF/QL	SP 418777	SF7(c)
		(g) Leamington Hastings	QL	SP 452680	SF7(a); M4; QF226(a)
8	Newport	(a) St Brides Wentloog	QL	ST 310829	—
		(b) Tredunnock	QL	ST 380958	—
		(c) Llangibby	QL	ST 379974	—
		(d) Llanwern	QL	ST 365866	SF21(a)
		(e) Bowleaze Common	QL	ST 374864	—
		(f) Caldicot	QL	ST 385864	—
		(g) Whitson	QL	ST 391838	—
9	Swansea	(a) Morfa	QL	SS 776858	SF18(e)

	(b)	Llantwit Lower	QL	SS 788980	SF18(d)
	(c)	Baglan Higher	QL	SS 775939	SF18(c)
	(d)	Bishopston	QL	SS 599902	SF18(a)
	(e)	Pwll	QF/QL	SN 461002	—
	(f)	Dowlais	QF	SO 011086	—
	(g)	Resolven	QL	SN 860026	—
	(h)	Clydach	QL	SN 722002	—
	(k)	Five Roads	QL	SN 487033	—
	(l)	Oxwich	QL	SS 510874	—
	(m)	Reynoldstone	QL	SS 500900	Q100(a)
	(n)	Wernddu	QL	SN 723015	—
10 Sheffield	(a)	Conisbrough	QL	SK 503965	—
	(b)	Kiveton	QL	SK 507838	—
	(c)	Norton	QF/QL	SK 369804	SF3(d)
	(d)	Eckington	QF/QL	SK 416799	—
	(e)	Ulley	QF/QL	SK 472886	SF3(f)
	(f)	Bramley	QF/QL	SK 504933	SF3(e)
11 Cardiff	(a)	Leckwith	QL	ST 140739	SF20(a)
	(b)	Lavernock	QL	ST 173689	SF20(b)
	(c)	Peterstone	QL	ST 261797	—
12 Newcastle	(a)	Whitburn	QL	NZ 395631	SF15(e)
	(b)	Springwell	QL	NZ 301592	—
	(c)	Beamish	QL	NZ 228554	SF15(b)
	(d)	Whickham	QF/QL	NZ 186592	—
	(e)	Medomsley	QL	NZ 135543	—

No.	Parent	Decoy(s)	Type	NGR	Co-located
12	Newcastle (continued)	(f) Ryhope	QL	NZ 419518	SF15(d)
		(g) Silksworth	QL	NZ 364516	—
		(h) West Herrington	QL	NZ 348542	—
		(i) Boldon Colliery	QL	NZ 332618	SF15(c)
13	Lancaster	(a) Overton	QF	SD 445581	= SF48(b)
14	Ashford	(a) Brabourne	QL	TR 109428	SF65(a)
15	Glasgow	(a) Renton	QL	NS 866004	SF13(a)
		(b) Auchenreoch	QL	NS 922007	SF13(j)
		(c) Edenbarnet	QF/QL	NS 496753	—
		(d) Douglas Muir	QL	NS 516751	SF13(b)
		(e) Craigmaddie	QF/QL	NS 576773	—
		(f) Craigend	QL	NS 584778	—
		(g) Craigmaddie	QL	NS 594759	SF13(c)
		(h) Peathill Wood	QL	NS 599760	—
		(i) Kilsyth	QL	NS 715799	—
		(j) Banton	QF/QL	NS 736815	—
		(k) Glennifer Braes	Q	NS 446600	Q83(a)
16	Leeds	(a) Thorner	QL	SE 386397	SF23(j)
		(b) Barwick in Elmet	QL	SE 399360	SF23(d)
		(c) Swillington	QL	SE 402309	SF23(h)
		(d) Wintersett	QL	SE 371162	SF23(a)
		(e) Chidswell	QL	SE 279234	SF23(k)
		(f) Emley	QL	SE 259138	SF23(b)

		(g)	Ingbirchworth	SE 197052	QL	SF23(m)
		(h)	Meltham Moor	SE 095083	QL	SF23(g)
		(i)	Cragg Vale	SE 004205	QL	SF23(f)
17	Derby	(a)	Swarkestone	SK 363299	QL	SF4(c)
		(b)	Thulston	SK 406305	QF/QL	—
		(c)	Ambaston	SK 437322	QL	—
18	Nottingham	(a)	Lowdham	SK 650455	QL	SF30(d)
		(b)	Cropwell Butler	SK 653364	QL	SF30(c)
		(c)	Clipston	SK 643337	QL	SF30(a)
		(d)	Barton in Fabis	SK 535314	QL	SF30(b); A41
19	Basingstoke	(a)	North Waltham	SU 576473	QL	SF57(a)
20	Gloucester	(a)	Longney	SO 774120	QL	SF14(d); Q204(b)
		(b)	Standish	SO 832085	QL	SF14(b)
		(c)	Brimpsfield	SO 927125	QL	SF14(c)
		(d)	Coberley	SO 972168	QL	SF14(a)
21	Preston	(a)	Clifton Marsh	SD 470288	QL	SF33(b); P6
		(b)	Farington	SD 523240	QL	SF33(a)
		(c)	Brinscall	SD 639202	QL	SF33(d)
22	Accrington	(a)	Haslingden	SD 763238	QL	SF35(a)
		(b)	Accrington	SD796279	QL	SF35(b)
		(c)	Burnley	SD 845288	QL	SF35(c)
		(d)	Worsthorne	SD 891325	QL	SF35(d)
		(e)	Hameldon Hill	SD 809287	QL	SF35(e)
23	Scunthorpe	(a)	Risby	SE 929158	QL	SF24(a)
		(b)	Twigmoor	SE 921058	QL	SF24(b)

No.	Parent	Decoy(s)	Type	NGR	Co-located
24	Peterborough	(a) Eye	QL	TF 264009	SF46(a); = A21
		(b) Stanground South	QF	TL 233958	= SF46(b)
25	Manchester	(a) Chat Moss	QL	SJ 695957	SF9(a)
		(b) Carrington Moss	QL	SJ 753919	SF9(f)
		(c) Astley Moss	QF/QL	SJ 719981	—
26	Kettering	(a) Cranford	QF/QL	SP 914784	—
		(b) Woodford	QL	SP 962761	—
27	Corby	(a) Stanion	QF/QL	SP 911854	—
28	Bedford	(a) Cople	QF/QL	TL 125480	QF220(a)
		(b) Mogger Hanger	QL	TL 126511	—
29	Luton	(a) Bendish	QL	TL 163205	SF44(a)
		(b) Flamstead	QL	TL 085127	SF44(b)
30	Yeovil	(a) Chinnock	QL	ST 496146	SF42(a); Q/QF208(a)
		(b) Closworth	QF/QL	ST 573120	—
31	Leicester	(a) Galby	QL	SK 694020	SF28(a)
		(b) Beeby	QL	SK 656076	SF28(b)
		(c) Newton Harcourt	QL	SP 635982	SF28(c)
		(d) Willoughby Waterless	QL	SP 577939	SF28(d)
32	Ipswich	(a) Shottisham	QL	TM 313427	SF38(a)
		(b) Bucklesham	QL	TM 238410	SF38(b)
33	Norwich	(a) Little Plumstead	QL	TG 299121	SF43(a)
		(b) Bramerton	QL	TG 305052	SF43(b)
		(c) Horning	–	Not traced	—

34	Doncaster	(a) Tickhill	SK 600947	QL	= A22
		(b) Armthorpe	SE 643043	QL	—
35	Stoke on Trent	(a) Caverswall	SJ 931542	QL	SF32(a)
		(b) Swynnerton	SJ 853361	QL	SF32(b)
		(c) Keele	SJ 813430	QL	SF32(c)
		(d) Beech	SJ 855371	QL	—
36	Cowley	(a) Denton	SP 605021	QL	SF36(a)
		(b) Sandford	SP 548010	QL	SF36(b)
37	Workington	(a) Siddick	NY 008318	QF/QL	—
		(b) Moresby	NY 011207	QF/QL	—
38	Ravenglass	(a) Bootle	SD 083879	QF/QL	—
		(b) Carlton	SD 071968	QF	SF37(b)
39	Northwich	(a) Little Budworth	SJ 610650	QL	—
40	Newark	*Cancelled?*	—	—	—
41	Brooklands	(a) Wisley	TQ 057589	QF	= QF202(a)
42	Hawarden	(a) Bretton	SJ 366629	Q/QF	= QF207(a)
43	Langley	(a) Longford	TQ 047778	QF	= QF211(a)
44	Woodford	(a) Mottram	SJ 866796	QF	= QF212(a); A44
45	Brigend	(a) Colwinston	SS 932763	QF/QL	= A5
46	Glascoed	(a) Coed-y-Paen	ST 346971	QF/QL	= A6
47	Hereford	(a) Holme Lacy	SO 549339	QF/QL	= A7
48	Pembrey	(a) Whiteford Burrows	SS 448956	QF/QL	= A8
49	Swynnerton	(a) Whitgreave	SJ 885293	QF/QL	= A9
50	Ebbw Vale	(a) Trefil	SO 129137	QF	= A11
51	Chorley	(a) Belmont	SD 658162	QF/QL	= A18

No.	Parent	Decoy(s)	Type	NGR	Co-located
52	Banbury	(a) Tadmarton	QF/QL	SP 401358	= A14
53	Carlisle	(a) Aglionby	QF/QL	NY 432571	= A15
54	Crewe	(a) Chorlton	QL	SJ 736504	= A16
55	Toton	(a) Diseworth	QF/QL	SK 463247	= A17
56	Blackburn	(a) Oswaldtwistle Moor	QF/QL	SD 736238	= A19
57	March	(a) Coldham	QF/QL	TF 452011	= A20
58	Poole	(a) Cranford Magna	QF	SZ 027963	= A27
59	Ardeer	(a) West Kilbride	QF	NS 200497	= A28
60	York	(a) Upper Poppleton	QL	SE 545548	= A30
61	Bridgwater	(a) Bawdrip	QF/QL	ST 351386	= A33
62	Mold	(a) Cilcain	QF	SJ 172635	= A34
63	Grantham	(a) Boothby Pagnall	QL	SK 953305	SF80(a); = A35
64	Marchwiel	(a) Worthenbury	QF	SJ 444471	= A36
65	Spennymoor	(a) Cornforth	QF	NZ 317326	= A37
66	Aycliffe	(a) Elstob	QF	NZ 323233	= A38
67	Thorpe Arch	(a) Wighill	QF	SE 481479	= A39
68	Ironbridge	(a) Leighton	QF	SJ 624057	= A40
70	Worcester	(a) Leigh	QF/QL	SO 770546	—
		(b) Kempsey	QF	SO 868474	—
71	Swindon	(a) Liddington	QL	SU 213790	SF41(a)
		(b) Barbury	QL	SU 149747	SF41(b)
72	Lincoln	(a) Branston Fen	QL	TF 078693	Q/QF20(b)
73	Nuneaton	(a) Shenton	QL	Not traced	—

74	Chelmsford	(a) Little Baddow	TL 758064	QL	SF64(a)
75	Colchester	(a) Great Bromley	TM 076257	QL	SF58(a)
76	Ayr	(a) Heads of Ayr	NS 285187	QF/QL	—
77	Irvine	(a) Drybridge	NS 348358	QF	—
78	Fort William	(a) Lundy	NN 156769	QF/QL	—
79	Kinlochleven	(a) Carnoch	NN 159615	QF	—
80	Dolgarrog	(a) Rowlyn	SH 742675	—	—
81	Waltham Abbey	(a) Epping	TL 431026	QF	—
82	Bristol	(a) Burrington A	ST 467578	QL	—
		(b) Burrington B	ST 465557	QL	—
		(c) Burrington C	ST 475574	QF/QL	—
		(d) Burrington D	ST 481575	QL	—
		(e) Burrington E	ST 482572	QL	—
		(f) Burrington F	ST 497570	QF/QL	—
83	Box Bridge	(a) Monkton Farleigh	ST 819659	QF/QL	= A1
84	Rugby	(a) Barby	SP 536712	QL	SF22(a)
85	Warrington	(a) Hatton	SJ 594821	QL	SF12(a)
86	Weston	(a) Bleadon	ST 310567	Q/QF	= Q158(a) & QF206(a)
87	Londonderry	(a) Glebetown	C 435131	QL	SF50(a)
88	Inverness	(a) Alturlie	NH 727489	QL	—
89	Perth	(a) Dow Hill	NO 153213	QL	—
90	Wellingboro	(a) Knotting	SP 990633	QL	—
91	Sussex Coast	(a) Alciston	TQ 504043	QL(S)	SF79(a)
92	Skinningrove	(a) Hinderwell	NZ 807169	QL	—

No.	Parent	Decoy(s)	Type	NGR	Co-located
93	Southampton	(a) Nutburn	QL	SU 392213	SF17(d)
		(b) Beaulieu	QL	SU 409038	SF17(b)
		(c) Botley	QL	SU 515116	SF17(g)
		(d) Durley	QL	SU 534162	SF17(f)
94	Dorset Coast	(a) Dawlish	–	Not traced	–
		(b) Dorchester	QL	SY 697978	–
95	Devon Coast	(a) Stanborough	QL	SX 775510	–
96	North East Coast	(a) Aldbrough	QL	TA 258373	SF31(d)
		(b) Sneaton Moor	QL	NZ 903029	SF10(e)
97	East Coast	(a) Huttoft	QL	TF 534773	SF51(a)
98	Wolverhampton	(a) Coven	QF/QL	SJ 894058	= QF224(a); M2
99	Hatfield	(a) Holwellhyde	QL	TL 296132	QF225(a); M3
		(b) Essendon	QF/QL	TL 264094	–
100	Not traced	–	–	–	
101	Hartlepool	(a) Hart	QL	NZ 494364	SF81(a)
102	Rochester	(a) Chatham	QF	TQ 779638	= QF223(a); M1

Table I.8 ASQLs for Operation *Starkey*

Area	Decoy	Replicating	NGR	Co-located
Southampton	Cadnam A	Dump/convoy	SU 274187	—
	Cadnam B	Camp (small)	SU 289157	—
	Cadnam C	Camp	SU 295174	—
	Lee *(Cancelled)*	Camp (small)	SU 354172	SF17(c)
	Sparsholt	Camp/convoy	SU 414291	—
	Durley	Standard QL	SU 534162	= C93(d)
	Brook *(replacing Lee)*	Camp (small)	SU 348281	—
Portsmouth	Meonstoke	Camp	SU 643169	—
	Ramsdean	Dump/convoy	SU 703205	—
	Stoughton A	Camp (small)	SU 794116	—
	Stoughton B	Dump/convoy	SU 816118	—
Newhaven	Brighton A	Camp	TQ 258087	—
	Brighton B	Camp	TQ 269085	—
	Brighton C	Camp	TQ 376076	—
	Brighton D	Camp (small)	TQ 400067	—
	Seaford	Camp	TQ 485067	—
	Alciston	Standard QL	TQ 504043	= C91(a)
Dover	Burmarsh B	Camp (small)	TR 091328	—
	Wigmore A	Convoy	TR 177485	—
	Wigmore B	Dump/convoy	TR 204449	—
	West Langdon A	Camp (small)	TR 316467	—
	West Langdon B	Camp/convoy	TR 333482	—

Table I.9 Naval Coast MQLs (NC Series)

Area	No	Decoy	NGR	Co-located
Plymouth Command	550	Helford	SW 744261	—
	551	St Mawes	SW 843348	—
	552	Ruan Lanihorne	SW 886413	—
	553	East Cornworthy	SX 844561	—
	554	Churston	SX 909571	—
	555	Menabilly	SX 103506	—
Portsmouth Command	600	Cobnor Point	SU 791020	—
	601	East Head	SZ 765987	—
	602	Itchenor	SU 784006	—
	603	Pagham Harbour	SZ 866964	—
	604	Cuckmere River	TV 508998	NH1
	605	Cuckmere Haven	TV 514986	NH1
	606	Sowley Pond	SZ 372964	—
	607	Chilling	SU 513038	—
	608	Crockford Bridge	SZ 362989	—
	609	Pennington Marshes	SZ 319923	—
	610	Dibden Bay	SU 403092	—
	611	Newton Bay East	SZ 422917	—
	612	Newton Bay West	SZ 415913	—
	613	Gravelley Marsh	SZ 414967	—
	614	Lynes Common	SU 445059	—

	615	Bembridge	*Not traced*	—
	—	Earth	SX 382557	—
Dover Command	650	Worth	TR 369563	SF78(a)
	651	Camber Castle	TQ 917183	—
	652	Sandwich Flats	TR 352608	—
	653	West Hythe	TR 147334	—
	654	Pett Level	TQ 895138	—
Nore Command	700	Kirton	TM 296416	—
	701	Long Reach	TM 225377	—
	702	Steeple	TL 909037	—
	703	Lower Hope Point	TQ 716788	—
	707	Breydon Water	TG 499069	—
	708	Oulton Broad	TM 518932	—
	709	Benacre Ness	TM 533833	—
	710	Whitehall Farm	TM 293433	—
	711	Falkenham Marshes	TM 313393	—
	712	Trimley Marshes	TM 254360	—
	713	East Tilbury	TQ 678757	—
	—	Canewdon	*Not traced*	—
	—	Burnham	*Not traced*	—
	—	East Mersea	*Not traced*	—

APPENDIX II

Decoy attacks

The following tables show the numbers of attacks on decoys recognised by Colonel Turner's Department during the Second World War, from the first in 1940 to the last in 1944. They are the audited figures collated by the Air Historical Branch at the end of the war, and occasionally differ slightly from those appearing in letters and reports compiled much closer to the event.* Attacks on army sites appear to be subsumed into the Air Ministry total.

* AIR 41/3

Table II.1 Attacks on day decoys

1940			*1941*		
July	K	6	January	K	1
	A	—		A	1
	D	—		D	—
August	K	2	February	K	2
	A	—		A	3
	D	1		D	—
September	K	7	March	K	1
	A	—		A	4
	D	4		D	—
October	K	10	April	K	1
	A	—		A	—
	D	3		D	—
November	K	4	May	K	—
	A	—		A	3
	D	1		D	—
December	K	1	June	K	1
	A	—		A	—
	D	—		D	—
Totals	K	36			
	A	11			
	D	9			
Key	K	K sites			
	A	Dummy aircraft displayed on real airfields			
	D	Dummy buildings			

Table II.2 Attacks on night decoys, 1940

	Type	*RAF*	*Naval*	*Total*
June	Q	36	—	36
	QF/QL	—	—	—
	SF	—	—	—
July	Q	11	—	11
	QF/QL	—	—	—
	SF	—	—	—
August	Q	28	—	28
	QF/QL	—	—	—
	SF	—	—	—
September	Q	37	—	37
	QF/QL	7	—	7
	SF	—	—	—
October	Q	23	—	23
	QF/QL	5	—	5
	SF	—	—	—
November	Q	28	—	28
	QF/QL	2	—	2
	SF	—	—	—
December	Q	11	—	11
	QF/QL	1	—	1
	SF	5	—	5
Totals	Q	174	—	174
	QF/QL	15	—	15
	SF	5	—	5

Table II.3 Attacks on night decoys, 1941

	Type	RAF	Naval	Total
January	Q	6	—	6
	QF/QL	1	—	1
	SF	5	—	5
February	Q	36	—	36
	QF/QL	—	3	3
	SF	2	—	2
March	Q	21	—	21
	QF/QL	—	1	1
	SF	14	2	16
April	Q	46	—	46
	QF/QL	1	—	1
	SF	13	—	13
May	Q	26	—	26
	QF/QL	—	—	—
	SF	4	—	4
June	Q	13	—	13
	QF/QL	—	4	4
	SF	3	—	3
July	Q	13	—	13
	QF/QL	—	—	—
	SF	6	—	6
August	Q	14	—	14
	QF/QL	3	—	3
	SF	1	—	1
September	Q	9	—	9
	QF/QL	2	—	2
	SF	—	—	—
October	Q	1	—	1
	QF/QL	10	1	11
	SF	—	—	—
November	Q	—	—	—
	QF/QL	—	1	1
	SF	—	—	—
December	Q	—	—	—
	QF/QL	1	1	2
	SF	—	—	—
Totals	Q	185	—	185
	QF/QL	18	11	29
	SF	48	2	50

Table II.4 Attacks on night decoys, 1942

	Type	RAF	Naval	Total
January	Q	—	—	—
	QF/QL	1	—	1
	SF	—	—	—
February	Q	—	—	—
	QF/QL	—	—	—
	SF	—	—	—
March	Q	3	—	3
	QF/QL	—	—	—
	SF	—	—	—
April	Q	8	—	8
	QF/QL	3	1	4
	SF	—	1	1
May	Q	3	—	3
	QF/QL	2	1	3
	SF	3	2	5
June	Q	2	—	2
	QF/QL	3	1	4
	SF	4	—	4
July	Q	9	—	9
	QF/QL	13	—	13
	SF	2	2	4
August	Q	9	—	9
	QF/QL	5	—	5
	SF	5	—	5
September	Q	2	—	2
	QF/QL	3	—	3
	SF	1	—	1
October	Q	—	—	—
	QF/QL	2	—	2
	SF	1	—	1
November	Q	1	—	1
	QF/QL	—	—	—
	SF	—	—	—
December	Q	—	—	—
	QF/QL	—	—	—
	SF	—	—	—
Totals	Q	37	—	37
	QF/QL	32	3	35
	SF	16	5	21

Table II.5   Attacks on night decoys, 1943

	Type	RAF	Naval	Total
January	Q	1	—	1
	QF/QL	2	2	4
	SF	—	—	—
February	Q	—	—	—
	QF/QL	1	—	1
	SF	—	—	—
March	Q	6	—	6
	QF/QL	12	2	14
	SF	3	—	3
April	Q	—	—	—
	QF/QL	—	—	—
	SF	—	—	—
May	Q	2	—	2
	QF/QL	2	—	2
	SF	—	—	—
June	Q	—	—	—
	QF/QL	—	—	—
	SF	—	1	1
July	Q	3	—	3
	QF/QL	1	1	2
	SF	1	—	1
August	Q	1	—	1
	QF/QL	2	1	3
	SF	—	2	2
September	Q	1	—	1
	QF/QL	1	—	1
	SF	—	—	—
October	Q	5	—	5
	QF/QL	1	3	4
	SF	—	1	1
November	Q	2	—	2
	QF/QL	1	1	2
	SF	—	1	1
December	Q	1	—	1
	QF/QL	—	—	—
	SF	—	—	—
Totals	Q	22	—	22
	QF/QL	23	10	33
	SF	4	5	9

Table II.6 Attacks on night decoys, 1944

	Type	*RAF*	*Naval*	*Total*
January	Q	3	—	3
	QF/QL	—	1	1
	SF	—	—	—
February	Q	10	—	10
	QF/QL	3	3	6
	SF	3	—	3
March	Q	5	—	5
	QF/QL	3	1	4
	SF	2	1	3
April	Q	3	—	3
	QF/QL	1	3	4
	SF	1	5	6
May	Q	4	—	4
	QF/QL	1	1	2
	SF	—	4	4
June	Q	—	—	—
	QF/QL	1	—	1
	SF	—	—	—
Totals	Q	25	—	25
	QF/QL	9	9	18
	SF	6	10	16

Table II.7 Attacks on night decoys: annual summary

	Type	RAF	Naval	Total
1940	Q	174	—	174
	QF/QL	15	—	15
	SF	5	—	5
1941	Q	185	—	185
	QF/QL	18	11	29
	SF	48	2	50
1942	Q	37	—	37
	QF/QL	32	3	35
	SF	16	5	21
1943	Q	22	—	22
	QF/QL	23	10	33
	SF	4	5	9
1944	Q	25	—	25
	QF/QL	9	9	18
	SF	6	10	16
Totals	Q	443	—	443
	QF/QL	97	33	130
	SF	79	22	101
Grand total	All types	619	55	674

APPENDIX III

The reckoning

We saw in Chapter 7 that the Air Historical Branch calculations pointed to a total draw-off by decoys of 2221.13 tonnes of bombs during the Second World War. This figure was calculated from the tally of day attacks maintained by Colonel Turner's Department, and those of night attacks derived by the Air Warfare Analysis Section. Table III.1 shows how it was arrived at.* The correction factor for Starfish – the additional 300 tonnes of bombs – was added because the AWAS average for their draw was based upon later attacks, and missed all the heavier operations in 1940–41.

Table III.1 AHB calculations of decoy effectiveness

Decoy type	Attacks	Average (tonnes)	Total (tonnes)	Source
K sites	47	2.50	117.50	Turner
Dummy buildings	9	1.30	11.70	Turner
Q sites	521	1.65	859.65	AWAS
QL and QF sites	173	1.53	264.69	AWAS
Starfish	119	5.61	667.59	AWAS
Additional correction factor for Starfish			300.00	
Total			2221.13	

* AIR 41/3, p 95.

Sources
and bibliography

References to primary sources drawn upon in research for this book are given in full among the notes, while secondary sources appear there using the 'Harvard' (author-date-page) system. The vast majority of primary sources used are papers held at the Public Record Office at Kew, whose standard group, class/piece referencing system has been followed. This being so, the only explanation required for use of the notes is a key to the group and class numbers which appear at the start of each reference.* These are listed below, together with a bibliography of published material.

ADM 1   Admiralty and Secretariat Papers
ADM 179   Portsmouth Station Records: Correspondence
ADM 199   Admiralty War History Cases and Papers
AIR 1   AHB Records, Series 1
AIR 2   Air Ministry Registered Files
AIR 5   AHB Records, Series 2
AIR 6   Air Council Records
AIR 8   Chief of the Air Staff Papers
AIR 14   Bomber Command Files
AIR 15   Coastal Command Files
AIR 19   Secretary of State for Air Private Office Papers
AIR 20   Air Ministry Unregistered Files
AIR 26   Operations Record Books: RAF Wings

* See further Cantwell 1993.

AIR 28   Operations Record Books: RAF Stations
AIR 29   Operations Record Books: Miscellaneous Units
AIR 40   Air Ministry Directorate of Intelligence Papers
AIR 41   Air Historical Branch Narratives and Monographs
AVIA 15   Ministry of Aircraft Production Files
BT 177   Board of Trade Papers
CAB 120   Minister of Defence Secretariat Files
CAB 121   Cabinet Office: Special Secret Information Centre Files
HO 186   Ministry of Home Security: Air Raid Precautions Registered Files
WO 199   Military Headquarters Papers: Home Forces

Bibliography

Anderton, M, 1999. Twentieth Century Military Recording Project: Bombing Decoys. English Heritage (Aerial Survey), unpublished report

Bekker, C, 1966. *The Luftwaffe War Diaries*. London: Macdonald

Brettingham, L, 1997. *Beam Benders: 80 (Signals) Wing 1940–45*. Leicester: Midland Publishing

Brunel, A, 1949. *Nice Work. The story of thirty years in British film production*. London: Forbes Robertson

Cantwell, J D, 1993. *The Second World War. A guide to documents in the Public Record Office*. PRO Handbook **15**. London: HMSO

Carrick, E, 1941. *Designing for Moving Pictures*. London: Studio Publications

Collier, B, 1957. *The Defence of the United Kingdom*. London: HMSO

Cooper, M, 1981. *The German Air Force, 1933–1945. An anatomy of failure*. London: Jane's

Cox, S, 1990. A comparative analysis of RAF and Luftwaffe intelligence in the Battle of Britain, 1940, *Intelligence and National Security*, **5(2)**, 425–43

Crawshaw, A, 1992. Aerial archaeology in Yorkshire: a 'Starfish' site, *Yorkshire Archaeological Journal*, **64**, 209–11

Cruickshank, C, 1979. *Deception in World War II*. Oxford: OUP

Cubbage, T L, 1987. The success of Operation Fortitude: Hesketh's history of strategic deception, *Intelligence and National Security*, **2(3)**, 327–46

Darvill, T C, Saunders, A D & Startin, D W, 1987. A question of national importance: approaches to the evaluation of ancient monuments for the Monuments Protection Programme in England, *Antiquity*, **61**, 393–408

Dewar, M, 1989. *The Art of Deception in Warfare.* Newton Abbot: David & Charles

Dobinson, C S, 1996. Twentieth-Century Fortifications in England, Vol III: Bombing Decoys of WWII. Unpublished report

Dobinson, C S, 1998. Twentieth-century Fortifications in England: the MPP approach, in English Heritage, 2–6

Dobinson, C S, Lake, J & Schofield, A J, 1997 Monuments of war: defining England's 20th-century defence heritage, *Antiquity*, **71**, 288–99.

English Heritage, 1998. *Monuments of War. The evaluation, recording and management of twentieth-century military sites.* London: English Heritage

Faithfull, H C T, 1958. Memoir: Colonel Sir John Fisher Turner, Kt, CB, DSO, *Royal Engineers Journal*, **72**, 301

Haigh, D, 1993. Local History from World War II: the 'Starfish' sites at Cragg Vale and Clifton, *Transactions of the Halifax Antiquarian Society,* **1** (New Series), 121–35

Handel, M I, 1982. Intelligence and deception, *Journal of Strategic Studies*, **5**, 122–54

Harris, A T, 1947. *Bomber Offensive*. London: Collins

Hartcup, G, 1979. *Camouflage. A history of concealment and deception in war.* Newton Abbot: David & Charles

Hinsley, F H, 1979. *British Intelligence in the Second World War. Its influence on strategy and operations, Vol 1.* London: HMSO

Howard, M, 1990. *British Intelligence in the Second World War, Vol 5. Strategic Deception*. London: HMSO

Hyde, H M, 1976. *British Air Policy between the Wars*. London: Heinemann

Jones, R V, 1998. *Most Secret War*. Ware: Wordsworth

Lloyd, M, 1997. *The Art of Military Deception*. London: Leo Cooper

Longmate, N, 1979. *Air Raid: The bombing of Coventry, 1940.* London: Arrow

Low, R, 1985. *Film Making in 1930s Britain*. London: Allen & Unwin

Meekcoms, K J & Morgan, E B, 1994 *The British Aircraft Specifications File. British Military and Commercial Aircraft Specifications, 1920–1949*. Tonbridge: Air-Britain

Motion, A, 1993. *Philip Larkin: a writer's life*. London: Faber and Faber

Müller, K-J, 1987. A German perspective on allied deception operations in the Second World War, *Intelligence and National Security*, **2(3)**, 301–26

Myerscough, J, 1985. Airport provision in the inter-war years, *Journal of Contemporary History*, **20**, 41–70

Nash, F, 1999. Secrets of the bombing decoys, *Essex Past & Present*, **1**, 4–5

Nieke, M R, 1997. Ten years on: the Monuments Protection Programme, *Conservation Bulletin*, **31**, 10–12

O'Brien, T H, 1955. *Civil Defence.* History of the Second World War, United Kingdom Civil Series. London: HMSO

Pye, A, & Woodward, F, 1996 *The Historic Defences of Plymouth*. Truro: Cornwall County Council

Redfern, N, 1998. Twentieth Century Fortifications in the United Kingdom. Unpublished report

Reymond, J, 1994. *Fortitude South: Kent's wartime deception*. Maidstone: Kent County Council

Richards, D, 1953. *Royal Air Force 1939–1945, Vol I: The fight at odds*. London: HMSO

Robinson, M, 1937. *Continuity Girl*. London: Robert Hale

Saward, D, 1985. *Bomber Harris*. London: Sphere

Schaffer, R, 1985. *Wings of Judgement. American bombing in World War II*. Oxford: OUP

Schofield, J & Lake, J, 1995 Defining our defence heritage, *Conservation Bulletin*, **27**, 12–13

Smith, M, 1984. *British Air Strategy between the Wars*. Oxford: OUP

Smith, D J, 1989. *Britain's Military Airfields 1939–1945*. Wellingborough: Patrick Stephens

Sturtivant, R, Hamlin, J & Halley, J J, 1997 *Royal Air Force Flying Training and Support Units*. Tonbridge: Air-Britain

Thetford, O, 1995. *Aircraft of the Royal Air Force since 1918*. London: Putnam

Threadgall, D, 1994. *Shepperton Studios: an independent view.*
London: British Film Institute

Wakefield, K, 1981. *The First Pathfinders. The operational history of Kampfgruppe 100, 1939–1941*. London: William Kimber

Whaley, B, 1982. Toward a general theory of deception, *Journal of Strategic Studies*, **5**, 178–92

Wheatley, D, 1980. *The Deception Planners: my secret war*. London: Hutchinson

Wright, R, 1970. *Dowding and the Battle of Britain*. London: Corgi

Index